Community Fieldwork in Teacher Education

In teacher education, fieldwork in community-based spaces (including foster homes and programs for homeless youth) is frequently contrasted with 'traditional' field experiences in classroom settings, where beginning teachers are immediately introduced to teacher-centered models of instruction. This volume works against such a model, presenting a counter-narrative of new teachers' understanding of the act of teaching. By exploring their work with at-risk youth in community-based sites, the authors uncover how nontraditional spaces for teaching and learning have the potential to open new doors for reimagining the teaching act and teacher identity.

This volume examines how prospective teachers have used writing within unconventional spaces as catalysts for considering what it means to become a teacher, as well as how the work of teaching can be conceptualized. It unites the practical aspects of fieldwork and with theoretical conceptions of teaching, and envisions how the work and the definition of 'teaching' can be broadened.

Heidi L. Hallman is an associate professor in the Department of Curriculum and Teaching at the University of Kansas. Her recent work has been published in *English Education* and *Teaching Education*, among others. In 2010, she received a grant from Conference on English Education for her research on prospective teachers' work with homeless youth.

Melanie N. Burdick is an assistant professor of English and director of composition at Washburn University. Her work has appeared in *English Education* and *The Journal of Teaching Writing*. In 2012 she was awarded a grant from the Council of Writing Program Administrators to study high school teachers' perceptions of college-level writing.

Routledge Research in Teacher Education

The Routledge Research in Teacher Education series presents the latest research on Teacher Education and also provides a forum to discuss the latest practices and challenges in the field.

Books in the series include:

Preparing Classroom Teachers to Succeed with Second Language Learners
Lessons from a Faculty Learning Community
Edited by Thomas H. Levine, Elizabeth R. Howard, and David M. Moss

Interculturalization and Teacher Education
Theory to Practice
Cheryl A. Hunter, Donna K. Pearson and A. Renee Gutiérrez

Community Fieldwork in Teacher Education
Theory and Practice
Heidi L. Hallman and Melanie N. Burdick

Community Fieldwork in Teacher Education
Theory and Practice

Heidi L. Hallman and
Melanie N. Burdick

NEW YORK AND LONDON

First published 2015
by Routledge
711 Third Avenue, New York, NY 10017

and by Routledge
2 Park Square, Milton Park, Abingdon, Oxon OX14 4RN

Routledge is an imprint of the Taylor & Francis Group, an informa business

© 2015 Taylor & Francis

The right of Heidi L. Hallman and Melanie N. Burdick to be identified as authors of this work has been asserted by them in accordance with sections 77 and 78 of the Copyright, Designs and Patents Act 1988.

All rights reserved. No part of this book may be reprinted or reproduced or utilised in any form or by any electronic, mechanical, or other means, now known or hereafter invented, including photocopying and recording, or in any information storage or retrieval system, without permission in writing from the publishers.

Trademark notice: Product or corporate names may be trademarks or registered trademarks, and are used only for identification and explanation without intent to infringe.

Library of Congress Cataloging-in-Publication Data

Hallman, Heidi L., 1976–
  Community fieldwork in teacher education : theory and practice / by Heidi L. Hallman, Melanie N. Burdick.
    pages cm. — (Routledge research in teacher education)
  Includes bibliographical references and index.
  1. Teachers—Training of. 2. Children with social disabilities—Education. 3. Non-formal education. I. Burdick, Melanie N., 1970– II. Title.
  LB1707.H34 2015
  370.71'1—dc23   2014048439

ISBN: 978-1-138-01378-0 (hbk)
ISBN: 978-1-315-79506-5 (ebk)

Typeset in Sabon
by Apex CoVantage, LLC

Printed and bound in the United States of America by Publishers Graphics, LLC on sustainably sourced paper.

Contents

List of Tables and Figures   vii
Foreword   ix
Acknowledgments   xiii

Introduction: Beginning at the Margins   1

1. Community Fieldwork in Teacher Education and Composition Studies   14

2. Composing Teachers, Teachable Students, and Teachable Spaces   46

3. Questioning through Writing: Writing as Dialogic Response   73

4. Questioning Teaching: Disrupting a Teaching Mythology   90

5. Questioning Curriculum: Reenvisioning Assumptions about Curricular Control and Expectations   108

6. Questioning Normal: Composing Ethical Representations of At-Risk Youth   123

7. The Promise of Work at the Margins: Community Fieldwork in Teacher Education   138

   Appendix A: Syllabus for Curriculum and Instruction in Middle School/Secondary English Language Arts Classrooms   151

*Appendix B: Syllabus for Advanced
   Composition—Teaching Emphasis*   155

Appendix C: Henry Taylor's Life Graph   159

Appendix D: Anne Chisholm's Life Graph   161

References   163

Index   175

Tables and Figures

TABLE

1.1 Participants, institutions, community sites, placement in book, and year of participation in study.   34

FIGURES

5.1 Models of English language arts curriculum   113
5.2 The concept of Reciprocal Transformation   119

Foreword

We talk often in teacher education about how things have changed—how today's students are different from those of the past, how new teachers must be prepared differently than their predecessors were. Knowledge is expanding exponentially, gaps are widening between in and out-of-school literacies, and social issues such as poverty and racism continue to plague communities and families. There is much debate about what teacher education reforms might be best and how to better prepare teachers for increasingly complex and diverse classrooms. How exactly can we improve what we do? Do we make student teaching internships longer? Require co-teaching with school-based mentors? Ensure placements in urban (or rural) schools? Create methods course assignments that address social justice and equity? All of these approaches have merit, and many have been implemented in teacher preparation programs. They all arise from teacher educators' desire to see their teacher candidates more prepared, emotionally and intellectually, for their new profession. Developing a satisfying teacher identity has always been difficult, but how do we best facilitate this process in a world that seems to be changing so rapidly that unexpected challenges are the norm?

Other proposals for change come straight from policy makers or external stakeholders who see teacher education as more of an obstacle to good teaching than a help, who wish to do away with traditional teacher education in favor of short-term workshops or intense summer programs providing quick overviews of research and theory prior to dropping candidates into real schools to learn 'on the job.' These stakeholders tend to value accountability over reflexivity, assessment over connection. However, one thing we all have in common is that we believe teacher education could do a better job preparing new teachers for contemporary education settings and the effective teaching of 21st-century students. But how do we best make these improvements?

Heidi L. Hallman and Melanie N. Burdick provide a possible answer. Why not ask preservice teachers to move outside the traditional classroom walls and interact with young people in community settings, settings many of them might find unfamiliar: group homes for abandoned youth, day centers for homeless families, and charter schools for 'at-risk' youth, to name a few targeted by Hallman and Burdick. Often called 'volunteerism' or 'service-learning,' Hallman and Burdick conceptualize preservice teacher work in these settings as that and much more; they see it as reciprocally beneficial and genuinely transformative for the teacher education students they interviewed and followed in their 5-year study. Work in these non-traditional contexts allowed the preservice teachers to rethink stereotypes, assumptions, and mythologies about teaching and learning born from their own life experiences and prior education. These field experiences, while at first almost dismissed by some of the teacher education students as simply tutoring or volunteering, ended up helping them experience the borderland between their own subjectivities and the real lives of the students with whom they worked. No longer could these kids be labeled as disadvantaged, as unintelligent, or as troublemakers. With time and commitment, as well as written and oral reflection, the teachers-to-be saw these children and teens as real people, with strengths and problems and lives and relationships and worries and joys. They were no longer the 'other' to be avoided, or even feared. They were young people with whom the teacher candidates developed relationships resulting in mutual understandings. Stereotypes were broken down. Myths were dissolved. Boundaries were overcome. Tensions were addressed head on, leading to richer conceptualizations of what school is and perhaps could be.

This book moves past superficial, general discussions of what can or should be done to improve urban education or rural education, or education of students who are apparently nonreaders or addicted to technology or without a family structure or whatever other issue is currently identified. Instead of generalities and empty euphemisms, Hallman and Burdick offer a possible, concrete solution for some of the challenges of teacher education in community fieldwork. And this solution is not offered simply in a practical 'how-to' way; it is richly theorized by scholars such as Bakhtin and Schön, Britzman and Bruffee, and Gee and Smagorinksy. Both teacher education and composition theorists and researchers are invited into the conversation, as Hallman and Burdick themselves engage in a dialogue, and just as they encourage their teacher education students to dialogue with their past and present selves and with their sometimes unrecognizable students living in often alien spaces. Such dialogue is not always easy or comfortable and sometimes demands foundational epistemological shifts, as identity work often does. Becoming a teacher is an identity process that benefits from such confrontation and negotiation, as the new teachers quoted in the book describe and exemplify.

Hallman and Burdick have written a book that makes a strong, engaging argument for the use of community spaces in teacher education—an argument that incorporates theory, research and the unforgettable words of preservice teachers themselves, such as Kelly, Katherine, Henry and Anne, who are changed in powerful, yet very different, ways by their fieldwork. I hope this book will be read by many and, more important, will prompt some to attempt such community connections in their own teacher education courses, as the quest continues to make teacher education more relevant, memorable, informative, and even transformational. Perhaps it is time to revision the traditional teacher education field experience, to expand the experiential options for preservice teachers learning what it means to teach. If students and schools have changed as much as we believe they have, a change in how we prepare new teachers seems a necessity. *Community Fieldwork in Teacher Education: Theory and Practice* offers a vision for such change.

—Janet Alsup, Purdue University

Acknowledgments

This project started with a desire to learn more about the education of youth who were deemed marginal—homeless youth, foster youth, and youth who were moved from one school to another with the hope that their 'marginal' status would be softened. As teachers, we also knew that the so-called marginal students in our classrooms often had valuable perspectives from which others could learn. As we entered the three community-based field sites that we feature in our book, Family Partnership, the Lodges, and Mettle Street School, we encountered families, young people, and educators who possessed a willingness to work alongside us. They also welcomed the beginning teachers in our teacher preparation programs with enthusiasm. We see that the families, youth, and educators constitute the critical fabric of this book, for their voices are what has made this book possible. We extend a heartfelt thank you to these individuals.

We acknowledge that aspects of our work have been shared at conferences, including the American Educational Research Association, Feminisms and Rhetorics, and the National Council of Teachers of English. We appreciate the professional support these organizations have provided us, and thank the Conference on English Education for the research initiative grant that helped propel this work forward. A thank you to those at Routledge who saw potential in our work and helped it move forward into publication. We thank the reviewers who provided us feedback on our work and saw the glimmers of a finished product in our initial manuscript. Finally, we thank the institutions at which we work, the University of Kansas and Washburn University, for the support they have shown us as our project emerged and evolved. We would like to share our particular appreciation for Dr. Danny Wade and Dr. Laura Stephenson at Washburn University who advocated for institutional support towards the research and writing of this book. Thank you to Dr. Richard Ellis and Kristine Hart in Washburn's Learning in the Community office for your wise counsel and your gifts of inspiration to pursue this project. We would also like to acknowledge the research support that the University of Kansas's School of Education Research Support Program provided as ongoing sponsorship of this project.

We are deeply grateful for the support of our friends and colleagues, Mary Louise Gomez, Terri Rodriguez, Melissa Schieble, Deana Bindel, Tom Pankiewicz, and Sarah Smarsh. Your honesty and integrity is something rare in this world, and without you, our work would feel flat. You help us see the beauty within the work, even when we struggle to see it, and give us the inspiration to continue. To our parents, Jim and Lynn Hallman and Richard and Janet Keeney, who affirmed our hard work. Thank you for always believing in us.

To our husbands, John Mattes and Robert Burdick who cheerfully took over the bulk of home and child care when deadlines loomed. You have always provided us the space and freedom to pursue our academic work, and for this, we are grateful. And, lastly, we thank our children, Ari, Helena, Sigrid, and Nico Mattes and Charlie, Simon, George and Peter Burdick. Your minds, hearts, and dreams are constant, living reminders of the importance of connection, relationship, and teaching.

Portions of Chapter 1 and 6 are reprinted from "Community-Based Field Experiences in Teacher Education: Possibilities for a Pedagogical Third Space," by Heidi L. Hallman, 2012, *Teaching Education*, 23(3), 241–263, Taylor & Francis Ltd, www.tandfonline.com. Reprinted with permission of publisher.

Portions of Chapter 1 are reprinted from "Service Learning and the Preparation of English Teachers," by Heidi L. Hallman and Melanie N. Burdick, 2011, *English Education*, 43(4), 341–368, copyright 2011 by the National Council of Teachers of English. Reprinted with permission.

Portions of Chapter 3 are reprinted from "Shifting Genres: A Dialogic Approach to Reflective Practice in Teacher Education," by Heidi L. Hallman, 2011, *Reflective Practice: International and Multidisciplinary Perspectives*, 12(4), 533–545, Taylor & Francis Ltd, www.tandfonline.com. Reprinted with permission of publisher.

Introduction
Beginning at the Margins

At the heart of this book is an exploration of the self–other relationship present in the teaching act. Throughout the book, prospective teachers reflect on their perceptions of working with students who are labeled 'at-risk' of school failure, as well as how these perceptions affect their ability to become teachers of such students. Teachers' stories of negotiating a pedagogical space with at-risk students are explored throughout the book as more than just stories about the work of teaching but as negotiations of what it means to inhabit the role of teacher.

This is the culmination of research that took place over 5 years at two universities and in three community-based field sites. Although we had several cohorts of prospective teachers who participated in our study over these years, we draw specifically, in this book, from the experiences of 12 beginning teachers. Teaching and tutoring at-risk students within their prospective communities, we draw on the stories of these 12 aspiring educators as way to illustrate the potential that community-based field sites have as field placements within teacher education programs. Through prospective teachers' journal and essay writing, as well as through their participation in focus group interviews and discussions, we feature the value of such community field placements for the training of future teachers.

In the chapters that follow, we introduce readers to the dynamics of what we call non-traditional spaces for teaching and learning. These spaces include a day center for homeless families, a group home where beginning teachers and adolescents worked together in the after-school hours, and an alternative school that invited beginning teachers to tutor students. Such contexts can be viewed as spaces on the margins, for these are not traditional schools or traditional learning spaces. We describe how these sites, over time, influenced teachers' understandings of the work they would undertake with students and presented us, as researchers, with considerations of the ethical dimensions of conducting research in such spaces.

The teachers' stories that we draw from over the course of 5 years were generated as a result of an aim to study prospective teachers' experiences working with at-risk students within non-traditional learning spaces. The term *at-risk*, throughout this book, is highly contested, as it suggests framing students through deficit orientations. As other terms situate students through similar lenses, including the terms *struggling, urban*, and *diverse*, we remain cognizant that all such framings label and categorize students. We see that we must disrupt these framings at the same time that our book is premised specifically on working with students deemed 'at the margins.' The marginal status of both students and spaces explored within this book asks teacher educators and beginning teachers to think more carefully and consciously about what constitutes good teaching.

Although prospective teachers came to this study as part of their university course work, their work in these nontraditional spaces encouraged them to question their emerging teaching practice. In some cases, prospective teachers offered rebuttals to the ideologies about homelessness and poverty expressed by their peers. Such challenges to "the perceived wisdom of those at society's center" (Yosso, 2006, p. 14) appeared throughout conversations with prospective teachers in seminar meetings and interviews. As our research unfolded, we began to view these stories, or narratives, as functioning in teachers' writing and talk as *counterstories* (Yosso, 2006). Counterstories synthesized teachers' perceptions of their own past and therefore allowed them to assert new identities as beginning teachers. Yosso (2006) describes the purpose of counterstories as being to "build community with those at the margins," to "challenge the perceived wisdom of those at society's center," to "nurture community wealth, memory, and resistance," and to "facilitate transformation in education" (pp. 14–15). Prospective teachers used the counterstories they crafted as responses to their work with students and viewed counterstories as enabling them to negotiate and embrace the new identities they wished to assume as teachers.

In other cases, prospective teachers' stories resonated with Yosso's (2006) definition of counterstories as "facilitating transformation in education" (p. 15). Tangible acts undertaken by some of the teachers, such as frequently providing books for the youth with whom they worked, confirmed a commitment to transformation in a very concrete way. Beginning teachers' reflections on their work with students, in these cases, produced action that was recognized in the community as being beneficial to students.

The chapters of the book, collectively, view prospective teachers' stories through two complementary theoretical lenses: the lenses of dialogism and spatiality. We consider these lenses to be especially important in today's educational context. Dialogism, as a concept, is premised on the idea of response to others, to texts, and to the larger community and highlights the negotiations beginning teachers make in contending with issues framing the current era of teaching. Spatiality is an important lens from which to consider the act of teaching, as the spaces in which students inhabit are changing. Because many more students now come from nontraditional homes and backgrounds, prospective teachers need to experience teaching within nontraditional spaces in order to better understand students' first learning spaces and how out-of-school spaces influence their in-school interactions.

Still, because we know that most teachers come from traditional spaces and are comfortable within traditional school spaces, allowing them the opportunity to work with at-risk youth in nontraditional learning spaces assists them in questioning and critiquing assumptions about the spaces of schooling and the interactions between teachers and at-risk youth. Beginning teachers must also participate consciously in the dialogic act of becoming a teacher in order to more thoroughly embrace a teacher identity that can weather the current storms of de-professionalization and accountability. Together, spatiality and dialogism are threaded throughout our analysis as ways to penetrate prospective teachers' views of teaching.

DIALOGISM AND TEACHING

Throughout our work with prospective teachers, we considered the tools by which teachers understood their relationship with students, and saw that teachers formed narratives of their work, in part, as responses, to the students whom they taught. Russian philosopher Mikhail Bakhtin's (1990) understanding of the relationship between self and other provides a framework for understanding the impetus for teachers' questioning of self in relationship with students, and tenets of a Bakhtinian dialogic perspective illuminate important considerations in understanding teachers' work as 'response.' Conceptualizing teachers' narratives through a Bakhtinian framework is premised on a *dialogic* approach to studying the relationship between self and other. A dialogic approach bridges the self-other divide and views all iterations of self as response to an intended other. A focus on the relationship between speaker and intended 'other' is particularly relevant to the study of teaching as dialogic. Teachers shape responses to students in order to act—either on themselves, on others, or on their practice. Therefore, teaching is viewed as always in relation to and in response to an intended 'other.' Bakhtin (Holquist, 1990) believed that we, as humans, are always intimately connected to the spatial and temporal contexts in which we live, and these connections are how we articulate who we are as well as our relationship to others.

Throughout our book, we illustrate how a Bakhtinian framework has implications for the study of teaching. Through elaboration of prospective teachers' work in nontraditional field sites, we explore the ways that teachers' approaches to the work of teaching provided a forum for investigating how teachers' responses changed over time. We explore Bakhtin's concept of dialogism as a way to conceptualize the relationship between self and other, and we delineate the *heteroglossic*, or the many-voicedness, nature of the act of teaching. In a Bakhtinian sense, then, teachers involved in the teaching act author themselves as future teachers, in part, through authoring the relationship they have with the 'other'—the students with whom they work. They create reciprocity within their relationships with students, allowing them to continually negotiate who they are in the moment.

A Bakhtinian conceptual framework is synonymous with what many have come to know as *dialogism*, or the premise that 'utterances' (Bakhtin's term), are always responsive in nature. Dialogism is primarily concerned with the idea that *all* language is produced as response to other language. Thus, a central tenet of viewing text as dialogic highlights the action utterances within one text make in relation to other texts. Nystrand, Gamoran, Kachur, and Prendergast (1997) articulate a dialogic view of text and utterances as

> fundamentally different from the common view that utterances are the independent expressions of thoughts by speakers, an account that starts with thoughts and ends with words and verbal articulation. Rather, because they respond to at the same time that they anticipate other utterances, they are 'sequentially contingent' upon each other. (p. 10)

Nystrand et al. (1997) emphasize the responsive, and therefore, dialogic quality of all text. The responsive nature of utterances situates all language in a chain of response and focuses on the contingency of all utterances. Bakhtin (1986) notes this when he states that "the single utterance, with all its individuality and creativity, can in no way be regarded as a completely free combination of forms of language" (p. 81). Utterances, then, respond to and adhere to various language forms, or genres, and at the same time, remain active agents in reshaping these genres.

Throughout our book, a Bakhtinian conceptual framework assists us in more fully recognizing teachers' response to 'others'; furthermore, we consider what a dialogic view of teaching might offer the field of teacher education by acknowledging how Bakhtinian theoretical tools highlight an explicit connection between the local-level influences on teachers and larger, historical influences that have shaped teachers' perceptions of what constitutes 'teaching.' A study of the connection between the local and the global is expressed by Bakhtin (1981) when he discusses the conflict between two forces inherent in discourse: the centripetal force which works at centralizing and unifying meaning and the centrifugal force (what Bakhtin calls the force of heteroglossia) that fragments ideological thought into diverse and multiple views. Sometimes referred to as a push–pull relationship between speaker and intended 'other,' recognizing this quality of heteroglossia as an inherent feature of language and language use removes expectation that teachers' negotiations of teaching must be tidy. In fact, the heteroglossic quality of language underscores all text as in relation with an intended 'other,' and therefore, is, at times, messy. Holquist (1990), in pointing to Bakhtin's notion about using language to achieve understanding writes that "all meaning is achieved by struggle" (p. 39). Bahktinian tools (Bakhtin, 1981, 1986) articulate an epistemology by way of articulating a theory of language. Teacher educators and researchers taking up a Bakhtinian conceptual framework are able to understand teachers' rhetorical moves in their thinking and teaching as purposeful.

SPATIALITY AND TEACHING

Investigating prospective teachers' work in nontraditional spaces has tremendous potential to encourage teacher candidates to learn about their students' capabilities, strengths, and interests (Sleeter, 2008) early in their education. Most convincingly, work in such spaces encourages teachers to deconstruct the assumed binaries of school–community, self–other, and teacher–student that so frequently limit beginning teachers' conceptualizations of teaching and learning.

School is not one homogenous and replicable space that is identically arranged and inhabited. The faulty reasoning that school is a uniform space that is duplicated throughout diverse communities is a dangerous one that leads to misunderstanding of educational processes. If schools are identical, then learners are identical, and teachers identical; under this premise, standardization makes sense and logically should be used to improve student learning. In fact, here is where much of the conflict between educators and reformers often occurs. Those who work on a daily basis within schools work among the variances, complexities, and ranges of classroom settings, of schooling, and of learners. The myth of standardization's good is even faultier now that schooling has become further complicated by the rise of movements such as charter schools, virtual schooling, early college schools, un-schooling, and homeschooling. Schooling may have been at one time more homogenously imagined if we hearken back to the one-room schoolhouse and consider what groups were likely to attend school; such students came from similar cultures and backgrounds. Today, as our society has become more heterogeneous, so has our schooling. As our students have become more diverse, so have we begun to experiment more with what schooling should entail. We can no longer assume that there is a singular way to teach and a singular type of learner, nor can we assume that the spaces of school look and behave identically.

Thus, it is important that we help prospective teachers understand this early in their education. Through fieldwork in nontraditional settings and with learners who may be labeled at-risk students, prospective teachers can begin to question and create counterstories that challenge the mythology that schooling is a defined and homogenous, replicable space.

Based upon theories of spatiality in *The Production of Space* by Henri Lefebvre (1991), we frame our research within the assumptions that changes in schooling are based on the individuals and groups of individuals who are participating in the spaces of the school. When we consider "spaces of schooling," we mean this in both a concrete and abstract sense. There is the brick-and-mortar school space in which students sit within walls and listen to teachers or discuss lessons with each other. This is also the space where parents can participate in conference with administrators, and janitors can work to make the school space attractive and safe. But there is also the abstract space of school that is made up of curriculum, relationships, and politics. Spaces of schooling, then, are created by a school's culture and the inhabitants of that space. This abstract notion of space is constructed socially and emphasizes relationships within particular school cultures, which, therefore, render the concept of 'space' as one that is created metaphorically through constructions of power, identity, and agency

Especially pertinent to our discussion is Lefebvre's (1991) distinction between dominated and appropriated space. Lefebvre describes dominated space as the space that is "invariably the realization of the master's project" which is "usually closed, sterilized, emptied out" (p. 165). Appropriated space, on the other hand, is defined by Lefebvre as built by the group rather than by the 'master.' Lefebvre's discussion of appropriated space includes the idea that "a natural space modified in order to serve the needs and possibilities of a group . . . has been appropriated by that group" (p. 165). Therefore, public schools are inherently dominated spaces, and at times, schools, and especially classrooms, can become appropriated spaces within the dominated space. This is done through acts of resistance and negotiation, through stories, and through constructed and contextualized curriculum carried out within such appropriated spaces.

Also applicable to our inquiry is the idea of movement within an edifice of space, identified as "fractured" by Lefebvre:

> It is impossible to overemphasize either the mutual inherence or the contradictoriness of these two aspects of space. Under its homogenous aspect, space abolishes distinctions and difference, among them that between inside and outside, which tends to be reduced to the undifferentiated state of the visible-readable realm. Simultaneously, this same space is fragmented and fractured, in accordance with the demands of the division of labor and the division of needs and functions . . . each spatial interval, is a vector of constraints and a bearer of norms and 'values.' (1991, pp. 355–356)

As prospective teachers must work within various curricular constraints, the counternarratives they author allow them to make sense of constraints and better fragment or fracture the dominated space for their own needs and the needs of their students.

Massey (1999) builds upon Lefebvre's work and encourages us to consider space through the following three proposals: "space is a product of interrelations . . . space is the sphere of the possibility of the existence of multiplicity . . . [space] is always in a process of becoming" (p. 2). Through Massey's suggestions, then, school spaces can be those created between teachers and students, between administration and teachers, and among parents and teachers. The many interrelations that take place create the space within which teachers teach and students learn. The individuals are both affected by the space as well as create it through their relationships. The lack of, or absence of, relationships can also change the content of the space. For example, the lack of some parental relationships with teachers, the lack of parental relationships with students, and absent or incomplete relationships between teachers and administrators can affect the space of schooling as much as their presence would. Popkewitz (1998) notes how such absences, in urban and rural schools, are sometimes viewed as the "presumed routes of salvation for the child" (p. 41). Referring to these absences as 'doublets,' Popkewitz asserts that the "negative, oppositional poles of what is absent in the child . . . are [recast] as positive poles to find personal redemption" (p. 42). Attributes such as 'poverty' or 'urban' are remade as attributes that can be 'cultivated' through teachers' watchful eyes. Prospective teachers grapple with such doublets in decision-making about how best to serve at-risk youth.

It is through relationships that the "sphere of possibility of the existence of multiplicity" occurs (Massey, 1999, p. 2). As relationships move and connect or disconnect, they create an actively fluctuating space. Teachers must be sensitive to these fluctuations and must learn to teach within the fluctuations and within the shifting relational spaces. By providing prospective teachers with fieldwork in a single, traditional type of school space—fieldwork often comes in the form of student teaching in a single classroom—we believe that beginning teachers are constrained in learning how multiplicity is created among varied relationships.

Finally, Massey's (1999) proposition that space is always "in a process of becoming" is one that seems especially relevant within the spaces of schooling and teacher education. Most educators see learning as a space of becoming, where students can be nurtured and led to become more knowledgeable, skilled, and fully human. Teacher education also sees the work of teaching as a space where individuals become teachers. In this space, individuals take on a teacher identity little by little and create an identity that further defines their individual space and the relationships they foster with students.

TEACHING AND TEACHER IDENTITY

Alongside other scholars who study teacher identity (e.g., Alsup, 2006; Zembylas, 2003), we understand that teachers are produced as *"particular types of professionals"* (Zembylas, 2003, p. 124, italics in the original), and take up their teacher identity as a project of continuous 'becoming' (Gomez, Black, & Allen, 2007) over time. Furthermore, teachers mediate their stories of self with the cultural and institutional expectations of what it means to be a teacher. *Identity*, as a theoretical concept, has been discussed in the research literature as fluid and complex, as well as inherently social (e.g., Alsup, 2006; Gee, 1999, 2001). D. Holland, Lachicotte, Skinner, and Cain (1998) discuss the premise that "identities, the imaginings of self in worlds of action, [are] . . . lived in and through activity and so must be conceptualized as they develop in social practice" (p. 5).

8 *Introduction*

Bakhtin's understanding of the relationship between self and other also assists us in recognizing the impetus for teachers' ongoing quest for a "teacher identity," and Bakhtin (Holquist, 1990) referenced this when he said,

> In order to see ourselves, we must appropriate the vision of others . . . I see myself as others might see it. In order to forge a self, I must do so from outside. In other words, I author myself. (p. 28)

In a Bakhtinian sense, then, teachers involved in the teaching act author themselves as future teachers, in part, through authoring the relationship they had with the other—the students with whom they worked—and their teacher identity is continually negotiated throughout their work with students. The questioning of the relationship between teacher and students found throughout teachers' experiences with at-risk youth encourages teacher educators to see that nontraditional spaces of teaching can be, with guidance and reflection, a conduit by which individuals understand who they are and how they perceive others. Bakhtin believed that humans are always in the process of negotiating with others—how they address each other as well as how they answer each other. Because we use the contexts in which we live to do this negotiation, it is important that these contexts be selected to provide such opportunities.

SPACES OF SERVICE AND SCHOOLING

Community-based field placements for prospective teachers offer potential sites for beginning teachers' growth, for such sites allow prospective teachers to consider how schools reside in the context of a community, and this awareness can broaden beginning teachers' understandings of where learning takes place (Rogers, Marshall, & Tyson, 2006). Throughout the book, we explore the potentials of extending teacher education programs' commitments to preparing teacher candidates for a broader understanding of students' learning and lives. In the chapters that follow, we specifically explore prospective teachers' work in three distinct field sites: *Family Partnership*, a day center for homeless families; *the Lodges*, a group home where beginning teachers and adolescents worked together in the after-school hours; and *Mettle Street School*, an alternative school that invited beginning teachers to tutor students.

Family Partnership Day Center for Homeless Families

Family Partnership is a national organization framed by a model with a successful history. A nonprofit organization committed to helping low-income families achieve lasting independence, Family Partnership is oftentimes contrasted with a 'shelter model' of assisting homeless individuals and families, as the program is founded on the premise of assisting homeless families through providing "an integrated approach that begins with meeting immediate needs but reaches much further to help people achieve independence and to alleviate the root causes of poverty" (Family Promise, n.d.). Family Partnership works with a small group of families over the course of a period of 3 to 4 months with the intention of fostering lasting independence. In Cedar Creek, the community in which our research took place, Family Partnership was one of several programs serving homeless individuals.

Cedar Creek, a community of approximately 90,000 people, is classified as a suburban community. The suburban nature of the community, as well as the presence of Green State University, the state's flagship institution, within the community of Cedar Creek, challenges the idea that homeless individuals and families exist in such communities. Yet, the face of homelessness has changed considerably in the past few years, and continues to change throughout the United States. It is now estimated that 14 out of every 10,000 people are 'rural' or 'suburban' homeless (as compared to 29 out of every 10,000 people who are 'urban' homeless) (National Alliance to End Homelessness, 2014).

Jackson City and the Lodges

Jackson City has a population of 234,000 made up of 85% Caucasian residents. The median income in 2009 was $46,000, and the city has poverty rates of approximately 27%. The Lodges is an organization that oversaw group homes for youth who had either been abdicated by their parents or who had been held within the juvenile detention system and placed at the Lodges as part of their case plans. The Lodges is open for youth ages 6 to 18, but the majority of residents are 15 to 18. The group homes serve up to 10 youth at a time, and each home has two house parents and a social worker assigned. The Lodges is situated less than 5 miles from the downtown area of Jackson City. Adolescents are referred to the Lodges for various reasons, but most are there because they have become wards of the state but without a foster family placement. A number of kids live at the Lodges following time at a juvenile detention center or because of drug related conflicts. All attended a local public school, where they are quickly and solidly labeled as 'Lodges kids' by faculty and other students.

The Lodges was selected as one of our research sites for several reasons. Although the kids at the Lodges are not homeless in the same way as those who were involved with Family Partnership, they are living in a nontraditional home situation in which the house parents and other children in the home were not in any way related. While the living situation is intended to provide stability for the kids involved, there is still much transition and insecurity in the kids' lives; kids at the Lodges know they are living in an environment that is nontraditional and assumed to be inferior to the homes most of their school peers inhabit. We hoped that working with at-risk students at the Lodges would allow prospective teachers from Wilkerson University to see that not all of their students will come from 'normal' family backgrounds, or backgrounds even remotely similar to their middle-class, White backgrounds. Prospective teachers had the chance to glimpse into the worlds of students' lives and create relationships with them instead of speculating and assuming where and how these kids resided outside of school.

Mettle Street School

Mettle Street School is also located in Jackson City and is a charter school that serves students within and outside the Jackson City School District. In 2012, the school reports having 148 students, just over 70% of whom qualify for free and reduced-price lunch. Mettle Street is a racially diverse school, with 43% White, 28% African American, and 23% Hispanic.

Elementary through high school students attend Mettle Street School. The elementary students who attend the school often have severe behavior issues that prevent them from attending traditional schools. The middle school and high school students who attend Mettle Street are there for a variety of reasons: some have not been successful in traditional school settings; others are teen parents who attend the school for its parent–child learning center.

The class sizes are small at Mettle Street, and in elementary classrooms, there are often enough para-educators and aides to give students one-on-one attention. Secondary students participate in many hands-on learning programs, such as the school-to-work program and various science and environmental projects. The school also has its own writing lab, where peer tutoring occurs. Because many of the students at Mettle Street are viewed as high-risk students, teachers are allowed freedoms to experiment with instructional methods that are often discouraged in traditional schools.

Prospective teachers who worked at Mettle Street School worked during the school day but in the school's writing center. Here they were able to work one-on-one with student writers and to help mentor the high school's own peer tutors. Because the prospective teachers were providing tutoring outside of a classroom construct, they were able to build relationships with students and better understand these students who were labeled as at-risk.

In the chapters that follow, we further elaborate how these field sites influenced teachers' understandings of the work they undertook with at-risk students. We highlight how prospective teachers grappled with concepts such as 'learning' and 'curricula,' as well as how they questioned the role that curriculum played in the relationships among teacher, students, and schooling. As teacher education programs and university-level courses continue to grapple with decisions about what field experiences matter for beginning educators' growth, they must look beyond traditional school placements that offer a direct pathway to the role of teacher. Instead, embracing alternative, nontraditional sites for teacher learning can foster broader contemplation of students' learning and lives and can lead teachers early in their career to view teaching as a process of inquiry rather than a predefined assemblage of techniques. Learning teaching is, indeed, a process of inquiry (Hollins, 2011). Viewing schooling as a complex arena where students' social, cultural, and economic backgrounds have play begins with fostering such understandings with new teachers from the beginning of their teaching careers.

In the following chapters we discuss in more detail the process of doing our research, as well as the findings of our research. In Chapter 1, "Community Fieldwork in Teacher Education and Composition Studies," we provide an explanation of our research questions, as well as outline procedures and descriptions of the participants and sites of our research. Chapter 2, "Composing Teachers, Teachable Students and Teachable Spaces," includes a theoretical overview of our book, including more background in Bakhtinian understandings of identity and dialogism as it relates to teacher education and theories of spatiality as they relate to community-based field sites.

The next four chapters feature our findings and analysis. Chapter 3, "Questioning Through Writing: Writing as Dialogic Response," focuses on three participants, Rhonda, Kelly, and Katherine, and their work at Mettle Street School. This chapter specifically highlights the work that prospective teachers do through the act of writing. Chapter 4, "Questioning Teaching: Disrupting a Teaching Mythology," focuses on the questions that two prospective teachers had as they worked with homeless youth through Family Partnership. This chapter grapples with what we call a 'mythology of teaching' and seeks to understand how beginning teachers negotiate the role of a teacher. Chapter 5, "Questioning Curriculum: Reenvisioning Assumptions About Curricular Control and Expectations," follows participants working with youth at the Lodges. This chapter also shows how prospective teachers began to understand teaching and curriculum through personal relationships with the youth at the Lodges and how curriculum became a space of interaction rather than prescription. Chapter 6, "Questioning Normal: Composing Ethical Representations of At-Risk Youth," looks closely at prospective teachers at both Family Partnership and the Lodges and analyzes their understandings of at-risk students. This chapter raises questions about the nature of research with populations of students often deemed the most marginalized.

Finally, the last chapter, "The Promise of Work at the Margins: Community Fieldwork in Teacher Education," presents an overview of our findings yet also circles back around into the college classroom. In doing so, it aims to focus once again on the work of teacher educators, who are often in a position to develop community-based field placements that provide valuable experiences for prospective teachers. We include, in this book, classroom resources in the form of syllabi and writing and discussion prompts in order to encourage others to engage in similar projects within the context of methods or composition courses. Several appendices at the end of the book, as well as detailed prompts within the final chapter, provide teacher educators with our classroom materials and some of our participants' actual classroom artifacts.

We hope that our book, *Community Fieldwork in Teacher Education: Theory and Practice*, provides readers with a rich understanding of what community-based field experiences can offer teacher candidates in terms of opening their identities as teachers to include students who are often left at the margins. We feel that this topic, in addition to being important and timely, ultimately invites readers into a deeper understanding of how and why community-based sites offer important learning spaces for teachers.

REFERENCES

Alsup, J. (2006). *Teacher identity discourses: Negotiating personal and professional discourses*. Mahwah, NJ: Erlbaum.

Bakhtin, M. (1981). *The dialogic imagination: Four essays* (M. Holquist, Ed). Austin: University of Texas Press.

Bakhtin, M. (1986). *Speech Genres and Other Late Essays* (C. Emerson & M. Holquist, Eds.) Austin: University of Texas Press.

Bakhtin, M. (1990). *Art and answerability: Early philosophical essays* (M. Holquist, Ed., & V. Liapunov, Trans.). Austin: University of Texas Press.

Family Promise. (n.d.). Our work. Retrieved from www.familypromise.org/our-work

Gee, J.P. (1999). *An introduction to discourse analysis: theory and method*. New York, NY: Routledge.

Gee, J.P. (2001). Literacy, discourse, and linguistics: Introduction. In E. Cushman, M. Rose, B. Kroll, & E.R. Kintgen (Eds.), *Literacy: A critical sourcebook* (pp. 525–544). Boston, MA: Bedford/St. Martin's.

Gomez, M.L., Black, R.W., & Allen, A. (2007). "Becoming" a teacher. *Teachers College Record, 109*(9), 2107–2135. Retrieved from www.tcrecord.org.www2.lib.ku.edu/library/Issue.asp?volyear=2007&number=9&volume=109

Holland, D. Lachicotte, W., Skinner, D., & Cain, C. (1998). *Identity and agency in cultural worlds*. Cambridge, MA: Harvard University Press.

Hollins, E. (2011). Teacher preparation for quality teaching. *Journal of Teacher Education, 62*(4), 395–407. doi:10.1177/0022487111409415

Holquist, M. (1990). *Dialogism*. New York, NY: Routledge.

Lefebvre, H. (1991). *The production of space*. Malden, MA: Blackwell.

Massey, D. (1999). Philosophy and politics of spatiality: some considerations. The Hettner-Lecture in Human Geography. *Geographische Zeitschrift, 87*(1), 1–12.

National Alliance to End Homelessness. (2014). Snapshot of homelessness. Retrieved September 22, 2014, from www.endhomeslessness.org

Nystrand, M., Gamoran, A., Kachur, R., & Prendergast, C. (1997). *Opening dialogue: Understanding the dynamics of language and learning in the English classroom*. New York, NY: Teachers College Press.

Popkewitz, T.S. (1998). *Struggling for the soul: The politics of schooling and the construction of the teacher*. New York, NY: Teachers College Press.

Rogers, T., Marshall, E., & Tyson, C. (2006). Dialogic narratives of literacy, teaching, and schooling: Preparing literacy teachers for diverse settings. *Reading Research Quarterly, 41*(2), 202–224.

Sleeter, C. (2008). Equity, democracy, and neoliberal assaults on teacher education. *Teaching and Teacher Education 24*(8), 1947–1957. doi:10.1016/j.tate.2008.04.003

Yosso, T. (2006). *Critical race counterstories along the Chicana/Chicano educational pipeline*. New York, NY: Routledge.

Zembylas, M. (2003). Interrogating 'teacher identity': Emotion, resistance, and self-formation. *Educational Theory, 58*(1), 107–127. doi:10.1111/j.1741-5446.2003.00107.x

1 Community Fieldwork in Teacher Education and Composition Studies

FIELDWORK IN TEACHER EDUCATION

Teacher education programs have identified early and diverse field experiences as one of the keys to successful teacher education (Darling-Hammond, 2006; Feiman-Nemser & Buchmann, 1987; Sleeter, 2008; Zeichner, 2010). Holistically, such field experiences exist to foster teacher candidates' understanding and practice of culturally relevant pedagogy (Ladson-Billings, 2001), as well as assist beginning teachers' understanding of the constructs of theory and practice (Shulman, 2005). Although field experiences have been acknowledged as an important component of teacher education programs, little work has explored the unique qualities of community-based settings as potential sites for teachers' learning (see Coffey, 2010). Suggesting that community-based settings have the power to transform the ways that beginning teachers think about the effects of schooling in their students' lives, Coffey (2010) also suggests that community-based sites can encourage beginning teachers to examine the extent to which social factors influence students' success in school. Community-based settings offer sites for beginning teachers to consider how schools reside in the greater context of a community, and this can potentially broaden beginning teachers' understandings of where learning takes place (Rogers, Marshall, & Tyson, 2006). Extending teacher education programs' commitment to preparing teacher candidates for environments that not only are part of schools but are also situated within communities, becomes a commitment to preparing beginning teachers for understanding that teaching and schooling extend beyond the walls of the classroom and into the world.

Some scholars (e.g., Coffey, 2010; Rogers et al., 2006) have suggested that community-based field experiences can potentially work on multiple levels to enhance beginning teachers' insight into both students' lives outside of school and the ways in which the institution of school responds to students. Community-based field sites, often contrasted with traditional 'apprenticeship of observation' models of fieldwork (Lortie, 1975) within classrooms and schools, work toward the goals of broadening beginning teachers' conceptions of where student learning takes place as well as support the idea that teachers are not only part of a school but part of a larger community. Community-based field experiences encourage beginning teachers to contextualize students' lives as part of the fabric of the larger community, and emphasize that familiarity with students' communities is important to the work of teaching.

Service-Learning in Teacher Education

In recent years, there has been an increased interest in what is known as *service-learning* in teacher education (e.g., Carter-Andrews, 2009). Service-learning has also been applied to many different disciplinary domains within teacher education, and most recently, service-learning has been highlighted with its application to literacy teacher education (e.g., Kinloch & Smagorinsky, 2014). Practitioners in the PK–12 context, as well as teacher educators, have benefited from this connection, which focuses on how service-learning can be integrated with disciplinary knowledge. Smagorinsky's (2014) efforts to connect service-learning to the English education program at the University of Georgia serves as a model for our work, and Smagorinsky states that the goal for the service-learning project that he initiated was to "place each of [his] students in a one-on-one tutoring relationship with a student who came from a radically different cultural environment in terms of race, ethnicity, social class, educational aspiration, family situation, and other such factors" (p. 92). In doing so, he hoped to provide beginning teachers and students in the community a mutually beneficial educational experience. Our book begins in the space of also aiming to create an experience both youth in the community and teachers in our university programs that would be mutually beneficial.

As Moore (2014) states, the concept of service-learning has been fraught with "mixed messages" (p. 109) and in common parlance is sometimes referred to as volunteerism. Yet, service-learning's relationship with and history of the concepts of *server* and *served* demand a more complex and nuanced understanding of service-learning's goals. Service-learning, a component of the educational system in the United States since the 1800s, is, as Eyler and Giles (1999) state, concerned with the "links between personal and interpersonal development and cognitive, academic development" (p. 9). Community service, Flower (2008) notes, brings "idealism and social consciousness into the academy. It brings a human face and complex lives into discussion of ideas and issues. But it can also plunge teachers and students into its own set of contradictory and sometimes profoundly conflicted social and literate practices" (p. 153). As service-learning situates itself with both the notions of 'service' and 'inquiry,' scholars (e.g., Flower, 2002, 2008; Schutz & Gere, 1998) have debated the balance act that service-learning must strike between the two;

as Kaufman (2004) observes, "English education students often arrive in Methods classes eager to learn the ins and outs of lesson plans, but, through service-learning, they also discover that they need to understand something more about themselves; the question of what they need to be effective about is a crucial one" (p. 178).

Being effective in the act of service-learning means being open to inquiry and reflection. Short stints of 'service' in the community, such as forays into soup kitchens and homes for the elderly, referred to by Mertz as "guerrilla service" (Mertz & Schroerlucke, 1998, as cited in Flower, 2002, p. 181), have been criticized for being superficial acts of service lacking opportunities for critical reflection about such experiences. Furthermore, these short service acts reinforce the distance between the 'giver' and the 'receiver' in the service act, thereby reinscribing the server–served dichotomy.

Flower's (2002, 2008) exploration of service-learning problematizes the server-served dichotomy that service-learning often creates, and articulates a more complex picture of the potential role reversals present in the act of service-learning. Her work features *reciprocity*—a concept that refers to both the interchange in roles between teacher and student as well as the interchange between university and community partnerships—as central to service-learning's definition, thus seeking to reverse the long-standing practice of the academy using the community for the academy's own ends (Zlotkowski, 1996). As Flower (1997) notes, some people in the service-learning act have been continually cast as "the knowledgeable servers, while [others are cast] as the clients, patients, or the educationally deficient—the served" (p. 96), and a server-served dichotomy is often perpetuated in service-learning's connotation. Flower's (2008) recent work, however, theorizes service-learning as having the capacity to break this dichotomy through an exploration of the relationship between 'self' and 'other.'

We view our work as squarely inhabiting the tenets of service-learning, yet we also seek to distinguish it as primarily residing within the realm of teacher education. Our term, *community fieldwork*, seeks to reconcile a need to be both service-learning and teacher education fieldwork and subscribes to Flower's conclusion that the primary goals of service-learning are twofold. First, service-learning must have a goal of viewing self and other as ultimately intertwined. A breaking of the self-other dichotomy through the act of service-learning is essential for participants' reflection on self as well as for participants' recognition of their prior, and perhaps limited, understandings. Second, the act of service-learning must be pursued alongside a process of inquiry. Flower (2008) notes that inquiry must begin by "confronting the conflicts within the everyday practice of outreach" (p. 154). These two tenets, as applied to the field of teacher education, are embodied within the community fieldwork experience. Community fieldwork, as inquiry, becomes not a series of interventions or programs but, instead, is treated as a situated sociocultural activity—an activity that is always socially, culturally, and historically located.

More than Technical Rationality

Schön (1987) used the concepts of 'artistry' and 'reflection-in-action' to move the discussion about competence away from reliance solely on what is known of as technical rationality, or the idea that competence is based only on systematic, scientific knowledge. When applied to teaching, or what Schön refers to as the "swampy zones of practice" (p. 3), artistry in teaching urges the teacher to reshape practice while engaged in practice. Hence, the term *reflection-in-action* seeks to keep the flow of practice intact while encouraging teachers to reshape practice. Schön stresses that different types of reflection serve different purposes in acquiring artistry.

Like the goals of service-learning and reflection-in-action, community fieldwork has the potential to disrupt deficit theorizing on the part of teachers (Sleeter, 2008, p. 1948), thus encouraging teacher candidates to critically question schooling and patterns of inequity. Because we know that many preservice teachers learn to teach by teaching their university peers in mock teaching environments (Shrofel, 1991), many beginning teachers have little direct, field-based experiences working with youth before student teaching. Therefore, the attitudes that beginning teachers express early in their careers may influence how they will develop as teachers.

Tenets of service-learning are useful in describing how community-based field experiences can be theoretically situated within teacher education programs (e.g., Anderson & Erickson, 2003; Boyle-Baise, 2002). Service-learning, as applied to teacher education, has been conceptualized as more than volunteerism, and Feinstein (2005) states that "the broad intended outcome of service-learning is to blend service and learning so that the service reinforces the college students' understanding of the learner and educational practices, and in return the learning improves and strengthens the service they can provide as teachers" (p. 3). Service-learning offers the possibility of reenvisioning the relationship between teacher and students, therefore becoming a site where teacher candidates can mitigate and reevaluate their prior beliefs (Feiman-Nemser, & Buchman, 1987).

Service-learning in teacher education is frequently contrasted with 'traditional' field experiences in classrooms where beginning teachers are immediately socialized into the role of teacher as 'expert' (Cuban, 1993; Lortie, 1975). Portes and Smagorinsky (2010) have noted that teacher candidates are still by and large socialized into traditional, teacher-centered models of instruction, composed, in part, of "a conception in which a teacher stands before students who face forward in seats and who are supposedly poised to listen and learn" (p. 236). Service-learning, and community-based fieldwork, works against this model, thereby becoming both a counter-narrative and conduit for beginning teachers to reconsider the relationship between teacher and students. The work that teacher candidates do in community-based field sites, then, can be conceptualized as service-learning for prospective teachers. Because the role of teacher as expert is put into question in the service-learning act, beginning teachers are prompted to critically examine the relationship between teacher and students, something that is often ignored in more 'traditional' field placement or practicum/student-teaching experiences.

Teacher Education as a Process of Socialization

Developing as a teacher inherently invites a process of socialization. Participating in fieldwork within teacher education is influenced by the process and structure of teacher education, more broadly, and being and becoming a teacher, Britzman (1991) argues, is part of a process of socialization influenced by *chronologies*. The concept of chronologies conveys a simultaneity of time, place, events, and the meanings that we give to them (Britzman, 1991, p. 55). Britzman acknowledges that beginning teachers are influenced by at least four chronologies during the process of becoming teachers and each chronology makes available a different range of voices and discourses. As beginning teachers move through these four chronologies, they encounter discourses that have shaped the chronologies, yet, at the same time, they bring their own experiences to the process of becoming a teacher.

Beginning teachers bring the first chronology with them, which is their educational biography and the synthesis they have created to make sense of the rules that govern schools, the nature of knowing, and the purpose of schooling. The second chronology involves the beginning teachers' experiences in the university and teacher education. The third chronology is the student teaching experience, where Britzman argues that beginning teachers begin to become privy to aspects of the teacher's world and departmental politics, and the fourth chronology begins when the teacher becomes a new, first-year teacher. The fourth chronology, as Britzman describes it, invites a teacher's newfound contemplation and understanding of the influences of "the school system, students, the teacher union, the community, public policy, professional organizations, and the cumulative experience of their classroom lives" (p. 56).

Our work seeks to uproot the assumption that the chronologies that Britzman (1991) describe must be solidified. Instead, we embrace the possibility that facets of the awareness and knowledge that teachers gain in the fourth chronology (first year teaching) can be introduced earlier. Britzman notes that the "sense we make of each chronology depends on the discourses we take up" (1991, p. 56). We see that taking up particular discourses—such as deliberating the nature of students' learning in 'nontraditional' spaces of learning and teaching—can be beneficial for teachers before they enter the first year of their teaching career. Furthermore, using the first chronology, one's biography, as a site for dialogue with the process of teacher education, student teaching, and in-service teaching, is viewed as a continual process and one that can be fostered throughout the development one undergoes while in a teacher education program.

We also see that teacher education must capitalize on helping students understand from early in their teacher education program that schools exist as part of a larger community. We imagine that community-based field placements can assist in the disruption of normative discourses. Britzman (1991) writes that the "normative discourse in teacher education reduces the complexity of competing chronologies by authorizing a functionalist version of socialization that is incapable of attending to the site of socialization as contested terrain, and the ways in which the individual becomes the site of struggle" (p. 56). The individual as a the site of struggle, to us, produces the possibility for agency, and this agency gives rise to the potential that beginning teachers may rethink prior assumptions and may question the normative discourses at work. In the next chapter, we discuss the relationship between the agency that teachers have and the discourses in which they participate.

We are cognizant that the way we position agency does not mean self-actualization in the sense that individuals operate free from context. Instead, we recognize the cultural contexts in which teachers work always push back on teachers' ability to possess agency. At times, this pushback may be rather indoctrinating, and may cause beginning teachers to resist seeking a voice that contradicts the cultural context in which they find themselves. Other times, the cultural context pushes beginning teachers to act and question. In many ways, this dialogic relationship between the self and the context mirrors the relationship between self and other, as both seek to position the teacherly self as existing within a multiplicity of competing ideologies and discourses. The dialogic relationship between self and context, and between self and other, constitutes the theoretical backbone of our book. Rather than seeing this continual back and forth as antagonistic, we see this relationship of negotiation and change as productive.

FIELDWORK IN COMPOSITION STUDIES

Traditionally, composition classes have been designed to teach students the basics of writing within the academy. Correspondingly, education classes have traditionally been designed to teach students the basics of instruction within a traditional K–12 classroom space. These courses often apprentice students into the status quo, without asking them to question or interact critically in their learning. Bartholomae (1986), in his seminal work of composition theory, encourages instructors to allow access by inviting students to "Invent the University" themselves. In order to learn to write within the university, students must appropriate (or be appropriated by) a specialized discourse, and they have to do this as though they were easily and comfortably one with their audience, as though they were members of the academy, or historians or anthropologists or economists; they have to invent the university by assembling and mimicking its language, finding some compromise between idiosyncrasy, personal history, and the requirements of convention, the history of a discipline. They must learn to speak our language. Or they must dare to speak it, or to call off the bluff, since speaking and writing will most certainly be required long before the skill is 'learned.' (pp. 4–5)

In the process of invention, students are not invited to re-invent; rather, they are encouraged to invent it in their minds through participating within conversations in which they aren't yet adequately prepared to engage. Bartholomae states that through writing, students can invent a context as they learn the context. They can understand the rules of academic discourse as they invent within these rules, not only through trial and error but also as an active participant.

So, too, this relates to the use of writing about community fieldwork. By reflecting on and critiquing their experiences, prospective teachers better understand and find access to the roles they will later take on as classroom teachers. When prospective teachers are able to learn from and invent their identity in writing as they learn the rhetorical context of classroom work, they gain a more powerful and flexible access into the existing conversations.

In the field of composition and rhetoric, the idea of fieldwork and writing instruction are a predictable combination. In the late 1980s and early 1990s composition studies took what is now defined as the 'social turn' (e.g., Bartholomae, 1986; Bizzell, 1994; Bruffee, 1984). At that point in the scholarship, there was a turning away from the idea that texts were written in vacuums, where a writer sits alone isolated with little contact or understanding of his audience. The social turn also dismissed that the main goal of writing was 'correctness.' Through the social turn in composition, we have come to see how texts are created within social contexts and that these differing contexts compel writers to make choices about the how, what, and why of their writing. In the 1980s, the field also began to recognize that a writer's identity (including race, class, gender, sexual orientation, etc.) influence one's writing of a text. Composition studies broadened to include the perspectives of critical theory and feminist theory, and the rise of critical pedagogy (e.g., Shor, 1996) urged students to recognize how individuals are connected to systems and institutions.

From the social turn emerged the idea that classroom writing is usually a simulated act and teachers must search out ways to make their writing instruction more authentic. As Bacon (1997) writes, "the classroom is such a contrived and atypical rhetorical environment . . . where the reader often has more knowledge about the topic than the writer, where she reads not to learn, but to evaluate so that the writer may learn, where the purpose of communication is easily subordinated to the purpose of demonstrating mastery or satisfying a requirement" (p. 42). Writing, then, must be connected to other experiences in order to solve problems that students name as 'real' and apart from the classroom. This "extracurriculum of composition" (Gere, 1994) means studying the literacy practices of local communities.

Related to the social turn in composition and rhetoric, there has been the 'public turn' in the field. Many scholars (e.g., Rose, 2010) have discussed the importance of public intellectuals, or academics, who can write to and share their ideas with the public rather than sustain their conversations only within the walls of academia. The idea of the community intellectual is of one who can address the needs and purposes of the community at any point. Farmer's (2002) vision of the community intellectual gives a humanness to intellectual work, and, as Farmer says, this is a face that is able to "confront the human faces of our neighbors and citizens in a cooperative spirit of making communities better—more hopeful, more sustainable, more just places to live" (p. 210).

There has also been an interest in creating more community-based literacy projects: service learning opportunities connected to composition coursework (Mathieu, 2005; Mikolchak, 2014), and community-based writing projects (Goldblatt, 2007; Flower, 2008) that allow university students and faculty to engage in literacy practices within off-campus communities. Students work in the community and then use this experience as fodder for their writing. This pedagogy is undergirded by the idea that students will learn more about writing if they are writing about topics that are authentic and connected to their own experiences.

Community-based writing embedded within a composition class allows students to create meaning in public spaces and move beyond the university. They learn to converse within academic contexts but also begin to learn to be "public intellectuals" (Cushman, 1999; Mathieu, 2005; Rose, 2010). Cushman (1999) writes that "when public intellectuals not only reach outside the university, but actually *interact* with the public beyond its walls, they overcome the ivory tower isolation that marks so much current intellectual work. They create knowledge with those whom the knowledge serves" (p. 330, italics in original).

Most community-based writing encourages students to work within an experience that they may not ever incorporate into their work or life outside of school. The hope is that through such an experience, students will become more politically engaged and more community-minded. Providing such an experience is also intended to help students see their writing in a real world setting, as an authentic opportunity rather than a mere exercise within classroom walls.

CHALLENGES OF UNIVERSITY/COMMUNITY COLLABORATION

Mathieu's (2005) work raises important questions about the possibility of meaningful collaboration between universities and the *streets*. Mathieu purposely names the outreach often done between the university and the community through using the word *street* because this term signifies the places that are sites of "research, outreach, service, or local learning" beyond the university (p. xii). *Street* is also noted as a problematic term and contrasts the term *street* with *community*, noting the term *community's* resonance with a 'persuasive warmth,' and its difficulty to reenvision as "uncommunal, complex, or conflictual" (p. xii). Mathieu adopts the term *street* as a spatial metaphor for outreach and service-learning in composition studies.

While we find ourselves sympathetic and concerned with the complexity of terminology, we choose to suggest that there are possibilities for positive collaboration between universities, schools, and community-based sites. We also see education itself as a communal good, one in which there are—and should be—a variety of stakeholders. We see that the world beyond the walls of the university must be connected and engaged with issues about education, as the broader world will be where our future teachers do their work.

Yet, the university cannot reign in this larger world for its own need or use; rather, it must build relationships with the community so that these collaborations can be sustained. Mathieu (2005) describes the development of service-learning and collaborations between the university and community partners as tactical, suggesting that successful service projects do not position the university as controlling the needs of the community. Rather, a tactical approach to service in the community seeks to allow for the development and sustainability of service projects.

Logistical challenges have been documented in much of the literature surrounding the integration of service-learning into university classes, such as freshman composition (e.g., Mintz & Hesser, 1996). Mikolchak (2014) recalls that her first service-learning teaching endeavor was difficult due to the specifics and logistics of the project. Although she found an ideal site for service-learning, a shelter for battered women, she notes that it was also a place with limited access to the public, "with a strict security system and a number of other regulations that are necessitated by the very sensitive nature of the site" (2014, p. 214). Mikolchak writes that challenges included "time management, transportation, work supervision, providing lunch, and other such details" (2014, p. 215).

Our experience with integrating community fieldwork into teacher education resonates with many of these challenges. We have found that, over time, some of these obstacles turned into routines that became cemented in the course structure. In the following sections, we describe how our community fieldwork aimed to work within the confines of the university, yet provide meaningful service to people in our communities. We describe how our project emerged and how, in some ways, the university structure has helped it be sustained for over five academic years. Our goal, through the description that follows, is to provide others who teach within teacher education programs and composition programs ideas for integrating community fieldwork into these disciplines.

RESEARCH SITES

Our research originated in two different undergraduate courses in two different institutions. Green State University's (GSU) secondary English Language Arts teacher education program is housed within the state's flagship institution, a large, research-oriented university in the Midwest United States. Green State University is located in a community of 90,000 people yet is only 45 miles from Marshall City, a large metropolitan area of just over 2 million. The relative proximity of Marshall City to GSU offers teacher education students the ability to attend the state's flagship institution yet, if they wish, complete their student teaching experience in schools located in the state's largest metropolitan center.

Cedar Creek, the community surrounding GSU, is a Midwest college town. Framed by a rural landscape, Cedar Creek is often described as a liberal college town in a conservative state. Green State University is the largest public institution in the region and its total undergraduate and graduate population exceeds 25,000 students. Although Wilkerson University in Jackson City is only 30 minutes by car, GSU operates in a world of its own and the culture and community of Cedar Creek is heavily influenced by GSU. Prospective teachers at GSU who are placed in Cedar Creek for their field and student-teaching experiences believe that they will have a generally good experience and will experience mentor teachers and classrooms that are open to pedagogical innovation.

Cedar Creek is also largely a middle class and White community. According to the 2010 census, 82% of Cedar Creek's population is White. Although the White community of Cedar Creek perceives Cedar Creek as a diverse community with understanding of diverse communities, it is apparent that Cedar Creek is not racially or ethnically diverse. We note this amid a changing demographic backdrop in U.S. schools, where statistics predict a rise in the number of immigrants in the U.S., as well as an increase in the number of students of color in U.S. classrooms (Rich, 2000).

The second institution involved in our research is Wilkerson University, a midsized public institution in Jackson City. Wilkerson is a municipal university. This means that although it receives some state and private funding, much of its funding comes from a citywide tax. Because of this unique relationship with Jackson City and the city's residents, Wilkerson University has multiple community-focused programs and initiatives. The campus is situated within an urban area, and approximately 90% of Wilkerson's students come from within its home state. The student body of approximately 7,000 represents the demographics of the city itself as well as the surrounding rural areas. Several of these neighboring rural communities are home to Native American reservation land. Jackson City itself is a somewhat diverse, small midwestern city. According to the 2010 census, the population is 70% White, 12% African American, and 13% Latino. The city's Latino population is currently growing, and Wilkerson University has created several diversity initiatives to respond to this change in the university's and the city's demographics.

University Course Work

In the context of this book, the students portrayed have already determined that they want to work in education. They want to be teachers. The community fieldwork encourages them to learn through their interactions with the community, as well as through their writing about the community, what it will mean to be a teacher. The students involved in the community fieldwork initiative are developing, through their writing, what their teacher identity will be and are learning how to work closely with individual students, most of whom are classified as 'at-risk' students, and see these students in a different light before standing in front of a classroom.

As we previously mentioned, research described in this book originated in two different undergraduate courses at two different institutions. One course, *Curriculum and Instruction in Middle/Secondary English Language Arts Classrooms*, was a secondary English language arts methods class held in a School of Education (syllabus in Appendix A). The other course, *Advanced Composition—Teaching Emphasis*, was an advanced composition class designated for junior and senior education majors held within an English department (syllabus in Appendix B). Central to the study is the use of writing within the field placement experience. Because one site of the study took place within a composition class, we were also able to frame assignments and tasks through composition theory.

Curriculum and Instruction in Middle/Secondary English Language Arts Classrooms

At GSU, prospective middle and secondary English teachers enroll in a course called *Curriculum and Instruction in Middle/Secondary English Language Arts Classrooms* during the academic year prior to student teaching. When we began the project, we envisioned that, as part of the course, a service-learning experience would present beginning teachers with opportunities to tutor youth in reading and writing, better understand youth's in-school and out-of-school literacies, and provide a context for preservice teachers' ongoing identity formation.

Curriculum and Instruction in Middle/Secondary English Language Arts Classrooms is part of a teacher education program within the School of Education at GSU that is designed to educate preservice teachers to understand the context of schooling in the United States; the relationships among schools, society, and families; knowledge about curriculum and pedagogy within the field of English language arts; and knowledge about oneself as a teacher. During the first semester that we included community fieldwork within the methods course in the teacher education program at GSU, we co-taught the methods course and implemented the service-learning component with several options. Family Partnership, the program for homeless families, was one option in year one. However, Family Partnership became the sole community fieldwork partner for the methods course at GSU, and this book draws from the experiences of five cohorts of prospective teachers who participated with the Family Partnership program. These cohorts ranged from 7 to 10 students and were composed of a subset of the students enrolled in the methods class. From the beginning of the project, the community fieldwork option has been posed as a contrast to the option of a traditional, classroom field placement. Therefore, in some years, approximately half the methods class would participate in a 'traditional' field placement in an English classroom, and the other half of the students would participate in community fieldwork.

We recognize that, in making this choice to contrast community fieldwork with traditional classroom placements, we automatically set up the binary of community fieldwork/traditional classroom placements. In some ways, this goes against our aim to move beginning teachers into thinking about the value of community fieldwork as contributing to knowledge about teaching rather than contributing a contrasting knowledge about teaching to that gained within a classroom. As we move forward with the project in current and future years, we've considered having all students participate in both experiences: community fieldwork and fieldwork in English classrooms.

Logistics of Participation: Family Partnership

Prospective teachers were posed with this option early in the course. Part of their process in deliberating which field placement they elected to participate in was hearing the community outreach director from Family Partnership discuss the program. Martha Lions, the community outreach director for Family Partnership, visited the methods class early in the semester. She opened her presentation with statistics about homelessness and how the program served local families. After this, Martha passed around framed photos of families who were currently in the program or families who had recently finished the program and had moved into permanent housing. Martha always delivered a vibrant and engaging presentation and was able to prompt students to ask questions about the causes of homelessness. She showed students a short video about the history of the Family

Partnership organization, and her visit each semester prompted students to gain a perspective on homelessness in their particular community and surrounding area.

Family Partnership's day center, the site of the tutoring and teaching work that beginning teachers undertook in Years 1 through 3 of the program, was located in a nondescript residential house in the center of downtown Cedar Creek. Martha, the director of Family Partnership, let volunteers know that the day center was unmarked so as not to draw attention to the purpose of the house when the morning bus picked up children for school. Families involved in the Family Partnership program spent their days (7 a.m.–5 p.m.) at the day center and then rotated between participating congregations in the evening hours. In Cedar Creek, thirteen congregations were participants in the Family Partnership program. The congregations' role was to provide an evening meal and sleeping arrangements for the families. The role of the day center was to provide computer access and a stable place for families to reside during the daytime hours. The work that prospective teachers undertook at the day center was arranged on a Monday/Wednesday, 3:30 to 5:00 p.m., schedule. This arrangement allowed youth who were part of the Family Partnership program to arrive at the day center after school in time to meet prospective teachers for tutoring and homework help.

In years four and five of the project, the structure of when prospective teachers worked with youth at Family Partnership changed. Because of scheduling issues, Martha advised GSU students that the best time for tutoring and teaching work with youth at Family Partnership would be after the dinner hour (6:00–7:00 p.m.). Family Partnership is based on a model that works with local congregations to arrange to host the families in the program for 1 week of each quarter of the year. This meant that families ate dinner and slept overnight at local congregations and moved each Sunday to a new congregation. Prospective teachers, then, drove to local congregations and worked with youth from 7:00 to 8:30 p.m. Sometimes this change of venue caused tensions for prospective teachers who felt uncomfortable working within the confines of a place of worship. In this arrangement, several prospective teachers felt that the meeting of the spaces of home and school became more pronounced.

Opportunities for Reflection Within the Course
As with all service-learning initiatives, opportunities for reflection on the experience must be paired with the experience itself. It is important during field experiences in diverse settings to provide opportunities for reflection on new information and experiences. As Richardson (1990) notes, teacher cognitions may be influenced by experience, but that experience is educative only with time for reflection. When those experiences are in unfamiliar settings with diverse student populations, without structured reflection, prospective teachers' negative stereotypes can be reinforced rather than challenged (Causey, Thomas, & Armento, 2000).

In the first year of the project, and in subsequent years, Heidi presented the concept of service-learning to students in the methods course through a discussion of service-learning based on Flower's (2008) work. In the discussion of service-learning through this framework, Heidi emphasized the importance of pairing observation with inquiry as well as grappling with the roles of server and served. Heidi also invited a representative from GSU's Center for Service Learning to speak with the students enrolled in the course. The center was a pivotal force in identifying organizations in the community that expressed a clear need and/or desire for a relationship with the university. This, in turn, allowed for the initial relationship with Family Partnership to be fostered.

Prospective teachers reflected on their community-based experience through weekly journaling and discussions in class. As the semester drew to a close, participants took part in a group interview that Heidi conducted with them about their experience. Finally, as a culminating activity of the semester, teachers were asked to complete 'life graphs' (Burke, 2007), a visual timeline of events that detailed how their perceptions of the Family Partnership experience changed over the course of the semester.

Advanced Composition—Teaching Emphasis at Wilkerson University

Wilkerson University's education program is housed in the department of education, located within the College of Arts and Sciences. The research data from Wilkerson University come from students enrolled in a junior-level advanced composition class for education majors, titled *Advanced Composition—Teaching Emphasis*. At Wilkerson, all students are required to enroll in a freshman composition course their first year and an advanced composition course their junior or senior years. The advanced composition course that education majors take is a combination writing course and writing pedagogy course that concurrently satisfies the university writing requirement as well as the state certification requirement for literacy pedagogy instruction. The advanced composition course for education majors therefore is made up of prospective teachers within a variety of emphases. One section of *Advanced Composition—Teaching Emphasis* would typically include students from both secondary and elementary education programs as well as secondary emphases ranging from secondary English, social studies, math, physical education, science, art and music.

The class is designed so students begin to see themselves not only as strong academic writers, but also as teachers of writing. Students write daily and have four formal papers for which they write multiple drafts working within a writer's workshop format. Students are also asked to begin the process of classroom inquiry through learning and questioning educational theory within areas such as writing across the curriculum, writing as a process, writing to learn, and writing assessment. The culminating project for the course is an analytical paper in which they synthesize their community field experiences with the theories read and discussed in class.

Logistics of Participation: The Lodges and Mettle Street School

The Lodges is a community of five group homes located in a wooded area secluded right outside an urban area where Wilkerson University is located. The homes are arranged in a horseshoe with a grassy field and open activity space on the inside of the horseshoe and a gravel road encircled by a forest surrounding the outside of the horseshoe. The forest area is lush and beautiful, and there is a feeling of quiet on the grounds. The Lodges provides a unique program for children and adolescents who have been referred by the state juvenile justice system or Division of Family Services. Surrounded by nature, the Lodges works to help residents find some support and comfort in a natural setting and through the love and structure of a family-based living situation. Many of the residents have been abused, and therefore, there is a dual focus of both healing and structure within the institution. Although the forested grounds are beautiful, the houses themselves appear to be utilitarian, 1970s' split-level constructions, each with the same exact layout and floor plan. At any one time there are approximately 50 residents between the ages of 6 and 18. There are three male-only houses, and two coed. Each house has live-in houseparents who oversee the residents' schedules, schoolwork, activities, and meals. The residents themselves share rooms, bunk beds, and common spaces. There are regular tutoring sessions and free time scheduled. The Lodges is situated within a fairly affluent suburban school district. The residents ride the school buses to and from the group homes and are known as 'Lodges kids' within their middle and high schools.

Residents are placed at the Lodges for a variety of reasons. Some have been taken from their parents or have become wards of the state for other reasons. Some residents have been in juvenile detention centers, and the Lodges is identified by the court as a required 'halfway house' for them to readjust to living outside of the detention center.

At this placement, prospective teachers facilitated a Sunday afternoon creative writing workshop for any interested residents. The workshop took place during Sunday afternoon free time, so there was modest, but not overwhelming, interest. The workshop took place outside at a picnic table when the weather was nice or in the common area of one of the group homes when the weather required indoor meetings.

Working at this community field placement site allowed prospective teachers to see some fairly troubled and at-risk students outside of the classroom setting. Prospective teachers also were able to work closely with students on their writing and to create writing curriculum outside of the bounds of state, district, or school mandated requirements.

One participant, Jacob Downing, coincidentally served as a houseparent at the Lodges. With his wife alongside him in this role, Jacob's experience at this site was invaluable in helping encourage Lodges kids to participate in the creative writing group. He also helped other prospective teachers understand the context of the Lodges. The partnership with the Lodges unfortunately fell through the second semester of the research, and this is likely because Jacob was no longer employed as a houseparent there. He moved on to other work, and we lost our liaison who was able to advocate for our project among the Lodges kids and other houseparents.

The second site of our research in Jackson City took place within a writing center in an urban charter school. Placements here occurred over two semesters involving two different classes of *Advanced Composition—Teaching Emphasis* students. Mettle Street School is a charter school in a medium-sized urban school district that consists of three other, large traditional high schools. Most of the students who attend Mettle Street School have not been successful at other, traditional high schools. It is a smaller school, with only 142 students and 24 faculty and staff. The state reports that 67% of the student body is 'economically disadvantaged' and that 50% of the students come from a minority background. The school building itself is tucked away in a residential area not far from Wilkerson's campus. It was easy for prospective teachers to ride bikes or make the short drive to Mettle Street School in order to meet their field placement hours. The building is a former junior high and does appear smaller and less intimidating than the large high schools in the district. Mettle Street is only two stories high and has an outdoor schoolyard reminiscent of younger children's recess playground. Because many of Mettle Street's students transfer to the school after having been unsuccessful at the district's traditional high schools, it has a reputation in the area for being a 'tough' school with problem students. Realistically, the demographics of the school are not so different from the other high schools in the area, and faculty we spoke with at the school are frustrated at times by the school's reputation. The class sizes are small, and the faculty are given some freedoms with their curriculum that may not be as possible in the district's other traditional high schools. This made Mettle Street and its writing center a unique community field placement opportunity for Wilkerson University's students. Because Mettle Street is a school, it was 'traditional' in a way that the Lodges and Family Partnership were not. Yet, because it was known as an alternative school in the Jackson City community, and it carried this definition, it was not situated as a traditional high school like the other comprehensive high schools in the city. Furthermore, the prospective teachers who worked at Mettle Street School worked outside of a traditional classroom, and within the school's writing center where they worked one-on-one with students and their writing.

The writing center is overseen by Dr. Sally Cacho, who is also curriculum coordinator and vice principal of the school. Dr. Cacho teaches the college writing course, and students in this class serve as peer tutors in the writing center. The writing center is located in a common space between administrative offices. While students can make arrangements to have one-on-one tutoring, many students at Mettle Street utilize the writing center by dropping off a draft of their writing for tutors to read and respond to. Then, students can pick up their drafts at a later time and revise based on tutor written feedback. The prospective teachers who were placed at Mettle Street had the opportunity to practice responding to high school student writing, as they at times served as tutors, alongside the high school peer tutors. They also established working relationships with the students who worked in the writing center as tutors. They were able to, at times, work one-on-one in face-to-face tutoring sessions with students. Finally, they were able to experience a charter school and a high school writing center and how these nontraditional educational entities worked.

Opportunities for Reflection within the Course
Throughout the semester, students in Advanced Composition were assigned a journal in which they were to reflect on course readings and discussions. When participating in field placements, students were asked to summarize their work each visit to their site and to relate their experiences to what they were learning in the course. Students were told that the purpose of their community field placement was to participate in the following: to work closely with students before stepping into a student-teaching role, to begin to develop a teacher identity, to experience working with a more diverse student population, and to provide practical application of theories and ideas we discuss in class. Therefore, students were expected to focus their journal reflections upon these goals. Most students did focus on working with diverse learners and their roles as teachers (teacher identity). The journals were turned in three times during the semester, and Melanie provided inquiry-based feedback that encouraged further student reflection. On the days when journals were due, students were also asked to spend class time in small groups sharing and discussing their field placement experiences.

Toward the end of the semester, students were assigned a 'life map' (similar to the "life graph" [Burke, 2007] that GSU students completed) in which they provided a reflective timeline of their work at the field placement. This life map served as a tool for reflection and as a prewriting exercise before students drafted their final papers. This final paper assignment asked students to reflect on and analyze experiences in their site. Students were given the following questions to help brainstorm a direction for their final papers, but the main goal was to bridge the theory they had learned in the course with the experiential learning of their community field placement work:

- How does what you experienced connect to, contrast with, clarify, or complicate the things we have read and discussed in class?
- How does theory hold up with real, live students?

- How did you experience the role of tutor or teacher and how did this experience compare to other times you have held this role, or imagined yourself within such a role?
- What is the state of literacy instruction for the population you worked with in your site?
- What individuals and experiences stood out for you, and why do you think these in particular were memorable?
- Has any part of this experience pushed you to reconsider what it means to teach? The relationship between teacher and student? What authority you will have in your future students' literacy experiences?

Drafts of these final papers were shared in response groups, so students were able to also learn from each other's experiences. During finals week, Melanie held focus group interview sessions with students to more informally discuss their experiences and to learn from students how to make the field placements more educable experiences in the future.

OUR PROJECT AS RESEARCH

Our accounts of the prospective teachers we feature in this book are embedded within a 5-year project that investigated the integration of community-based fieldwork in teacher education and composition studies. Following others (e.g., Moore, 2014; Smagorinsky, 2014), we view this teaching-focused aspect of our work as beneficial to prospective teachers, community members with whom they work, the university at large, and also to instructors such as ourselves. Yet, we also situate our work as research, and one could say that our work has both a 'practice' and a 'theory' dimension. One could also say that the 'practice' and the 'theory' dimension are one in the same as they complement each other and help articulate the goals of each. The beauty of the fields in which we work is, in part, because of the intense merging of theory and practice. We seek, however, to outline for our readers a methodological framework from which we work, as we see this as interacting closely with the theoretical platforms that inform our work.

Throughout our study, we draw upon narrative methodologies (e.g., Bruner, 2002; Clandinin & Connelly, 2000; Mishler, 1999; Reissman, 2008) as methods appropriate for investigating the tensions within and between teachers' narratives and their work in community-based field sites. We explore prospective teachers' experiences of community-based fieldwork through their stories of self, as we view these stories as important windows into understanding beginning teachers' relationships with students. Mishler (1999) notes that the stories we, as people, tell about our lives are the ways we "express, display, [and] make[s] claims for who we are—in the stories we tell and how we tell them" (pp. 19–20). Therefore, the stories that prospective teachers told us were identity claims about who they were during the time they worked in community-based sites. We feature prospective teachers' stories, as told to us within reflective journals, interviews, life graphs, and other artifacts that were part of our courses. Throughout the community-based experience, we prompted students to focus on the self as a way to situate teacher identity as a gradual formation of 'becoming' (Gomez, Black, & Allen, 2007).

Because we agree that research interviews are politically mediated events (Flannery, 2008), we see that constructing stories for analysis from interview transcripts involves difficult interpretive decisions (Reissman, 2008, p. 42). We use the term *narrative* interchangeably with *story* and distinguish between 'seeing data as story' (narrative analysis), which can be understood as a situated interpretation of events, and 'seeing stories in data' (analysis of narratives; Clandinin & Connelly, 2000). Throughout the book, we employ analysis of narratives co-constructed through individual and group interviews, seminar meetings, or what we collectively view as 'storytelling events.'

We also recognized narratives within the texts that prospective teachers produced. Whether these texts were reflective journal entries or final papers, we sought to uncover narratives within prospective teachers' texts. We consider narratives to contain the following textual elements: (a) temporal sequencing of remembered events, (b) narrative point of view (the 'I' or 'we' of the story; the teller), (c) setting, (d) characters (who may be portrayed as protagonists/antagonists in relation to the teller), (e) plot (sequencing of events, but also a complication in the action), (f) stance toward the subject (how the teller feels about the subject), and (g) theme. At times, we selected titles for the narratives that come from the narratives themselves and represent the theme under discussion. In coding for narrative themes, we attended to our perceptions of the 'what' (content) as well as the 'how,' 'to whom,' or 'for what purposes' of the storytelling event (Reissman, 2008, pp. 53–54), based on the research goals and our own situated interpretations. We pursued a case-centered analysis, with the case being a community fieldwork project over a period of 5 years, with the aim of theorizing from the case (Stake, 1995).

It was through the interplay of undertaking both an inductive and deductive coding process (Strauss & Corbin, 1998) that central themes were illuminated with regard to prospective teachers' work in community field sites. The central themes spoke to ideas of the role of teacher and student, as well as the place of pedagogy and curriculum in the work that prospective teachers undertook. Most importantly, the themes reiterated to us that teachers were theorizing agents (Britzman, 1991) who enact theories of teaching and learning in their everyday practice. They are bodies through whom theory and practice were united, and a theory and practice unification was born through teachers' lived experience. Through our emphasis on teachers' narratives, we emphasize the importance of Clandinin's (1985) "personal practical knowledge" in the everyday experiences of teachers:

Personal practical knowledge is knowledge which is imbued with all the experiences that make up a person's being. Its meaning is derived from, and understood in terms of, a person's experimental history, both professional and personal. (p. 361)

Emphasizing personal practical knowledge through teachers' narratives sheds light on the dilemmas that arise from social practice, and teachers are presented as complex beings who are trying to make sense of their teaching work.

PORTRAITS OF PROSPECTIVE TEACHERS AND COMMUNITY CONTEXTS

As mentioned, our work was situated in two university contexts as well as in three community-based sites. In the following section, we provide an overview of these community sites and the prospective teachers who we focus on throughout the book. In the following we have included a chart (Table 1.1) to provide a summary of the participants, their placements, and their participation in the study.[1]

Family Partnership for Homeless Families and Research on Homelessness

To contextualize the rise in homelessness in the United States, it can be noted that "on a single night in January 2013, there were 610, 042 people experiencing homelessness in the United States" (U.S. Department of Housing and Urban Development's [HUD] 2013). HUD also states that, in 2013, nearly 36% of people experiencing homelessness were families, with families constituting 50% of all homeless people living in sheltered locations. Homelessness among families rose significantly after the great recession of 2008, and in 2009, the United States Conference of Mayors (2009) reported that U.S. cities saw "the sharpest increase in the demand for hunger assistance since 1991" (p. 1) and saw an increase in homeless families. Two years later, the United States Conference of Mayors (2011, p. 3) reported that U.S. cities saw an average of a 6 % increase in homelessness and a 16 % increase among families with children experiencing homelessness. Together, these statistics suggest a national portrait where family homelessness has increased. Homelessness among youth has also risen since 2008, and it is now estimated that approximately 550,000 unaccompanied, single youth and young adults up to age 24 who experience a homelessness episode of longer than 1 week (National Alliance to End Homelessness, 2014). Homelessness is a difficult issue to document, as counting individuals who constitute the homeless population in the United States demands accounting for both sheltered and unsheltered individuals. An accurate portrait of

34 *Community Fieldwork in Teacher Education*

Table 1.1 Participants, institutions, community sites, placement in book, and year of participation in study.

	Green State	Wilkerson University			
	Family			Included in	
Participant	Partership	Lodges	Mettle St.	Chapter	Year of Study
Ming	X			2, 6	1
Sarah	X			2	1
Tara	X			2	1
Rebecca	X			2, 6	1
Henry	X			4, 6	3
Anne	X			2, 4	4
Geneen		X		5, 6	4
Jacob		X		5	4
Sharon		X		5	4
Rhonda			X	3	5
Kelly			X	3	5
Katherine			X	3	5

the homeless population also does not typically account for families and individuals who have 'doubled up,' or taken shelter with relatives or other families.

Most typically, the homeless youth population has been represented as residing in the inner-city with single-parent-(female-)headed families. Yet, the face of homelessness has changed considerably in the past few years, and continues to change. It is now estimated that 14 out of every 10,000 people are "rural" or "suburban" homeless (as compared to 29 out of every 10,000 people who are "urban" homeless; National Alliance to End Homelessness, 2014). Similar structural issues that are linked to urban homelessness (e.g., lack of affordable housing) are also linked to rural/suburban homelessness. One significant difference that has been noted between urban and rural/suburban homelessness is the lack of resource and access to services in rural areas (National Alliance to End Homelessness, 2014). Cedar Creek adopted the Family Partnership model in 2008, and, in 2011, served 18 families, the most served in 1 year in the Cedar Creek community (Family Promise of Lawrence, n.d.).

Family Partnership is a national organization, and currently has affiliates in 41 states. The organization works with a small group of families over the course of a period of 3 to 4 months, providing families with a comprehensive approach to sustaining independence (Family Promise, n.d.). Through specific features of the program, including an Interfaith Hospitality Network and Family Mentorship, Family Partnership is built around a premise that supporting and nurturing families through the challenging circumstance of homelessness will foster lasting independence. In Cedar Creek, Family Partnership is one of several programs serving homeless individuals, although it is the only program that specifically works with families. In fact, in the other shelters available within the Cedar Creek locale, sleeping arrangements for individuals over the age of 12 are strictly by gender. In this regard, families are sometimes divided when residing at shelters.

In the United States, homeless children have been labeled as being the most invisible others in school, whose position of marginality has been reinforced by a blaming the victim mentality and a society that remains class-stratified (Diver-Stamnes, 1995). Barton (1998) notes that

> the transient lifestyle led by homeless children and their families engenders feelings of not belonging . . . this is often due to the fact that homeless families lack the resources needed to provide their children with educational daycare, private education and tutoring, and private instruction in sports and the fine arts. These kind of inequalities lead homeless children to feel that their own life experiences are somehow inferior to those of normal children. (p. 381)

As a result, scholarship (e.g., McChesney, 1993; Quint, 1994) has noted that homeless children tend to experience more depression and feelings of mental anguish than children who do not experience homelessness in their childhood.

Prospective Teachers Who Worked at Family Partnership

This book draws on particular cases of beginning teachers' work at Family Partnership throughout the 5 years of our project; some teachers were individuals who felt highly committed to the Family Partnership program and stayed on as volunteers with the program for months after the semester ended. Other teachers, once beginning their work with youth, opted to complete the required hours as quickly as possible, deeming that they were not doing 'real' teaching work when tutoring youth in the program. Here, we introduce the prospective teachers that our book highlights.

Ming Nguyen, Sarah Emerson, Tara Stance, and Rebecca Avery
Ming Nguyen, a student in her early 20s, was one of two non-White students in her cohort of English language arts education majors. Unlike many of the students enrolled in the teacher preparation program at Green State University, Ming, a self-identified Chinese American student, lived with her extended family in a community 40 miles from the university. This community, a suburb of Marshall City, afforded more diversity as well as more employment opportunities for others in Ming's family. Most days, Ming took

the university bus back and forth from Marshall City to Cedar Creek. Ming struggled in many of her English content area courses, as well as in courses that required her to lead presentations or discussions with large groups of students. Ming expressed her discomfort with taking such roles in the classroom with me. During the course of the year of the study, other instructors in the School of Education asked me about my perceptions of Ming's ability to be a future classroom teacher. Ming often appeared to be quite nervous in front of her college-age peers and this may have prompted instructors to express concern about her ability to lead a classroom of adolescents.

Sarah Emerson, a student in her early 20s and a native of the state in which GSU was located, was representative of the majority of Green State University's teacher candidates in several ways. Sarah was White, middle class, and well prepared in her content area, English, and her plans for after her graduation from the teacher education program included residing within a 1-hour driving proximity to both GSU and the Marshall City metropolitan area. Sarah intended to continue pursuing graduate course work that would lead to the completion of her master's degree while beginning her first teaching position the year following the completion of the teacher education program. Sarah's intent was to teach middle or high school English, and she was, at the time of the study, completing an endorsement in TESOL (Teaching English to speakers of other languages). Sarah saw preparation for teaching diverse students through a lens that emphasized the short-term possibilities such training might have on her career as a teacher.

Tara Stance, a student in her early twenties, was an out-of-state student from a neighboring state. Tara is White and was considering teaching in an international context after the completion of the teacher education program at GSU. Tara cited her semester-long study abroad experience to Ireland as a catalyst for this interest. Tara was a confident young woman who looked favorably on new experiences. She was the first student to express interest in working with homeless youth. This, to us, demonstrated a disposition to work with new cultures and people. Tara, a leader among her peers, was optimistic about the confronting any challenges she might face.

Rebecca Avery, a White student in her early 20s, was overt about her commitment and adherence to teaching practices framed by tenets of social justice. She specifically cited the book *Reading, Writing, and Rising Up: Teaching About Social Justice and the Power of the Written Word* by Linda Christensen (2000) as espousing an ideology she wished to embrace in her teaching. Rebecca was a student attending GSU from a neighboring state and intended to secure a teaching position in her home state on completion of the teacher education program. Rebecca and Tara tended to pair up for activities in class, and signed up to participate at Family Partnership during the same time frame each week.

Henry Taylor and Anne Chisholm
Henry Taylor was a white student in his early 20s. He grew up in Marshall City and attended a diverse school for most of his K–12 schooling

experience; however, during his high school years, his family moved to the most affluent suburb of Marshall City, a city called Rose Park. In discussions with Henry, he repeatedly contrasted his experience in Marshall City schools with his experience in the wealthy suburb of Rose Park. He said, "I relate to the kids in Marshall City. I am one of them. I know what it is like to not be perceived of as the kid with advantages. And, when you are not the kid with advantages, people tend to write you off. I don't think any of my former teachers thought I'd make it to GSU." Henry was a tenacious individual. Coincidentally, Henry was placed for his student teaching experience in a school in Rose Park. The teacher who Henry was placed with was skeptical of Henry's innovative teaching style and his awareness of and comradery with students who were deemed 'nonmainstream.' Henry clashed with his mentor teacher and eventually was placed in another school. GSU had determined that Henry was not at fault in these altercations; rather, he was the product of overt discrimination. Henry was the student that we developed a long-term relationship with and had the most contact with years after he finished the English education program. This book draws from conversations with Henry that extend past his time working with youth at Family Partnership.

Anne Chisholm grew up in the community of Cedar Creek and graduated from high school in the late 1980s. Anne was a nontraditional student who had returned to GSU in her late 30s to pursue obtaining her teaching license. Now in her early 40s, Anne expressed resonance with the kind of diversity she viewed as present within the community. Although she described it as mainly "economic diversity," she noted that she was not surprised that homeless families resided in Cedar Creek, but noted that the families were likely more 'hidden' in a college town than they might be in other communities. Because Anne attended one of the city's local high schools over two decades ago, she expressed comfort and awareness with the resources available in the community. For example, Anne was aware that Cedar Creek had a homeless shelter and a women's shelter in addition to the Family Partnership program. Particularly, she noted that because Cedar Creek was a midsized college town, most people in the state had always perceived the community as more expensive, more educated, and more competitive in terms of job prospects than other towns throughout the state. This, in turn, had perpetuated a notion that issues such as homelessness were not present or critical in Cedar Creek. Anne's life experiences had helped her be open to the possibility of learning more about her community, particularly the Family Partnership organization.

The Lodges and Research on the Education of Foster Children

Research has provided powerful explanations as to why foster children require special treatment within an educational setting. Not only are these students at-risk of school failure (Blome, 1997; Zetlin, MacLeod, & Kimm, 2012), but they are also at-risk of other societal dangers when they become emancipated. Herrington, Kidd-Herrington, and Kritsonis (2006) estimate that within a year of emancipation, one third of these individuals will have "an encounter with the law" (p. 2), 40% will face homelessness, 40% of the females will become pregnant, and more than half will be without employment. School is one institution that is positioned to make an impact on these individuals, but often their vulnerabilities are unknown or misunderstood. Because of the instability of these students' early lives, there is more uncertainty, distrust, trauma, rejection, and sorrow. These students have difficulties keeping up in school because they are coping with many emotional issues, and they have trouble connecting with other students and teachers because of past traumas and rejections. The presence of foster children in our schools calls for focused intervention (Herrington et al., 2006). However, few teachers are supported, notified, or trained to work with these youth (Zetlin et al., 2010). As more and more of these students enter our schools, we must find ways to better prepare teachers to deal with the special needs of these students.

The Lodges provides a space where prospective teachers can work closely with foster children and develop relationships with them. We hope this will be a start to beginning teachers' understanding of this vulnerable and misunderstood group of students.

Prospective Teachers Who Worked at the Lodges

We feature three beginning teachers who worked at the Lodges. One of these individuals, Jacob Downing, also was a houseparent at the Lodges during his time of participation in our study. We recognize how Jacob's dual role as both student at Wilkerson University and houseparent at the Lodges facilitated a deeper relationship with the Lodges during this particular semester.

Geneen Sandovar, Jacob Downing, and Sharon Burns

Geneen Sandovar, a student in her early 20s, was from a small midwestern town and was majoring in secondary social studies education. Geneen had a young 2-year-old daughter, and her husband was serving in the military. She was an enthusiastic student who embraced the opportunity of working with students at the Lodges. Following the semester in which she worked at the Lodges, she stopped by Melanie's office and shared her idea for working on a grant to purchase e-notebooks for Lodges students because she was concerned that the students lacked access to digital resources.

Jacob Downing was in his early 30s, and throughout the project, he served as a valuable liaison for the Lodges. Jacob was a serious and pragmatic student who had previously earned a business degree. After being laid off, he decided to follow what he described as his calling to work with kids and become a teacher. At the time of the study he was a secondary social studies major. He and his wife were houseparents at the Lodges and were expecting their first child. Jacob worked hard during the semester to 'work ahead' on many assignments because his baby was due during the last few weeks of the semester. Although he found his work at the Lodges fulfilling, he and his wife resigned from their jobs as houseparents, leaving after the current school year because they had a child of their own. Because of his work as houseparent, Jacob educated his classmates as well as his instructor on the best ways to set up the fieldwork at the Lodges. His perspective was indispensable throughout the course of the semester's work.

Sharon Burns, a secondary math major who was in her early 20s, was a student who excelled in her course work. She worked in the campus learning center as a peer tutor in math, so she was already comfortable teaching and tutoring in a one-on-one setting. At graduation, she earned a prestigious award from the College of Arts and Sciences given to one exceptional graduate each semester, and part of her application for the award included her work at the Lodges. She was president of the university's honor society and participated in several extracurricular service projects at the university. Sharon embraced the work she did at the Lodges and in many ways modeled the experience that we hope to provide through community fieldwork.

Mettle Street School and High School Writing Centers as Nontraditional School Spaces

Writing centers have been in existence for many years at the post-secondary level, but in the last decade there has been a new interest in high school writing centers (Childers, Fels, & Jordan, 2004; Fels & Wells, 2011; Kent, 2006). In the realm of writing center theory, writing centers are often envisioned as an out-of-school space even though they exist within college campuses or actual secondary school buildings. In his seminal work, *The Idea of a Writing Center*, Stephen North (1984) began the discussion that continues today about writing center theory and how it can be seen as a nontraditional school space. The space of the writing center also facilitates a nonauthoritarian relationship between tutor and tutee, where

> any plan of action the tutor follows is going to be student-centered in the strictest sense of that term. That is, it will not derive from a generalized model of composing, or be based on where the student ought to be because she is a freshman or sophomore, but will begin from where the student is, and move where the student moves. (North, 1984, p. 439)

The writing center is a space that is outside of teachers' authority in many ways, freeing students to take more control over their writing. With peer tutoring and an absence of authoritarian, traditional instruction, the writing center becomes a community space among students and peer tutors. We also see writing as a space for peer feedback, rather than a space solely intended for teacher evaluation.

Prospective Teachers Who Worked at Mettle Street School

Finally, in the next section, we describe the three participants in our book who worked at the writing center at Mettle Street School. Through their work in the writing center space, these three individuals began to question the teacher–student relationship and used writing as a space within their own emerging teaching practice to challenge long-held assumptions about teaching and learning.

Rhonda Jackson, Kelly Leponte, and Katherine Sternmeister

Rhonda Jackson was an elementary education student from a small town. She saw her identity as being a part of that small town, and she planned to return to her own elementary school as a teacher after graduation. As she reflected on her work at Mettle Street School she began to see that she could also be a part of a very different school setting. Rhonda was a serious student who had little patience when one of her classmates complained or diverted classroom discussions in nonproductive ways. She would roll her eyes and patiently wait for the teacher to get us all back on track.

Kelly Laponte, a quiet and easygoing student, found confidence as she worked with the students at Mettle Street School. As she looked back at her experiences, Kelly was positive and enthusiastic. She wore a small diamond nose ring and was always smiling and making eye contact with whomever she engaged. In many ways, Kelly was representative of many students at Wilkerson University, in that she grew up not far from the campus, was in her early 20s, and is White and middle class. She was studious and reserved, portraying a stereotypical rural, midwestern work ethic.

Another prospective teacher, Katherine Strenmeister, was a nontraditional student in her thirties who was majoring in secondary math education. Throughout the semester, she became concerned for the students she came in contact with, and over time, she was able to see how her presence, even for a short period, made a difference in their writing and confidence. She was petite and soft-spoken, and an excellent, detail-oriented student who questioned in careful yet strong ways. She was regularly the first student to arrive for class, and would occasionally wait after class until her classmates had gone in order to talk with the professor, quietly clarifying assignment details.

LOOKING AHEAD: PROSPECTIVE TEACHERS AS BOUNDARY SPANNERS

As instructors, we developed relationships with the prospective teachers we feature. Over time, we began to see changes in how they thought about and enacted new relationships between teacher and students. We saw an emergence of what some scholars, including Howey and Zimpher (2006), have viewed as alternative conceptualizations of the work of teachers. Howey and Zimpher use the term *boundary spanners* to refer to individuals who "[blur] the lines of responsibility between traditionally assumed by those in universities, schools, and school districts" (2006, p. 5). As we saw the prospective teachers with whom we worked challenge the roles in which they were being socialized into, we sought to study how they negotiated these roles. We found that beginning with the question, "What does it mean to be a teacher?" helped us see the process of teacher identity unfold for our students. In the next four chapters, we explore the how the process of questioning one's role of 'teacher' drew our students into the community experience, and into a deeper reflection on the relationship between self/other, or teacher/student. This work is the foundation of the work of 'boundary spanners,' as we see a parallel between teachers' identity formation and the work that composers do as they participate in the act of writing. As beginning teachers, they must learn to assemble and mimic the work of being a teacher without yet knowing what fully what that work is. As Bartholomae (1986) notes, through writing, students can invent a context as they learn the context. Likewise, beginning teachers can invent themselves as boundary spanners as they learn what the act of teaching entails; they can challenge and invent as they learn the rules of the discourse.

In the following chapter, we engage in further discussion of the role of teacher, students, and pedagogy. We then turn to explore more specific examples in the chapters that follow, seeking to outline the processes by which prospective teachers learned about their role as teachers and the act of teaching through community fieldwork. In the closing chapter, we build an explicit discussion of the practical and future applications of our work and how these ideas can be integrated into already existing education and writing programs.

NOTE

1 To protect the confidentiality of participants in the study, all names are pseudonyms.

REFERENCES

Anderson, J., & Erickson, J. (2003). Service-learning in preservice teacher education *Academic Exchange Quarterly, 7*(2), 111–115.

Bacon, N. (1997). Community service writing: Problems, challenges, questions. In L. Adler-Kassner, R. Crooks, & A. Watters (Eds.), *Writing the community: Concepts and models for service learning in composition* (pp. 39–55). Washington, DC: American Association for Higher Education.

Bartholomae, D. (1986). *Inventing the university*. New York, NY: Guilford.

Barton, A. C. (1998). Teaching science with homeless children: Pedagogy, representation, and identity. *Journal of Research in Science Teaching, 35*(4), 379–394. doi:10.1002/(SICI)1098-2736(199804)35:4<379::AID-TEA8>3.0CO;2-N

Bizzell, P. (1994). "Contact zones" and English studies. *College English, 56*(2), 163–169.

Blome, W. W. (1997). What happens to foster kids: Educational experiences of a random sample of foster care youth and a matched group of non-foster care youth. *Child and Adolescent Social Work Journal, 14*(1), 41–53. Retrieved from http://link.springer.com/article/10.1023/A:1024592813809

Boyle-Baise, M. (2002). *Multicultural service learning.* New York, NY: Teachers College Press.

Britzman, D. P. (1991). *Practice makes practice: A critical study of learning to teach.* Albany: State University of New York Press.

Bruffee, K. A. (1984). Collaborative learning and the "conversation of mankind." *College English, 46*(7), 635–652. Retrieved from www.jstor.org/stable/376924

Bruner, J. (2002). Narratives of human plight: A conversation with Jerome Bruner. In R. Charon & M. Montello (Eds.), *Stories matter: The role of narrative in medical ethics* (pp. 3–9). New York, NY: Routledge.

Burke, J. (2007). *The English teacher's companion* (3rd ed.). Portsmouth, NH: Heinemann.

Carter-Andrews, D. J. (2009). "The hardest thing to turn from": The effects of service-learning on preparing urban educators. *Equity & Excellence in Education, 42*(2), 272–293. doi:10.1080/10665680903060261

Causey, V., Thomas, C., & Armento, B. (2000). Cultural diversity is basically a foreign term to me: the challenges of diversity for preservice teacher education. *Teaching and Teacher Education, 16,* 33–45. doi:10.1016/S0742-051X(99)00039-6

Childers, P. B., Fels, D., & Jordan, J. (2004). The secondary school writing center: A place to build confident, competent writers. *Praxis: A Writing Center Journal, 2*(1). Retrieved from http://projects.uwc.utexas.edu/praxis/?q=node/91

Christensen, L. (2000). *Reading, writing, and rising up: Teaching about social justice and the power of the written word.* Milwaukee, WI: Rethinking Schools.

Clandinin, D. J. (1985). Personal practical knowledge: A study of teacher's classroom images. *Curriculum Inquiry, 15,* 361–385. Retrieved from www.jstor.org/stable/1179683

Coffey, H. (2010). "*They* taught *me*": The benefits of early community-based field experiences in teacher education. *Teaching and Teacher Education, 26,* 335–342. doi:10.1016/j.tate.2009.09.014

Cuban, L. (1993). *How teachers taught: Constancy and change in American classrooms, 1890–1990.* New York, NY: Teachers College Press.

Cushman, E. (1999). The public intellectual, service learning, and activist research. *College English, 61*(3), 328–336. Retrieved from www.jstor.org.www2.lib.ku.edu/stable/379072

Darling-Hammond, L. (2006). *Powerful teacher education.* San Francisco, CA: Jossey-Bass.

Diver-Stamnes, A. C. (1995). *Lives in the balance: Youth, poverty, and education in Watts.* Albany: State University of New York Press.

Eyler, J., & Giles, D. E. (1999). *Where's the learning in service-learning?* San Francisco, CA: Jossey-Bass.

Family Promise. (n.d.). About us. Retrieved from www.familypromise.org/About-Us

Family Promise of Lawrence. (n.d.). History timeline. Retrieved from http://lawrencefamilypromise.org/history-timeline/

Farmer, F. (2002). Review: Community Intellectuals. *College English, 65*(2), 202–210.

Fels, D., & Wells, J. (2011). *The successful high school writing center: Building the best program with your students*. New York, NY: Teachers College Press.

Feiman-Nemser, S. & Buchmann, M. (1987). When is student teaching teacher education? *Teaching and Teacher Education, 3*(4), 255–273.

Feinstein, S. (2005). *The spirit of generosity: Service learning in a pre-service teacher education program*. Retrieved from ERIC database. (ED490389)

Flannery, M. (2008). "She discriminated against her own race": Voicing and identity in a story of discrimination. *Narrative Inquiry, 18*(1), 118–130.

Flower, L. (1997). Partners in inquiry: A logic for community outreach. In L. Adler-Kassner, R. Crooks, & A. Watters (Eds.), *Writing the community: Concepts and models for service-learning in composition* (pp. 95–117). Washington, DC: American Association for Higher Education Press.

Flower, L. (2002). Intercultural inquiry and the transformation of service. *College English, 65*(2), 181–201. doi:10.2307/3250762

Flower, L. (2008). *Community literacy and the rhetoric of public engagement*. Carbondale: Southern Illinois Press.

Gere, A.R. (1994). Kitchen tables and rented rooms: The extracurriculum of composition. *College Composition and Communication, 45*(1), 75–92. doi:10.2307/358588

Goldblatt, E. (2007). *Because we live here: Sponsoring literacy beyond the college curriculum*. Cresskill, NJ: Hampton Press.

Gomez, M.L., Black, R.W., & Allen, A. (2007). "Becoming" a teacher. *Teachers College Record, 109*(9), 2107–2135. Retrieved from www.tcrecord.org.www2.lib.ku.edu/library/Issue.asp?volyear=2007&number=9&volume=109

Herrington, D.E., Kidd-Herrington, K., & Kritsonis, M.A. (2006). Coming to Terms with No Child Left Behind: Learning to teach the invisible children. *National Forum of Special Education Journal, 18*(1), 1–7.

Howey, K., & Zimpher, N. (Eds.). (2006). *Boundary spanners*. Washington, DC: American Association of State Colleges and Universities.

Kaufman, J.E. (2004). Language, inquiry, and the heart of learning: Reflections in an English methods course. *English Education, 36*(3), 174–191. Retrieved from www.jstor.org.www2.lib.ku.edu/stable/40173092

Kent, R. (2006). *A Guide to Creating Student-staffed Writing Centers, Grades 6–12*. New York, NY: Peter Lang.

Kinloch, V., & Smagorinsky, P. (2014). *Service-learning in literacy education: Possibilities for teaching and learning*. Charlotte, NC: Information Age Publishing.

Ladson-Billings, G. (2001). *Crossing over to Canaan: The journey of new teachers in diverse classrooms*. San Francisco, CA: Jossey-Bass.

Lortie, D. (1975). *Schoolteacher: A sociological study*. Chicago, IL: University of Chicago Press.

Mathieu, P. (2005). *Tactics of hope: The public turn in English composition*. Portsmouth, NH: Boynton/Cook.

McChesney, K. (1993). Homeless families since 1980. *Education and Urban Society, 25*, 361–379.

Mertz, J.S., Jr., & Schroerlucke, K. (1998). *Technology consulting in the community* (Carnegie Mellon Center for University Outreach Reports). Retrieved from www.cmu.edu/outreach/csinc

Mikolchak, M. (2014). Service-learning in English comp. In V. Kinloch & P. Smagorinsky (Eds.), *Service-learning in literacy education: Possibilities for teaching and learning* (pp. 211–224). Charlotte, NC: Information Age Publishing.

Mintz, S., & Hesser, G. (1996). Principles of good practice in service-learning. In B. Jacoby & Associates, *Service-learning in higher education* (pp. 26–52). San Francisco, CA: Jossey-Bass.

Mishler, E. (1999). *Storylines: Craftartists' narratives of identity.* Cambridge, MA: Harvard University Press.

Moore, M. (2014). Service-learning and the fields-based literacy methods course. In V. Kinloch & P. Smagorinsky (Eds.), *Service-learning in literacy education: Possibilities for teaching and learning* (pp. 105–115). Charlotte, NC: Information Age Publishing.

National Alliance to End Homelessness. (2014). Snapshot of homelessness. Retrieved from www.endhomelessness.org/pages/snapshot_of_homelessness

North, S. M. (1984). The idea of a writing center. *College English, 46*(5), 433–446.

Portes, P. R., & Smagorinsky, P. (2010). Static structures, changing demographics: Educating teachers for shifting populations in stable school. *English Education, 42*(3), 236–247.

Quint, S. (1994). *Schooling homeless children: A working model for America's public schools.* New York, NY: Teachers College Press.

Reissman, C. K. (2008). *Narrative methods for human sciences.* Thousand Oaks, CA: Sage.

Rich, M. F. (2000). America's diversity and growth: Signposts for the 21st century. *Population Bulletin, 55*(2), 1–43. doi:10.1598/RRQ.41.2.3

Richardson, V. (1990). Significant and worthwhile change in teaching practice. *Educational Researcher, 19*(7), 10–18.

Rogers, T., Marshall, E., & Tyson, C. (2006). Dialogic narratives of literacy, teaching, and schooling: Preparing literacy teachers for diverse settings. *Reading Research Quarterly, 41*(2), 202–224.

Rose, M. (2010). Opinion: Writing for the public. *College English, 72*(3), 284–292. doi:198.252.15.206

Shulman, L. (2005). Pedagogies of uncertainty. *Liberal Education, 91*(2), 18–25. Retrieved from http://search.proquest.com.www2.lib.ku.edu/docview/209812613/abstract?accountid=14556

Schutz, A., & Gere, A.R. (1998). Service learning and English studies: Rethinking "public" service. *College English, 60*(2), 129–149. doi:10.2307/378323

Schön, D. (1987). *Educating the reflective practitioner.* San Francisco, CA: Jossey-Bass.

Shor, I. (1996). *When students have power: Negotiating authority in a critical pedagogy.* Chicago, IL: University of Chicago Press.

Shrofel, S. (1991). Developing writing teachers. *English Education, 23*(3), 160–177. Retrieved from www.jstor.org/stable/40172760

Sleeter, C. (2008). Equity, democracy, and neoliberal assaults on teacher education. *Teaching and Teacher Education, 24*(8), 1947–1957. doi:10.1016/j.tate.2008.04.003

Smagorinsky, P. (2014). Service-learning in an alternative school as mediated through book club discussions. In V. Kinloch & P. Smagorinsky (Eds.), *Service-learning in literacy education: Possibilities for teaching and learning* (pp. 85–103). Charlotte, NC: Information Age Publishing.

Stake, R. (1995). *The art of case study research.* Thousand Oaks, CA: Sage.

Strauss, A. & Corbin, J. (1998). *Basics of qualitative research: Techniques and procedures for developing grounded theory* (2nd ed.). London, England: Sage.

The United States Conference of Mayors. (2011). *Hunger and homelessness survey: A status report of hunger and homelessness in America's cities.* Retrieved from http://usmayors.org/pressreleases/uploads/2011-hhreport.pdf

U.S. Office of Housing and Urban Development. (2013, June). *The 2013 annual homeless assessment report.* Washington, DC: HUD Office of Community Planning and Development. Retrieved from https://www.hudexchange.info/resources/documents/ahar-2013-part1.pdf

Zeichner, K. (2010). Rethinking the connections between campus courses and field experiences in college- and university-based teacher education. *Journal of Teacher Education, 61*(1–2), 89–99. doi:10.1177/0022487109347671

Zetlin, A., MacLeod, E., & Kimm, C. (2012). Beginning teacher challenges instructing students who are in foster care. *Remedial and Special Education, 33*(1), 4–13. doi:10.1177/0741932510362506

Zlotkowski, E. (1996). A new voice at the table? Linking service-learning and the academy. *Change, 28*(1), 21–27. doi:10.1080/00091383.1996.10544252

2 Composing Teachers, Teachable Students, and Teachable Spaces

Alongside other scholars who study identity, particularly teacher identity (e.g., Alsup, 2006; Britzman, 1991; Danielwicz, 2001; Zembylas, 2003), we understand teachers and future teachers as produced as *"particular* types of professionals" (Zembylas, 2003, p. 124, italics in the original) that form their teacher identity as a project of continuous becoming (Gomez, Black, & Allen, 2007) over time. Furthermore, teachers mediate their stories of self with the cultural and institutional expectations of what it means to be a teacher.

Identity, as a component of teachers' development, has been theorized as fluid and complex, as well as inherently social (Alsup, 2006; Bucholtz & Hall, 2005). Alsup (2006) defines identity as "general sense of selfhood or understanding of the self[,] a set of distinguishing characteristics of an individual that emerge from this sense of selfhood" (p. 205). Borrowing the concept of borderlands from Anzaldua (2007), Alsup emphasizes the fluidity of teacher identity through the concept of borderland discourse (2006, p. 5) and describes borderland discourse as a "transformative type of teacher identity discourse" which is "inclusive of the intellectual, corporeal, and the affective aspects of human selfhood" (2006, p. 6). Using Gee's (1999) theory of Discourse, in which Discourses act as " 'identity kits' and come complete with the appropriate costume and instructions on how to act, talk, and often write, so as to take on a particular role that others will recognize" (Gee, 2001, p. 526), Alsup positions teacher identity as a construct linked with larger disciplinary or social/ cultural discourses that affect people.

We recognize that teachers' identities are shaped by social systems of classification—what Gee (1999) would refer to as Discourses[1]—and use this as a premise from which to see how teachers perform identity. Moya (2006) asserts that social structures impose on one's social identity, thereby coming together in context-specific ways that have bearing on how one is treated by others. Social identities are often based on stereotypical notions and these notions can prevent others from seeing the self as one wants to be seen. The "visible self" (Alcoff, 2006) that is seen by others has an impact on one's lived experience; the visible self can include the color of one's skin, as well as other embodied features. Gee's (1999, 2001) work consistently stresses the agentive part of identity work in that we see how individuals shape and reshape Discourses at the same time that they participate in them. Discourses, rather than being solidified, are permeable constructs and individuals reshape them at the same time as they participate within them.

We are interested in the agentive self and in what it means for teachers to shape the Discourses in which they participate. How can we account for the participation of the agentive self within Discourse? We look to the work of philosopher Mikhail Bakhtin to assist us in illuminating teachers' active participation in shaping who they become as teachers.

COMPOSING TEACHERS: A BAKHTINIAN VIEW OF IDENTITY

Through the understanding of identity that we have just outlined, we see that teachers' identities can become texts in which teachers author themselves. Others, then, are positioned as readers of these texts. Through such a view, one's self, or identity, does not exist as an individually created entity but, rather, is formed within a nexus of social relationships and affiliations. Moreover, one's identity, because of being situated within a social context, is subject to change over time. As contexts and affiliations change, so does one's identity. Through dynamic interplay in discursive processes, identity is, as Jenkins (1996) notes, the direct result of the "dialectical interplay of processes of internal and external definition" (p. 25). In this way, identity has an individual aspect—an aspect that emphasizes how an individual internally and externally creates identity.

Yet, we have found that teacher identity must be theorized in a reciprocal relationship to others' identities, as teachers form their narratives of self as responses, in part, to the students they teach, the administrators with whom they work with, and the university-based faculty responsible for teacher training, among others. Identity, then, has to do with the social, or with groups other than oneself. When we speak of the 'self,' it is often our individual constitution, not just of how we see the self but also of how we are recognized as such. We must account for both dimensions of identity, and see Bakhtin's (1990) understanding of the relationship between self and other as providing a framework for understanding the impetus for teachers' questioning of self in relationship with other. We believe that a Bakhtinian perspective can illuminate important considerations in pursuing an ongoing understanding of teacher identity.

What does it mean to conceptualize teacher identity through a Bakhtinian framework? First, this conception is premised on a dialogic approach to studying the relationship between self and other. A dialogic approach bridges the self/other divide and views all iterations of self as responses to an intended other. Bakhtin's work (Holquist, 1990) outlines ideas that consider the relationship between speaker/writer, text, and audience, and these theoretical concepts are helpful in understanding the fluid and complex nature of identity itself. Dialogism, Bakhtin's conceptual framework, has been schematized by interpreter Michael Holquist (1990) as a way to understand Bakhtin's theories. We draw on these theories as a way to expand understandings of teacher identity.

Bakhtin believed that the self always resides in two spaces at once: the space that is 'I' and the space that is 'other.' These two spaces are always in relation to each other and are continually referenced in the creation of self. Bakhtin (Holquist, 1990) outlined this when he said that

> in order to see ourselves, we must appropriate the vision of others . . . I see myself as others might see it. In order to forge a self, I must do so from outside. In other words, I author myself. (p. 28)

In a Bakhtinian sense, then, teachers involved in the teaching act must author themselves as future teachers, in part, through authoring the relationship they have with the other—stakeholders involved in the teaching act. Teachers create reciprocity in relationships with others that allow them to continually negotiate who they are in the moment. Henry Taylor, a beginning teacher who worked with youth at Family Partnership, stressed the way in which he remembered his youth and how he perceived himself as a young person. Henry said, "I think about the way that I was when I was a kid and I try to understand that continuously as I make choices as a teacher. It wasn't so long ago that I was just like these kids."

By saying that he is "just like these kids," Henry sees the intertwining of the self and the other, or the teacher and the student. In occupying both positions of self and other, the teacherly self is able to reside in two places simultaneously—the space of 'I' and those who are different from the space of 'I.' Gomez and White (2010) refer to this relationship as "figure and ground—linked together as a fluid and changing set of events" (p. 1017), and Bakhtin referenced the relationship between self and other as an "excess of seeing" or a "surplus of sight" (Holquist, 1990) when he said,

> When I contemplate a whole human being who is situated outside and over against me, our concrete, actually experienced horizons do not coincide. For each given moment, regardless of the position and proximity to me of this other human being whom I am contemplating, I shall always see and know something that he, from his place outside and over against me cannot see himself . . . as we gaze at each other, two different worlds are reflected in the pupils of our eyes. (pp. 22–23)

Bakhtin's words require that we see another's viewpoint in order to recognize what we cannot see ourselves from our own positions. Not only are we participants in Discourses, but such Discourses are also complexly structured and mediated by numerous factors—the histories of our experiences growing up, our schooling experiences, and our cultural backgrounds, among others.

Alsup (2006) uses the concept of borderlands to explain the dissonances that beginning teachers encounter. We witnessed the concept of borderlands enacted when beginning teachers contrasted the ways in which they viewed literacy practices in the lives of homeless youth. Contrasting the practices they saw at the day center at Family Partnership with middle-class literacy practices (Compton-Lilly, 2003) of which they were more familiar, preservice teachers began to articulate dissonances. Sarah Emerson wrote about this in her journal:

> I am going to go out on a limb and say that I doubt any of the kids' parents [at Family Partnership] have ever read to them. I'm not judging this, but it is really different than my upbringing and kids that I'm used to being around. I think this is why I am kind of disoriented when I'm at Family Partnership. I'm sure these kids don't want to read with me because it is just a strange activity for them. I am struggling to see what I believe in this space where the practices are so different from what I am familiar with.

In the preceding journal entry, Sarah articulates the borderland space—a space that asks her to confront the 'different' and the 'new' and to act within the space at the same time.

We see the concept of borderlands as important to our work because it reinforces the importance of the other. Together, the frameworks we mention earlier serve as a corpus of work that moves the notion of teacher identity from a concept focused primarily on the self to one that integrates an understanding of the other. Although some (e.g., Bucholtz & Hall, 2005) have conceptualized teacher identity as the "social positioning of self and other" (p. 586), we have found that most recent work on teacher identity (Hong, 2010; Trent & Lim, 2010) stresses the development of self, sometimes without overt consideration of the other. In contrast, we view the intertwining of self and other as prompting prospective teachers' consideration of their own identity in productive ways early in their teacher education program and teaching career.

Dissonances in Teacher Identity

In studying work focused on teacher identity, we note that scholars (e.g., Alsup, 2006; Danielewicz, 2001) have found that oftentimes teachers' identities must have congruence with societal norms or tensions will arise that are often difficult for teachers to resolve. The greater the tension that exists between the composed identity of the teacher and the norms that society has historically created for the teacher, the more likely it is that the novice teacher will not make teaching a lifelong career (Alsup, 2006, p. 183). Alsup (2006) highlights case studies of beginning teachers and contrasts the identity formation process that several of these teachers undertook in relationship to the dominant teacher identity—one that resides in being middle class, White, female, and heterosexual. Alsup found that, although non-unitary subjectivities (Bloom, 1998) are necessary for holistic identity formation, teachers who experience what may be viewed as "discordant subjectivities" lessen the chance that they will develop a satisfying professional identity (p. 183). Alsup is careful not to suggest that tension is always bad, however, and views tension as potentially providing the impetus for important identity development. However, a cautionary tale is told that when tensions become too great and too little support is felt, prospective teachers were less likely to become in-service secondary teachers (Alsup, 2006, p. 183). Friesen and Besley (2013) and Chong (2011) discuss this idea through the concept of 'dissonances.' Chong notes that dissonances occur when there is a mismatch between students' idealized visions of the profession and the reality that confronts them when they become professionals. Idealized versions of the profession abound, especially with the proliferation of media caricatures (see Carter, 2009) of teachers.

In addition to mismatches between one's personal identity and a dominant or idealized version of teacher identity, we have also found that prospective teachers may experience dissonances (Hallman, 2007) in teacher identity as they move between university and school contexts. In the university, prospective teachers may be encouraged to embody a stance of inquiry, thereby questioning their practice and envisioning multiple possibilities for their work in the classroom. Yet, as they move to the school contexts, beginning teachers feel that a stance of mastery may be more appropriate. With a stance of mastery, beginning teachers assert more competence in their judgments of what they see as best practice. The dissonance they perceive between inquiry and mastery becomes problematic as they undertake the formation of their teacher identity.

Indeed, the idea of tension, or discord, may not be appealing to beginning teachers. Through inviting Bakhtin to speak back to prospective teachers' perceived dissonances in teacher identity, we recognize that a dialogic understanding of identity not just is the push and pull of individual conversations between speaker and intended other but also includes the polyphony of voices present in the D/discourses that surround all of us as actors in the world, or speakers of text. Understanding the ideological tension that prospective teachers feel in inhabiting both the spaces of inquisitive student and knowledgeable teacher may assist both teacher educators and beginning teachers in abandoning their hope for a unidimensional teacher identity.

Community-based field sites, in some ways, serve as challenging sites in which beginning teachers grapple with the ideas of inquiry and mastery. Anne Chisholm, a nontraditional prospective teacher who worked with youth at Family Partnership, questioned how she might define herself within the community-based context:

> ANNE: When I'm at Family Partnership, I do feel like I'm hanging out with the kids and they see me as a mentor, or a friend, or maybe they even see me as a mom. But, I am also seeing myself as a teacher. I don't think they'd call me a teacher, though.
>
> HEIDI: Do you think this is because of the space you are working in or the role you are taking?
>
> ANNE: It is both. Certainly they don't see the church basement as they see school—so, yes, it is the space. It is also that I don't really have a defined role with them. I am like a volunteer, a friend, a mentor, and an outsider all at once.

Anne articulates the dissonance she feels when working within the undefined role of her work at Family Partnership. She wants to assume a relationship with the students with whom she works but looks for assistance in defining what that role might be. Bakhtin (1981) explains this dilemma through the concepts of *authoritative discourse* and *internally persuasive discourse* and writes that, in our daily life, we are always persuaded by conversants who have authority—whether these authorities are in the form of another individual or the larger society. Bakhtin refers to this normalizing discourse as giving rise to internally persuasive discourse, thus establishing a dialectic between oneself and intended other. Bakhtin (1981) notes the shared sense of discourse between individual and conversant by stating,

> The word in language is half someone else's. It becomes 'one's own' only when the speaker populates it with one's own intentions, his own accent, when he appropriates the word, adapting it to his own semantic and expressive intention. (p. 293)

The relationship between authoritative discourse and internally persuasive discourse is always one of struggle and this relationship determines one's becoming—the "orientations, investments, beliefs, and dispositions that are already inscribed in the specific discourses we take up" (Britzman, 1991, p. 20). Bakhtin (1981) recognized that the tension between these two discourses produces an individual's ideological becoming:

> The ideological becoming of a human being . . . is the process of selectively assimilating the words of others . . . The tendency to assimilate others' discourse takes on an even deeper and more basic significance in an individual's ideological becoming . . . Another's discourse performs here and so forth—but strives rather to determine the very basis of our ideological interrelations with the world, the very basis of our behavior;

it performs here as authoritative discourse and an internally persuasive discourse. (pp. 141–142)

Authoritative discourse, according to Bakhtin, is a discourse that demands allegiance and is responsible for creating the normative discourse that organizes our perceptions of the world. In terms of becoming a teacher, the role of the teacher throughout history has significantly shaped authoritative discourse. Understandings of the teacher force as Warren (1989) describes—primarily female, transient, and academically underprepared compared to their more middle-class counterparts—still affects the way the profession is seen today. In discussing the concept of discourse in an individual's becoming, Bakhtin (1981) notes that there is a

> gap between . . . the authoritative word (religious, political, moral; the word of a father, of adults and of teachers, etc.) that does not know internal persuasiveness, and . . . [the] internally persuade word that is denied all privilege, backed up by no authority at all, and is frequently not even acknowledged in society. (p. 342)

In contrasting authoritative discourse and internally persuasive discourse, Bakhtin positions authoritative discourse as holding power over individuals as the discourses urge individuals to conformity.

Throughout our book, we view the trope of 'teacher as expert' as an authoritative discourse that has consistently shaped the expectations surrounding the role of the teacher. Anne Chisholm was searching for this trope throughout her work at Family Partnership. As Portes and Smagorinsky (2010) remind us, the dominant model of classroom teaching into which teachers are socialized is one that adheres to a role of teacher as authority. This role bolsters a teaching mythology that constrains beginning teachers' views of an appropriate teacher's role (Hallman & Burdick, 2011). Teacher as authority, which we discuss more at length in Chapter 4, remains a powerful force in beginning teachers' conceptualizations of themselves as future teachers.

Bakhtin describes internally persuasive discourse as pulling one away from the normative, authoritative discourse. Internally persuasive discourse celebrates non-unitary meanings and ambiguity and, therefore, is a discourse of becoming. Britzman (1991) writes that internally persuasive discourse is "opened during times of spontaneity, improvisation, interpretive risks, crises, and when one reflects upon taken-for-granted ways of knowing" (p. 22). Pointing to a need for teachers to inhabit a double consciousness in which teachers must have an understanding of not simply the structure of schools and the skills necessary to teach there, Britzman emphasizes the importance of one's identity construction as a teacher and teachers educators are charged with helping beginning teachers develop a double consciousness, thereby relating the people and places of schooling to schooling's "history, mythology, and discourses" (1991, p. 2).

Throughout the integration of community fieldwork in our university courses, we consistently asked prospective teachers to negotiate the push–pull between authoritative discourse and internally persuasive discourse. This required us to make explicit the tools for articulating this tension. In journal assignments and in interviews, we urged beginning teachers to identify what we saw as tensions between the expectations they had of themselves as teachers and how these expectations played out in the field site. We sought to undo the dichotomy of teaching as mastery and teaching as inquiry that was present in many beginning teachers' minds, instead emphasizing the process of inquiry as central to becoming and being a professional.

New Times and Teachers as Shape-Shifting Portfolio People

Commonly thought about as a dissonant dualism, perhaps it is possible to think about how mastery and inquiry can coexist and lead preservice teachers to productive talk about identity. Yet, to understand teacher identity, we also must situate it in what some (Luke & Elkins, 1998) have called *New Times*. New Times signifies that the era in which we now live. Competing forces of regulation, deregulation, and professionalization in education, as well as technological advancement, are continually changing what it means to teach and to be a teacher (Cochran-Smith, 2001). As a result, Clandinin et al. (2009) characterize these phenomena as producing a "shifting landscapes on which teachers live and work" (p. 142).

New Times also signifies an environment where ever-changing technological change has transformed society. Technological innovation, which often goes out of date quickly, has reshaped U.S. society and has reshaped work and workers (Gee, Hull, & Lankshear, 1996). We view that the tenets of New Times have not only affected schooling but have also had an impact on the role of the teacher and the expectations for teaching today. Because we live in a society that, in its past, was concerned with the production of material goods yet is increasingly reliant not on jobs and wages, but upon one's portfolio, or what Gee (1999) notes as "the skills, achievements, and previous experiences that a person owns and that he or she can arrange and rearrange to sell him or herself for new opportunities in changed times" (p. 97), a person's marketability is reliant on one's ability to switch between and among Discourses.

To highlight the ability to switch between D/discourses, Gee (1999, 2001, 2004) introduced the term *shape-shifting portfolio people* to refer to workers in New Times and states that "shape-shifting portfolio people see themselves in entrepreneurial terms. That is, they see themselves as free agents in charge of their own selves as if those selves were projects or businesses" (2004, p. 105). Shape-shifting portfolio people see their set of skills as capable of being rearranged to fit the job market and are fully willing to rework the presentation of themselves to shape-shift into something else. Although we recognize Bakhtin's assertion of the pull of authoritative discourses in shaping what it means to be a teacher today, we also see that living in New Times urges teachers—perhaps those who leave the profession or find it difficult to adopt a teacher identity—to imagine new possibilities for themselves. Therefore, we find the movement between the adoption of 'normalcy' in teacher identity to an identity as a 'nonteacher' more abrupt today than ever before. The prevalence of shape-shifting portfolio people in today's world allows beginning teachers who may be unsure of solidifying a teacher identity to be cautious about firmly rooting themselves in the teaching profession.

The idea that teaching is 'normal' has been problematized. Britzman (1991) comments on the idea of normalcy in teaching by describing the myth of normalcy in education as telling an uncomplicated tale of becoming a teacher: The teaching life is known and predictable. People who select it are often 'average' people who wish to maintain a 'stable' or 'regular' life and live in middle-class contexts. Similarly, Alsup (2006) notes that sometimes young people "choose to become teachers for that very reason—they think that teaching will allow them to concentrate on other parts of their lives, such as family" (p. 63). Alsup further notes that many young teachers believe that teaching is a "culturally and socially uncontroversial professional choice" (2006, p. 63). We found that prospective teachers took on the attitude that they could seamlessly adopt the uncontroversial role of teacher, and this view was held by both nontraditional students, like Anne, as well as by traditional students.

Nontraditional students, like Anne, acknowledged that teaching would be second careers for them, but they also felt that they knew what teaching was and what the work and the role entailed. For example, Anne still held onto the belief that she could make a unique contribution to the field through her entry into the profession as a nontraditional student. Although she knew that she may encounter dissonances on entering teaching as a profession, Anne produced a counterstory that contended with the dissonances she expected she might feel as she transitioned from her previous roles into the role of teacher.

Counterstories often synthesized teachers' perceptions of their own past and therefore allowed teachers to assert new identities as beginning teachers. Anne's counterstory drew on the idea that her life experience and stature as a mature individual would contribute in unique ways to the profession. In articulating this story of herself as teacher, Anne differentiates herself from other students—traditional students—in ways that affirm to her that the move into the role of teacher will be smooth despite the challenges she may face.

In other instances, we saw that prospective teachers acknowledged that they would change careers if teaching "didn't work out" as a viable career option. In a conversation with Henry, three years after his experience at Family Partnership, we learned that Henry was still searching for the teacher

Composing Teachers, Teachable Students, and Teachable Spaces 55

identity he thought he may find along the way. Henry had embedded his counterstory into his search for the role of 'teacher':

> HEIDI: It's been three years since you worked with the kids at Family Partnership. Do you see yourself in the same way as you did then?
> HENRY: Yeah, for the most part. But I always saw myself as questioning teaching. Like, if it didn't work out, I'd have to do something else. And, here I am, two years later, substitute teaching and getting my master's degree in education.
> HEIDI: You know, in some ways, I see your 'on the fringe' mentality as maybe why you are still committed to it—teaching.
> HENRY: [laughs]. I guess you could see it that way. I really see myself as working best with the kids from Marshall City [urban center]. That's where I'm from and ultimately those kids are my people. So, yeah, I probably see myself staying there.
> HEIDI: What about teaching itself? Are you thinking about a full-time position for next year?
> HENRY: That's a good question. I'm not sure. I've really enjoyed subbing so I could see myself doing that. But, if I find a full-time position, yeah, I could see myself doing that if it was in the right school for me. But, I just have a hard time seeing myself as really a teacher. You know, I'm just always learning.

In the preceding conversation, Henry privileges the context of the school/job over his desire to adopt the role of teacher. Henry, during his time as a student at GSU, was one of the university students most committed to the work at Family Partnership. Among the cohort of 10 college students that worked with youth at Family Partnership during the time he did, Henry consistently pursued additional opportunities—beyond the required course expectations—to work with youth at Family Partnership. In seeking these opportunities, Henry appeared led by his inner voice to act on his values and creative understandings.

The internal voice of Henry that we felt was so unique and inspiring presented a struggle for him. Britzman (1991) aptly locates internally persuasive discourse as "renegade knowledge," writing that the practices of internally persuasive discourse are "in opposition to socially sanctioned views and normative meanings. It is the language of subversion" (p. 21). Because internally persuasive discourse seeks to extend meaning and grapple with ambiguity, Henry was especially able, in his work at Family Partnership, to display a presence that other beginning teachers often struggled with. Even Anne, who was often able to articulate a broader understanding of the world because of her life's experiences, her role as a nontraditional student, and her commitment as a military spouse, was bound by the taken-for-granted ways endorsed by the authoritative discourse about teaching that she sought to embody.

In urging prospective teachers to embrace becoming a teacher through their experience working in community-based field sites, we saw our aim of encouraging beginning teachers to experience, and even encourage, a resonance with internally persuasive discourse. We viewed this 'renegade knowledge' as valuable to beginning teachers as they struggled to make sense of teaching. Yet, we take Bakhtin's warning to heart, as internally persuasive discourse is "denied all privilege" (Bakhtin, 1981, p. 342). Unlike authoritative discourse, internally persuasive discourse "pulls away from norms and admits a variety of contradictory social discourses"; it has "no institutional privilege, because its practices are in opposition to socially sanctioned view and normative meanings" (Britzman, 1991, p. 21).

Henry, who we feature further in Chapter 4, drew strength from his 'renegade knowledge' yet felt like a shape-shifter in that he tried to decide how best to position himself as a real teacher. In the methods course and beyond, we took on the work of supporting students in their negotiation of the interplay between authoritative discourse and internally persuasive discourse. We also saw the dichotomies of self/other, history/context, and teacher/student as discussion points aimed not at coming to a consensus or a unitary meaning but, rather, as a way to acknowledge the intentions and meanings of the other colliding with one's own intentions and meanings. Rather than merely seeing oneself as a shape-shifter, we intended for teachers like Henry to examine the reasons the dissonances they had existed, examining them as productive sites of struggle in the development of their own teacher identity.

COMPOSING TEACHING: PEDAGOGY, THE ALCHEMY OF SCHOOL SUBJECTS, AND THE TEACHER AS REDEEMER

Learning to teach not only involves contending with one's identity and role as a teacher and how one must position oneself this role but also learning to teach involves the concept of pedagogy. The issue of pedagogy sits at the crux of understanding the act of teaching. Pedagogy addresses the process by which teachers produce knowledge, and, in doing so, constructs the relationship between teaching and learning.

Scholars in education debate over the extent to which a secondary school subject, such as English language arts, can be considered specific to its discipline. School subjects can be viewed as domains where disciplinary knowledge has been translated into what we call the school subject of English language arts, and methods courses designed to teach have often included what Popkewitz (2009, 2010) refers to as the "psychologies of pedagogy," or strategies which govern who the child is and who he should be, including whether the child becomes a good citizen, a lifelong learner, or an appropriate problem solver. Viewing schooling as a process in normalizing behavior and preparing docile citizens, where contentious disciplinary content is transformed into unambiguous knowledge (Bernstein, 1996; Popkewitz, 1998) underscores the idea that schooling is not only about the biological qualities of children's growth, learning, and development, but also about the inscription of cultural and social principles related to the making of future citizens. Popkewitz (2010) refers to the translation of disciplinary knowledge into school subjects as 'alchemy,' which "provide[s] an analytic 'tool' to consider the processes of translation from disciplinary knowledge to teaching practices" (p. 413).

Pedagogy, through this lens, is a practice that converts the knowledge within a disciplinary field into practices that psychologize the learner. As with 16th- and 17th-century alchemists who sought to transform one type of metal into another, pedagogy is a process that seeks to move disciplinary knowledge into a new form. Becoming an English teacher, then, is more than teaching Shakespeare, for it asks that teachers teach Shakespeare in a manner that situates students as appropriate learners. Popkewitz (2010) argues that the tasks of learning across school subjects are not that different; although the content of mathematics and music may be different, students' participation in school subjects are generated historically through translation tools drawn from psychology.

Other scholars understand that the school subject reflects the epistemologies and discourses of the disciplines they arise from (Moje, 2008; Shulman, 2005). Gee (1996) points out that unless students are acquiring the discourse of the disciplines, they are unable to enter those communities as literate members. This line of thinking asserts that even if schools, because of their other goals related to producing certain types of dispositions in workers and citizens, have turned disciplines into subjects, the work of teacher educators consists of helping future teachers understand the disciplinary knowledge and discourses in the pursuit of student engagement and more equal life chances.

We would argue that, although teachers must have a deep understanding of disciplinary knowledge and its practices, uncovering the reasons why some schools are successful in recruiting what look like disciplinary practices while others are not is difficult for prospective teachers to comprehend. Instead, through introducing the notion of *alchemy*, prospective teachers may begin to question the complexity of knowledge as taught to students within the context of school; they may begin to question how schools serve differing populations of students and how schooling experiences affect children in much different ways. We agree with Popkewitz's (1998) assertion that the task of modern schooling is the deliberate design of a child's 'soul'—the "inner beliefs, feelings, and sensitivities that generate actions" (p. 50) rather than the consumption and/or acquisition of static knowledge. In relation to this, teachers are positioned as redeemers and a salvation narrative is composed that stresses the redemption of the child through the actions of the teacher. Through such a narrative teachers are, especially in relation to students who are disadvantaged or marginalized, invested in a social mission to right inequality.

Yet, as Popkewitz (1998) warns, such narratives of salvation create a "doubleness" in which the qualities that children possess that are viewed as 'negative' (such as homelessness) are recast to be seen as 'positive' work for the teacher; a child's disadvantaged home life is recast as an undertaking for teachers' 'success.' In doing such work to guide, rationalize, and recast, students' 'success' becomes more about teachers' 'success' than the child's growth, and teachers who monitor children to guide them toward success become uplifted through their work.

Such narratives were continuously present in our work with beginning teachers and we combatted this doubleness throughout the years of our study. At the same time, we encouraged teachers to explore ways of characterizing the youth with whom they worked, reflecting the real, and many times difficult, circumstances of children's lives. Perhaps the contrasts beginning teachers made most were within the stories they recounted that contrasted students' literacy learning outside of school with the practices they witnessed in English language arts classrooms. In the following vignette, Ming, Tara, and Rebecca question the practices they have seen in school and those they witness at the Family Partnership day center:

> MING: I am seeing that many of the kids really don't want to read when I encourage them to do so. Unless they come with a book, they'd rather play a game or just talk with me.
>
> TARA: I have seen this and I really think that picking up a book is pretty foreign to them [the youth at Family Partnership]. Their parents probably didn't read to them so we may be the only adults who've encouraged them to read.
>
> REBECCA: Other than their teachers.
>
> TARA: Well, yes. But even their teachers are doing in inside of the school day. It's different when you have a home environment that encourages you to read than if you don't.
>
> REBECCA: It must be hard for kids who have had the lives these kids have had to all of the sudden read in their spare time. But I think this is where we can come into their lives and make this impact.

Through discussion of the youth, Ming, Tara, and Rebecca cast themselves as providing positive guidance for the children. Yet, they also begin with the premise that the children's lives been not been 'normal.' As Popkewitz (1998) warns, the outcome of "turning [children's] negativities into positivities makes it not possible for the child to ever be normal or average" (p. 42), and this becomes the real danger in casting children into such roles.

In his book *Struggling for the Soul: The Politics of Schooling and the Construction of the Teacher*, Popkewitz (1998) writes that prospective teachers who were enrolled in a Teach for America (TFA) training institute constructed particular views about urban children that placed them outside of the norm for so-called normal development when they stated that the children with whom they worked had "no discipline" in their homes and lacked parental figures who read to them. Such classifications implied that the children lacked the norms to learn properly and psychologized the child as lacking the "self-esteem for success" (Popkewitz, 1998, p. 26). As with the prospective teachers with whom we worked, categorizations such as these worked in ways to predetermine who the child was and how teachers might be positioned in relation to the child.

We saw our work with prospective teachers as assisting beginning teachers with understanding the binaries they created in making categorizations of who children were. In creating these categorizations of homeless/non-homeless, White/Black, foster child/non–foster child, we urged beginning teachers to consider how their classifications placed limits on the possibilities they imagined for the children. Rather than become paralyzed in their approach, we also urged beginning teachers to marry contemplation of such ideas with action, specifically through applying Bakhtin's (1990) "excess of seeing." Empathy for those who were seen as others refined the idea that there really is no other, but rather the idea of the other means "not like I" (Boesch, 2007, p. 5). Boesch (2007) notes that, when we have interactions with those that we see as 'different' from ourselves, we must begin by becoming familiar with the cultural context inhabited by those we view as other (p. 7).

So, although we did not expect prospective teachers to immediately move to reside in a position of reciprocity in which they could seamlessly intertwine self and other; rather, through the exploration of contexts different from their own, we trusted that beginning teachers could move to position self, other, and pedagogy in a relationship that recognized the dependency of each tenet on one another. Our position, as teacher educators, was to assist prospective teachers in articulating how they viewed this triad, moving beginning teachers to question the linear hierarchy often assumed among knowledge, teacher, and student.

Our final point in emphasizing the inclusion of pedagogy within the sphere of teacher identity resonates with the fact that "discursive principles of teacher education and teaching provide few analytical tools with which to 'think' systematically about the production of power, knowledge, and subjectivities" (Popkewitz, 1998, p. 136). Although literature about teacher identity, teacher reflection, and teacher beliefs are abundant in the field of teacher education (e.g., Hong, 2010; Poulou, 2007) these works underscore the redemptive position of the teacher. Few understandings of teacher/student go the distance in redefining the roles of self/other to urge teachers to discard the promise of teacher as redeemer. In fact, some may argue that now, in the postindustrial era, we must pursue this promise with even more vigor as the relationship among knowledge, teacher, and student changes. We, however, come away with the understanding that a dialogic relationship of self/other must reside at the center of the teaching act.

COMPOSING TEACHABLE STUDENTS

Now, we turn to think further about the students with whom prospective teachers worked. Teachers in our study went about the work of 'composing' the students with whom they worked in an effort to understand them. In many ways, this was a deliberate attempt to help beginning teachers understand how difference resided not only in the material lives of the students (e.g., in their circumstances as homeless youth or foster children) but also in the ways that prospective teachers constructed the circumstances around these materialities.

Hacking (1990) introduces the concept of populational reasoning, a system by which populations of people came to be ordered through state reform tactics concerned with social welfare of the state. By classifying 'types' of people and ordering them into certain categories, human needs were seen in instrumental and empirical terms in relation to the functioning of the state. Hacking extends this into the realm of human biology by noting that certain diseases, categories, and states of being come into existence to measure, organize, and divide people. As a result, populational reasoning constructs our understanding of how children learn and of the reasons why certain groups of children are likely to 'succeed' or 'fail' in school. Defining how students fit into groups is more than just a way to classify students but is used as a way to normalize, individualize, and divide.

Hacking (1986, 1995) uses the phrase "making up people" to study the ways in which classifications affect people, and people, in turn, affect the ways they are classified (called the looping effect). In our subject area of English language arts, we have found that the concept of making up people has emerged in the teaching of our discipline in interesting ways, and see how the teaching of so-called classic texts has changed to assert such ideas. Take, for example, the construction of Holden Caulfield in Salinger's *Catcher in the Rye*. Holden was, in the past, seen as a troubled youth with teenage angst and rebellion but is now often cast and taught as a 'depressed youth.' We attribute this change to the emergence of depression as a disease so prevalent now in society yet once fairly absent from reasons of normalizing and classifying people.

Defining how people fit into groups is more than defining sets of characteristics and labeling people as such. It is, as Popkewitz (1998) notes, a system to delineate normal/abnormal, where the "normal is embodied in the individual, and the nonnormal is inscribed in populational discourses mobilized to characterize, examine, classify, and define the child who is outside of reason" (p. 55). One of the prospective teachers in our study, Ming, challenged herself when constructing the homeless students with whom she worked. Throughout the time she spent at Family Partnership, Ming worked extensively with Penny, a middle school student. Penny was drawn to Ming's reserved demeanor and was extremely talkative with Ming about her experiences in middle school. At the beginning of the school year,

Penny told Ming that she had recently been recommended to participate in the Gifted and Talented program at her school, and Ming shared this with her fellow prospective teachers in a seminar meeting. The conversation that ensued among the beginning teachers elicited questions and comments about students' abilities and economic class in ways that challenged previous perceptions:

> MING: Penny told me today that she is in the Gifted and Talented Program at her middle school.
> TARA: That is great.
> REBECCA: Wow! That is great.
> SARAH: That seems like something that you may not hear very often—a homeless student in Gifted and Talented. I mean, it is a stereotype that homeless students must not be very smart.
> TARA: But that is a stereotype.
> SARAH: Yes. But I bet a lot of people in the community I grew up in believe these kind of stereotypes. They can't imagine it would be any different.
> REBECCA: Like because the kids aren't coming from stable homes they can't succeed. I see what you are saying.
> TARA: And now we are seeing evidence that stereotypes aren't always true. They are stereotypes.

In the preceding conversation, prospective teachers use Penny's status as a gifted and talented student to challenge the construction of the 'homeless adolescent.' Using a concrete example by which to discuss preconceived notions of students and how teachers react to these preconceptions was important work in prospective teachers' act of 'composing' students. The example of Penny was recounted several times throughout the course of conversations in seminar meetings. Penny's student status appeared to be a powerful influence on beginning teachers' perceptions of students at Family Partnership.

Yet, Penny existed as a homeless student whose life was different from the life many prospective teachers had while growing up. Tara, although she remarked that stereotypes were broken through students like Penny, also lamented the fact that many students at Family Partnership did not have access to books or educational experiences outside of school. She said, "I do think that Penny is the exception. Most of the kids there [at Family Partnership] have had rough lives and this has really affected their schooling. Some of the kids have not had that consistency and they struggle in school because of it. Probably no one has been reading to them on a consistent basis throughout their lives."

Here, we wish to make note of beginning teachers' constructions of the student who is seen as 'abnormal,' or as having an existence that has not given them access to normalcy. We see this construction as embodied in both the concepts of the 'urban' and the 'rural' child—children who reside off the spectrum of what constitutes 'normal.' Children at the field sites were considered, by the prospective teachers, to be 'urban,' 'rural,' or 'at-risk' youth, and these terms were used in their discussion of the children. The terms *urban* and *rural*, Popkewitz (1998) argues, are used to produce children who are 'abnormal.' It is important to note that, although geographical distinctions have bearing on children's learning, Popkewitz writes that "the same systems of pedgagogical ideas circul[ate] in the two geographical locations. For this reason, I use the two words as one—urban/rural" (p. 3). The urban/rural child, then, is cast as not 'normal.' Although Penny, who was newly labeled as gifted and talented, was composed as being smart and able, she was, at the same time, the urban/rural child. The spaces of urban and rural worked alongside the spaces of normalcy.

COMPOSING THE SPACES OF SCHOOLING

When we discuss the 'spaces of schooling' in this book, we mean this in both concrete and abstract senses. There is the brick-and-mortar school space of school in which students sit within walls and listen to teachers or discuss lessons with each other. This brick-and-mortar space is also the space where parents participate in conferences with administrators, where janitors work to make the school space attractive and safe, and where students in hallways and cafeterias congregate, socialize, and grapple face-to-face with viewpoints and backgrounds other than their own. There is also the abstract, social space of school that is made up of curriculum, relationships, and politics. Spaces of schooling, then, are created and sustained by a school's culture and by both the creators and the inhabitants of that space. This abstract notion of space is constructed and cemented over time and emphasizes relationships within particular school cultures, which, therefore, render the concept of 'space' as one that is created metaphorically through constructions of power, identity, and agency. At the same time, the constructed social space can be changed and adapted; however, often, space is controlled by those who have the most power.

The ways in which space is created, both socially and concretely, is partly homogenized with regard to the ways in which we think about 'school spaces.' There are traditional school spaces that are architecturally typical: classroom spaces with a presentation space toward one end of the room for a teacher to stand and perform; office spaces for administrators and others who have authority over the space; common student spaces such as hallways and libraries and cafeterias that are large and allow for some adult observation and supervision of students. These spaces are expected and ingrained within the dominant culture in the U.S.

And yet, in other ways, we see that the space of school is not one homogenous and replicable space that is identically arranged and inhabited. There are schools whose classrooms have no windows and others with entire walls of glass. There are schools that have large open spaces for students to congregate and socialize by the front doors and others where students meet metal detectors and security guards when they enter the space. There are schools where the teachers are constantly moving about the building with the students, and there are buildings where teachers stay in their classrooms, rarely leaving their posts between the opening and closing bells. No matter the traditions or distinctions of school space, we see space not only as a geographical or architectural concept but also as a place of interrelations between people and within structures of power.

People and cultures invest places with meaning. From this, we can also see that those people and cultures who are in power are those who invest and dictate meaning in spaces; through these investments of meaning, those with power constrain other, less empowered individuals and cultures within the space. This limits those with lesser power from not only the ability to invest meaning in their place but often keeps them from becoming empowered because they are not able to interact with the place in alternate ways, and their identities become a part of a place that they cannot claim. There is no movement, and the places become inert, meaningless, and the individuals in the place become frozen and inert as well. Their identities become defined by the place instead of the individuals bringing their identities to the place to impact its meaning. At the same time, others with power are creating both meaning and identity.

When thinking about 'traditional' schools, Lortie's (1975) conception of socialization is at play; through such a view, socialization is "a subjective process—it is something that happens to people as they move through a series of structured experiences and internalize the subculture of the group" (p. 61). Traditional teacher education programs have already identified and claimed the meaning of the space and the teacher's identity within the space.

In community-based spaces, however, we see the possibility for teachers' socialization as potentially more dialogic. Following Bakhtin's understanding that a move to see others leads back to a turn on the self (Holquist, 1990), the spaces of the community ask prospective teachers to question the identity and role that they assume and position that alongside their expectations of what it means to be a teacher. When Bakhtin discusses a surplus of sight, he does not argue that we lose sight of ourselves; rather, we actively seek empathy with the other by turning toward the other and then back to ourselves. Allowing prospective teachers to begin to claim identity in a less defined space, less schooled space, allows them to create an identity that can, in turn, redefine the space of school. This allows a prospective teacher's identity to be flexible and responsive to the space in which it is situated, thus, offering the possibility that the constrained place of school may change over time.

We see place-based education (or PBE, as it is often referred to) as a movement resonant with our work in community-based spaces, for it is a movement in education that focuses upon students' understanding and interaction with place. Place-based education is a counter-development to both standardization and globalization and has its roots in multiple other movements such as service learning, eco-education, experiential education, and critical pedagogy. Whereas standards-based education focuses upon standardized 'truths' that are inflexible and concrete, Theobald (2006) explains the ways place-based education can be viewed as a response to standards-based education:

> Much more than the currently popular 'standards-based' educational movement, place-based education rests on recent developments in cognition theory concerning the nature of human understanding. Most significantly, place-based curriculum and instruction capitalizes on the crucial role of context in human learning. But more than just reaping the instructional benefits of embedding subject matter into the particularities of the place where students happen to live, place-based education intends to increase the motivation to learn among students, as this type of study enables them to see the value of greater intellectual leverage over their immediate environment. (p. 316)

Certainly one of the attributes heralded by place-based advocates is that it is a way to increase student engagement and agency (Gruenewald, 2003; McInerney, Smyth, & Down, 2011; Theobald, 2006), and this is because so much of our identity and learning is shaped by place. We continuously comprehend the world and create relationships based upon the places we inhabit. In place-based education, place is a lens through which we understand all learning, and place consists not only of geographical space but also of the social and the cultural constructs that inhabit a place. Cultural and social constructs that imbue a place are where identities are reworked and renegotiated.

Furthermore, place-based education demands a localism in response to the current influences of globalism and asks us to teach students to see the global through the lenses of the local of which they are a part and for which they can advocate. We see place-based education as a response to the erasing of the local in the New Times in which we now live. We see that the local must somehow engage with the global in order to counter the view that there is a monolithic, global culture that dictates what identities are possible. Like Bakhtin, we imagine that there is both an authoritative discourse and an internally persuasive discourse that are always in struggle with one another and at the same time both deeply influential in one's becoming. The 'space' of school becomes the site where these struggles are played out. Gruenwald calls our attention to geographical distributions of wealth and power. Within Gruenwald's work, and within this book, we consider how the concept of space affects the actions and conditions of teaching. Gruenwald (2003) writes that

> examining the many ways in which politics and place are entangled can inform educators with ideas about how people, places and cultures take shape. Beyond that, entering politicized space suggests political roles for educators as mediators in the construction of culture, identity and the places where they emerge. (p. 631)

Terms such as *annexation, segregation, exile,* and *absorption* are used to describe politicized space, and we, too, will consider how such terms influence our understandings of teaching, schooled and unschooled spaces, authority, and curriculum.

Finally, we note the influence of the work of Henri Lefebvre (1991) and his theories of spatiality. Gruenewald (2003) describes Lefebvre's work as fitting into an ideological dimension of place and states that "one function of space . . . is hegemonic: Domination is maintained not through material force but through material forms." Therefore, geographical space always reflects and reproduces relationships of power and ideologies. Lefebvre maintains that all social spaces produce the following relationships and interactions: space that is accessible for those who normally inhabit, spaces prohibited areas and their boundaries, places of 'abode' where one can create his or her own meaning, and 'junction points' that exist on the boundaries of the prohibited spaces.

We see that there are two spaces within Lefebvre's articulation of spatiality that encompass freedom—accessible spaces and places of abode—and these spaces are only 'free' within the constraints of the socially constructed domains. We see the spaces of community-based sites as what Lefebvre (1991) refers to as junction points, defined as "places of passage and encounter . . . [where] access is forbidden except on certain occasion" (p. 193). These spaces are often those that are only marginally (if at all) considered spaces of schooling. It is within these marginal places that our research portrays how prospective teachers can grow and develop in profound ways due to the freedom they experience from socially constructed school spaces.

Impacting Space at the Margins

As discussed earlier in this chapter, we draw on Anzaldua's (2007) understanding of borderlands, and Alsup's (2006) borderland narratives to help frame teacher identity in relation to students and traditional teaching roles. We extend this work by applying these theories to the relationships and identities within and beholden to inhabited spaces. In her book, *Yearning: Race, Gender, and Cultural Politics*, bell hooks (1990) discusses "marginality" as a place of particular openness. hooks states that being on the margin is "much more than a site of deprivation; in fact . . . it is also the site of radical possibility, a space of resistance . . . It offers to one the possibility of a radical perspective from which to see and create, to imagine alternatives, new worlds" (1990, pp. 149–150). In this way, through the stories of our research, the margin can be a space of hope and a space of movement and possibility. We see this hope in our understanding of community-based field placements in teacher education and now feature two vignettes about the 'marginality' of Mettle Street School, the Lodges, and Family Partnership.

The Marginality of Mettle Street School

The place of the writing center is in the common reception area in middle of the administrative suite in Mettle Street School. There is a computer desk and a chair on one side of the space where students can work with a tutor or a tutor can work alone with a piece of student writing. There is also a rocking chair in the space that the tutors use sometimes. The lighting is dim. There are no teachers in the space, but staff and administrators move through the space on their way to other spaces. The writing center is not a part of a classroom.

The place of the writing center is very different from a classroom, although it is still an institutional place. It also is not really a part of the administration of the school. The students who work as peer tutors in the writing center are out of place among the administration offices. In a traditional school space, these offices would rarely be inhabited by students, and if they were, it is likely that the students would be there because of some conflict within the school. There are also no teachers in this space. Therefore, the prospective teachers who are placed to work in the writing center work within a 'nonclassroom' space; it is a space that is rarely inhabited by teachers and students. For this reason, the teacher–student relationship can become less concrete. There is a possibility that it can be situated as a tutoring relationship, although it was created within a space claimed by administrators.

In many ways, working within the space of the writing center allowed prospective teachers to create valuable nontraditional relationships with students and administrators. The prospective teachers were also able to consider how particular spaces supported learning, and how such a space could portray institutional significance through its placement, activity, and relationships. Katherine Sternmeister, one of the prospective teachers placed at Mettle Street School, described the context of the school's writing center in this way: "The writing center was merely a computer on a table in the middle of the administrative offices. For one student, the noise and traffic that came with that setting at times hindered his efforts to write." Other prospective teachers commented in their journals about the space of the writing center being away from teachers and yet situated in a space of institutional authority.

The Marginality of the Lodges

The Lodges, a collection of group homes situated immediately outside of the urban vicinity in Jackson City, are surrounded by heavily wooded areas. The homes themselves sit in a horseshoe arrangement within a cleared space of the forest. From the outside these homes appear to be large, traditional single-family homes. On entering one of the group homes, one recognizes that they are home spaces but yet not exactly home spaces. Right inside the door exists a 'reception space' with several chairs, a desk, and a computer where guests can 'check in.'

The desk and the computer are usually staffed by one of the houseparents. After leaving this reception-like area, the rest of the home space appears more homelike except for the extensive amount of furniture in each room. There is a living room with a fireplace and a television, but the room has four sofas instead of one. The dining area off the kitchen does not have one dining table, but four tall tables, all with numerous high stools. On these stools residents sit to eat or do homework. The bedrooms, too, are filled with bunk beds. Outside each group home, there is a picnic table and a basketball goal. Within the horseshoe of houses, there is a large grassy field.

On warm days, prospective teachers who were placed at the Lodges would often take their writing workshop outside of the homes to write in the grassy area, or out to a picnic table under a tree. It seemed more profitable to them to work with students outside the group home setting. The place that the writing workshop met was within the forest, and the theory existed that in order 'to heal,' the kids at the Lodges must be a part of nature and learn from nature.

It was also assumed that kids at the Lodges needed to have the love and structure of a family. This assumption about what the kids at the Lodges needed was very different from what was assumed the space of school should provide for the kids. Prospective teachers implicitly understood that the focus of work at the Lodges was more about providing an emotionally supportive experience for the youth—something that was perhaps less measurable and more internal than what was expected of them in the traditional school space.

It was important for the prospective teachers to see that the kids were not in institutional-style buildings. They had their own space. There were comfortable places with couches, beds, fireplaces, carpets, televisions, kitchens, basketball courts, grassy fields, forests, and sky. The roads are gravel and there was not a view of buildings, concrete, or traffic. As a result, interactions became more community based than may have been possible in a school setting.

And yet, the Lodges is neither a school nor a home space. It is certainly at the margins of both of these spaces. The students who live at the Lodges are considered 'marginal' in that they are considered wards of the state. They either do not have or are not allowed to be in their original 'homes' and therefore are placed within a homelike institution. The homes are institution-like with their reception areas and lack of privacy. The natural world is a stark contrast to the spaces within the residents' homes.

Because this space was so far away from school space, was closer to a residential area, and the residents were labeled as 'marginalized,' the prospective teachers who worked with youth at the Lodges were able to experiment with curriculum. There was no list of student learning outcomes. There was no classroom. The 'teachers' showed up on Sunday afternoons and decided their main goal was just to help these students write, to find their voices and their creativity. In this case, the freedom of the margins was clearly beneficial to prospective teachers' understanding of learning and curriculum, as well as to their understanding of youth's motivation to participate in defining both what learning and curriculum meant to them.

The Marginality of Family Partnership

Family Partnership was the place most specifically defined; it stood as 'a place within a place.' The day center of Family Partnership was where individuals went after school but before they were transported to their dinner and sleeping space. The day center was in an old home, yet it had the feeling of an institution that was waiting for families to claim to the space as 'home.' Perhaps because the families had no place (a home) for themselves, the day center existed as a sparsely furnished series of connected rooms. The space, given to the families who were in the Family Partnership program, seemed to have an 'unclaimed' feeling.

The individuals in the program had rules that dictate the expectations and some of these include no use of alcohol or other substances, adherence to time of transportation to dinner at the congregation, and general guidelines governing appropriate use of the day center. Yet, families cannot make the place their own. Instead, the day center exists as a stopgap that is inherited for a time but is not owned by the inhabitants. The inhabitants are 'placed' there. This is an interesting phrase—'they are placed'—they are made a part of the place. They did not choose the place, but because they have no place, the kindness of the charitable institution places them.

The institution, then, gives them a place that then becomes part of their identity. Here they cannot claim the place, but the prospective teachers have some control over the behaviors of the students in the place. They have the authority of being a part of a helping institution. They have an authority in this place that they might not be able to claim in a school.

The relationships created as teacher and students through the Family Partnership program are still created as such but are much less defined because the space is much less constricted. In working with homeless youth after dinner in the space of a congregation, it was, at times, difficult for prospective teachers to see themselves and the youth as typical teachers and students. The combination of homelessness and work in the basement of a church, with the church space defined as a place of worship, presented concrete differences from the space of a school with traditional teachers and students. The people placed within the space of the church basement, however, were not expected to be 'worshipers' or to inhabit a traditional relationship to the space. Instead, they were within the space temporarily, and used it as a makeshift home. Placing prospective teachers in this temporary home–non-home space and asking them to establish teacher–student relationships with the children is an example of borderlands (Alsup, 2006; Anzaldua 2007). As a community field placement site, there are multiple spaces and borders coming together among community, religion, home, and with the introduction of prospective teachers into the space, but there was also the space of school at the margins. The Family Partnership space incorporated all of these and, at the same time, none of these traditional spaces. It was a church, but the children and their families were not worshippers. It was a makeshift living space, with beds and linens donated, but it was not a home. It was a community space, but the homeless children and their families were considered outsiders in the community. With the prospective teachers work as teachers/tutors in the space, borderlands of school are introduced, yet the traditional school boundaries and borders dissolve when they are pulled into such a nondefined (or multiply defined) space. The traditional relationships and behaviors of school between teachers and students then can be redefined and reexamined by the prospective teachers.

THE ACT OF COMPOSING AND THE PROMISE OF TEACHERS' AGENCY

Throughout our book, we work in the space where discourses circulate and produce particular types of people—including teachers and students. As researchers, ethical representation of our participants—particularly of those who are most stigmatized through labels such as being 'at-risk' of school failure—demands that we consider how participants enact agency. Although societal discourses about at-risk youth compose particular visions of these youth, we aim to recognize the agency that youth possess. Agency is often made visible through the stories that participants tell.

Through awareness of a dialectical relationship between participants' agentive selves and the discourses in which they operate, we can account for the back and forth between self and discourse, and we view this as working within the dialectic of "both ways" of ethnographic knowing (Luttrell, 2003). In the next chapter, we explore prospective teachers' writing and how writing became a site for inquiry as well as a site for 'composing' teachers and students. We approach writing through a framework of dialogism and outline the processes by which dialogism deliberates theories of personhood and agency within the local-level context. A focus on the dialogic helps us move beyond dualisms and instead focus on the polyphony of forces that challenge our 'composing.' As Britzman (1991) aptly states, retheorizing our practices in teacher education requires that we attend to the "double problem of changing ourselves and transforming our circumstances" (p. 239). Thus, we begin and end this chapter with an emphasis on the pinnacle of teacher identity and its effect and influence on the act of teaching.

NOTE

1 Gee's (1999) definition of Discourse ("big D" Discourse) refers to the combination of language with other social practices (e.g., behavior, ways of thinking, values, customs), whereas discourse ("little d" discourse) refers to language in use.

REFERENCES

Alcoff, L. (2006). *Visible Identities: Race, gender and the self.* New York, NY: Oxford University Press.

Alsup, J. (2006). *Teacher identity discourses: Negotiating personal and professional discourses.* Mahwah, NJ: Erlbaum.

Anzaldua, G. (2007). *Borderlands/La Frontera: The new mestiza* (3rd ed.). San Francisco, CA: Aunt Lute Books.

Bakhtin, M. (1981). *The dialogic imagination: Four essays* (M. Holquist, Ed.). Austin: University of Texas Press.

Bakhtin, M. (1990). *Art and answerability: Early philosophical essays* (M. Holquist, Ed., & V. Liapunov, Trans.). Austin: University of Texas Press.

Bernstein, B. (1996). *Pedagogy, symbolic control and identity: Theory, research, critique.* New York, NY: Taylor & Francis.

Bloom, L.R. (1998). *Under the sign of hope: Feminist methodology and narrative interpretation.* Albany: State University of New York Press.

Boesch, E. (2007). The enigmatic other. In L. Mathias & J. Valsiner (Eds.), *Otherness in question: Labyrinths of the self* (pp. 3–9). Charlotte, NC: Information Age Publishing.

Britzman, D.P. (1991). *Practice makes practice: A critical study of learning to teach.* Albany: State University of New York Press.

Bucholtz, M., & Hall, K. (2005). Identity and interaction: A sociocultural linguistic approach. *Discourse Studies, 7,* 585–614.

Carter, C. (2009). Priest, prostitute, plumber? The construction of teachers as saints. *English Education, 42*(1), 61–90. Retrieved from www.jstor.org.www2.lib.ku.edu/stable/40607917

Chong, S. (2011). Development of teachers' professional identities: From pre-service to their first year as novice teachers. *KEDI Journal of Education Policy, 8*(2), 219–233.

Clandinin, D. J., Downey, C. A., & Huber, J. (2009). Attending to changing landscapes: Shaping the interwoven identities of teachers and teacher educators. *Asia Pacific Journal of Teacher Education, 37*(2), 141–154. doi:10.1080/13598660902806316

Cochran-Smith, M. (2001). Reforming teacher education: Competing agendas. *Journal of Teacher Education, 52*(4), 263–265. doi:10.1177/0022487101052004001

Compton-Lilly, C. (2003). *Reading lives: The literate lives of urban children.* New York, NY: Teachers College Press.

Danielwicz, J. (2001). *Teaching selfes: Identity, pedagogy, and teacher education.* Albany: State University of New York Press.

Friesen, M. D., & Besley, S. C. (2013). Teacher identity development in the first year of teacher education: A developmental and social psychological perspective. *Teaching and Teacher Education, 36,* 23–32. doi:10.1016/j.tate.2013.06.005

Gee, J. P. (1996). *Social linguistics and literacies: Ideology in discourses* (2nd ed.). Philadelphia, PA: Falmer Press.

Gee, J. P. (1999). *An introduction to discourse analysis: theory and method.* New York, NY: Routledge.

Gee, J. P. (2001). Literacy, discourse, and linguistics: Introduction. In E. Cushman, M. Rose, B. Kroll, & E.R. Kintgen (Eds.), *Literacy: A critical sourcebook* (pp. 525–544). Boston, MA: Bedford/St. Martin's.

Gee, J. P. (2004). *Situated language and learning: A critique of traditional schooling.* London, England: Routledge.

Gee, J. P., Hull, G., & Lankshear, C. (1996). *The new work order.* Boulder, CO: Westview Press.

Gomez, M. L., Black, R. W., & Allen, A. (2007). "Becoming" a teacher. *Teachers College Record, 109*(9), 2107–2135. Retrieved from www.tcrecord.org.www2.lib.ku.edu/library/Issue.asp?volyear=2007&number=9&volume=109

Gomez, M. L., & White, E. (2010). Seeing one another as "other." *Teaching and Teacher Education, 26,* 1015–1022. doi:10.1016/j.tate.2009.10.044

Gruenewald D.A. (2003). The best of both worlds: A critical pedagogy of place. *Educational Researcher, 32*(4), 3–12. doi:10.3102/0013189X032004003

Hacking, I. (1986). Making up people. In T.C. Heller, M. Sonsa, & D. E. Weller (Eds.), *Reconstructing individualism* (pp. 222–236). Stanford, CA: Stanford University Press.

Hacking, I. (1990). *The taming of chance.* New York, NY: Cambridge University Press.

Hacking, I. (1995). The looping effects of human kinds. In D. Sperber, D. Premack, & A. Premack (Eds.), *Causal cognition: An interdisciplinary approach* (pp. 351–383). Oxford, England: Oxford University Press.

Hallman, H. L. (2007). Negotiating teacher identity: Exploring the use of electronic teaching portfolios with preservice English teachers. *Journal of Adolescent & Adult Literacy, 50*(6), 474–485. doi:10.1598/JAAL.50.6.5

Hallman, H.L., & Burdick, M.N. (2011). Service learning and the preparation of English teachers. *English Education, 43*(4), 341–368. Retrieved from http://search.proquest.com.www2.lib.ku.edu/docview/874324979?accountid=14556

Holquist, M. (1990). *Dialogism.* New York, NY: Routledge.

hooks, b. (1990). *Yearning: Race, gender, and cultural politics.* Boston, MA: South End Press.

Hong, J. Y. (2010). Pre-service and beginning teachers' professional identity and its relationship to dropping out of the profession. *Teaching and Teacher Education, 26*(8), 1530–1543. doi:10.1016/j.tate.2010.06.003

Jenkins, R. (1996). *Social identity.* London, England: Routledge.

Lefebvre, H. (1991). *The production of space.* Malden, MA: Blackwell Publishing.

Lortie, D. (1975). *Schoolteacher: A sociological study.* Chicago, IL: University of Chicago Press.

Luke, A., & Elkins, J. (1998). Reinventing literacy in new times. *Journal of Adolescent & Adult Literacy, 42*(1), 4–7.

Luttrell, W. (2003). *Pregnant bodies, fertile minds.* New York, NY: Routledge.

McInerney, P., Smyth, J., & Down, B. (2011). 'Coming to a place near you?' The politics and possibilities of a critical pedagogy of place-based education. *Asia-Pacific Journal of Teacher Education, 39*(1), 483–494. doi:10.1080/1359866X.2010.540894

Moje, E. (2008). Foregrounding the disciplines in secondary literacy teaching and learning: A call for change. *Journal of Adolescent & Adult Literacy, 52*(2), 96–107. Retrieved from www.jstor.org.www2.lib.ku.edu/stable/20111747

Moya, P. (2006). What's identity got to do with it? Mobilizing identities in the multicultural classroom. In L. M. Alcoff, M. Hames-Garcia, S. Mohanty, & P. Moya (Eds.), *Identity politics reconsidered* (pp. 96–117). New York, NY: Palgrave Publications.

Popkewitz, T.S. (1998). *Struggling for the Soul: The politics of schooling and the construction of the teacher.* New York, NY: Teachers College Press.

Popkewitz, T.S. (2009). Curriculum study, curriculum history, and curriculum theory: The reason of reason. *Journal of Curriculum Studies, 41*(3), 301–319. doi:10.1080/00220270902777021

Popkewitz, T.S. (2010). The limits of teacher education reform: School subjects, alchemies, and an alternative possibility. *Journal of Teacher Education, 61*(5), 413–421. doi:10.1177/0022487110375247

Poulou, M. (2007). Student-teachers concerns about teaching practice. *European Journal of Teacher Education, 31*(1), 91–110. doi:10.1080/02619760600944993

Portes, P.R., & Smagorinsky, P. (2010). Static structures, changing demographics: Educating teachers for shifting populations in stable schools. *English Education, 42*(3), 236–247. Retrieved from www.jstor.org/stable/40607989

Shulman, L. (2005). Pedagogies of uncertainty. *Liberal Education, 91*(2), 18–25. Retrieved from http://search.proquest.com.www.2.lib.ku.edu/docview/209812613/abstract?accountid=14556

Theobald, P. (2006). A case for inserting community into public school curriculum. *American Journal of Education, 112*(3), 315–334. doi:10.1086/500711

Trent, J., & Lim, J. (2010). Teacher identity construction in school-university partnerships: Discourse and practice. *Teaching and Teacher Education, 26*(8), 1609–1618. doi:10.1016/j.tate.2010.06.012

Warren, D. (Ed.) (1989). *American teachers: Histories of a profession at work.* New York, NY: Macmillan.

Zembylas, M. (2003). Interrogating 'teacher identity': Emotion, resistance, and self-formation. *Educational Theory, 58*(1), 107–127. doi:10.1111/j.1741-5446.2003.00107.x

3 Questioning through Writing
Writing as Dialogic Response

A month into the fall semester, beginning teachers from Wilkerson University had settled into their fieldwork and other course work. Kelly Laponte, who was working within an English classroom at Mettle Street School, had begun writing in her journal, capturing observations of the school and students as well as asking questions about her fieldwork. She had recently met a 17-year-old student, Carla, who had opened up to her and had told her about the pathway she had taken in coming to Mettle Street. As Kelly processed what Carla had told her, she wrote about it in her journal. Kelly circled around the concern she kept having about academic standards at the school and wrote:

> Carla told me that she has been at Mettle Street for two years. She used to go to Jackson City High. She said she wished she had tried harder when she was at Jackson City High, but that she liked Mettle Street because the teachers actually cared and wanted to help their students. This was so encouraging, but I wonder if academic standards are compromised for this.

Kelly's concern for what she viewed as a compromise of academic standards was an ongoing concern for her and one that she expressed throughout the semester. Using a journal to voice her concerns, she used writing as a tool to question her assumptions. Kelly's concern about Mettle Street School and Carla's pathway in arriving there was not the same concern other beginning teachers in her cohort expressed, and she rarely expressed these sentiments when speaking among her peers. We suspected that Kelly perceived that her views on the issue of standards were divergent from the views of her peers, and, for this reason, she felt a social obligation to keep quiet. Kelly's writing, on the other hand, became a space for her to explore divergent views. In this chapter, we explore the prospective teachers' work within the space of their writing and look directly at the writing prospective teachers produced throughout the community fieldwork experience. We consider how writing became a meeting place for the personal and the public and how beginning teachers learned to make meaning not within an isolated linguistic system but, rather, amid a cacophonous background of other utterances that were always pushing up against their own. Bakhtin's (1981, 1986) force of heteroglossia manifested itself in the writing of prospective teachers, as did the concept of *answerability* (Bakhtin, 1993). We look specifically at the writing of Rhonda Jackson, Kelly Laponte, and Katherine Sternmeister, and think about how a Bakhtinian view of writing disrupts the strict dichotomies of personal/public and self/other in prospective teachers' writing.

WRITING AS DIALOGIC RESPONSE

The concept of *dialogism* can be viewed as interchangeable with the notion of conversation, with the idea of conversation viewed as a "typical, social, human condition . . . in which social knowledge and selves are constructed" (Danielewicz, 2001, p. 145). Bakhtin considers that all language is inherently dialogic and writes that "life is dialogical by its very nature. To live means to engage in dialogue, to question, to listen, to answer, to agree" (Todorov, 1984, p. 97). Through these engagements, we form understandings of ourselves and of others and begin to see what possibilities are open to us.

Likewise, Bakhtin views writing not solely as a private reflection of one's experience or the public production of a finished text but, instead, as the meeting of reflection and production. Texts are an ongoing interplay between personal and public voices (Welch, 1993, p. 494), as well as part of a greater system than the words or sentences of which they are composed (Bakhtin, 1981, pp. 42–49). Like conversation, the act of writing is dialogic response, structured through the interplay of utterance and answer. Utterances are created, in part, to structure the self and to create knowledge. Knowledge, then, is intended and positioned as an answer to the other, and this cycle of utterance and answer continues in a dynamic fashion, imbued with one's beliefs and values.

Emig (1977) described the learning process through writing as an intrinsically dialogic one, and one in which the writer is both communicator and respondent, providing feedback and critique upon the communication. She calls this "a unique form of feedback, as well as reinforcement, [that] exists with writing, because information from the *process* is immediately and visibly available as that portion of the *product* already written" (Emig, 1977, p. 125, italics in original). She extends this thought by saying that "the importance for learning of a product in a familiar and available medium for immediate, literal (that is, visual) re-scanning and review cannot perhaps be overstated" (Emig, 1977, p. 125). Emig's work was groundbreaking, in that it articulated the recursive quality that writing possessed. Her work was also groundbreaking, however, because it essentially moved a theory of dialogism inside the writer him- or herself. Moving the cycle of utterance and answer inside oneself as writer stresses the power of the utterance. Utterances become, then, not single voices, but rather voices always animated by other voices. Bakhtin calls this animation the force of *heteroglossia*, and we view this many-voicedness, as articulating the exchange between a speaker and an intended other. Bakhtin suggests that all meaning is created through two parts—'utterance' and 'answer' (Bakhtin, 1986, p. 91) and that these two parts mutually respond to each other. Language always exhibits heteroglossic characteristics; this quality is not a dissonance, or unnatural but a part of language. Bakhtin (1981) writes that heteroglossia is alive as long as language is alive and states,

> But this occurs in the midst of heteroglossia, which grows as long as language is alive. Every concrete utterance of a speaking subject serves as a point where centrifugal as well as centripetal forces are brought to bear. The processes of centralization and decentralization, of unification and disunification, intersect in the utterance; the utterance not only answers the requirements of its own language as an individualized embodiment of a speech act, but it answers the requirements of heteroglossia as well; it is in fact an active participant in such speech diversity. (p. 272)

Although Bakhtinian concepts, including heteroglossia, have proven to be an important component of many sociocultural accounts of literacy learning (e.g., Graue, Kroeger, & Prager, 2001; Heath, 1982), Juzwik (2004) notes that Bakhtin's (1993) concept of *answerability*, or the ethical component of Bakhtin's theoretical framework, has been underexplored. Juzwik defines answerability as a "relational, participatory understanding of moral personhood that focuses attention on the authorial responsibility of individual speakers and writers and is thus concerned with the individual's capacity for good or harm, through responsive acts of language" (2004, p. 537). Viewing participants (teachers) as 'moral agents' (2007, p. 539) in the classroom, Juzwik writes that answerability provides "a mechanism for theorizing individuals as responsive *and* responsible moral agents in classrooms" (2007, p. 538). As participants in dialogue, participants strive to make meaning with others while, at the same time, offer judgment and evaluation about the meanings made. As moral agents, participants question or extend the argument with which they are presented, striving for an agreement between speakers. At other times, participants remain satisfied to continue to reside in a stance of disagreement between speakers.

As participants move to become both responders and moral agents within interaction with others, how do they do so within the space of the texts they produce? How does participants' writing serve as a site for deliberating one's own action and interaction with others? Through looking at the texts of three beginning teachers, Rhonda Jackson, Kelly Laponte, and Katherine Sternmeiser, we explore these questions.

RHONDA'S TEXTS: RECOGNIZING HETEROGLOSSIA

Rhonda Jackson was an elementary education student from a small town and saw her identity as being a part of that small town, planning to return to her own elementary school as a teacher after graduation. As Rhonda reflected on her experiences at the writing center at Mettle Street School, she showed her tough, rural background, and focused on the ways that working with students at Mettle Street School affected her energy levels as well as her perception of appropriate instruction.

In her first journal entry, Rhonda expressed her reservations about working at Mettle Street School, mainly because of the reputation of the school and the ways others reacted to her placement:

> I was a little nervous on my first day . . . I was a little intimidated. Whenever I told people that I was going to be working there for a while, I heard things like, "Ha, good luck!" or "betcha' that'll be interesting!" When I walked in, I was pleasantly surprised by the students . . . They were a far cry from the "problem kids" people made them out to be.

After being "pleasantly surprised by the students," Rhonda reflected upon reasons that the students were in this particular school (and not the school settings she grew up in and considered to be the norm). The fault was not that of the students, but Rhonda considered it a larger issue:

> It soon became clear to me that the . . . students were kids who'd slipped through the educational system. Somewhere along the lines they had been failed, either by their teachers, the school, and probably by their parents as well. . . . I left on my first day ready to tackle anything!

Rhonda's journal writings responded to the way that at-risk youth, as a group, were characterized by society, and she used the space of the journal to challenge the normal/at-risk dichotomy and how this framed academic success. At the same time, Rhonda's journal entries voiced a desire to grapple with the past and the present in the lives of youth at Mettle Street. Moving back and forth between strong assertions for new conceptualizations of at-risk youth and plans for how she might teach students at Mettle Street School, Rhonda's journal entries suggested that she was responding to multiple views about students at the school, teaching these students, and explaining to others the value of working with students at Mettle Street. These multiple views, or internally persuasive discourses, were acknowledged and presented in Rhonda's journal writing.

Although all texts respond to other utterances, Rhonda's journal writing stresses a dialogue with both herself and the larger society. In personal terms, she seeks to challenge the views she has held—the views that include how Mettle Street School is unlike her own educational background and the realization that the students at Mettle Street School were not seen as 'normal.' Here, we see what Bakhtin (1981, pp. 324–325) refers to as "double-voiced discourse." We hear not just Rhonda's words but also the words of many. These voices include a number of discourses about at-risk youth: the 'toughness' of teaching these youth, the characterizations society holds about youth who attend schools like Mettle Street, and the future possibilities for these youth. These discourses become part of the authoritative discourse with which Rhonda engages. Rhonda does not discard these multiple, and sometimes contradictory, discourses. Rather, she allows them to exist alongside her own assertions, thereby creating a tension against which her own words can resonate.

During her first day at her field placement at Mettle Street School, Rhonda goes through a transition of being nervous to being ready to work with the kids she views as having been failed by the adults and institutions in their lives. As Rhonda continued her placement, however, she reflected on other experiences that she described as affecting her energy levels and her understandings of what it means to be a teacher. She wrote,

> Then I read the student writing. That took the wind out of my sails... at the same time though, a little fire began to burn inside me, that made me want to really get to know these students struggles and become an advocate for them in some way.

Rhonda begins to see students' writing more complexly. Although she is discouraged by what she perceives of as a lack of quality in student writing completed for a school assignment, when she read a piece of student writing that wasn't written for school, she reflected on this writing and wrote, "The author had a real knack for writing, but that wasn't being conveyed in her weekly senior composition essays. It got me thinking, 'How can two opposite ends of the spectrum exist in one student's writing?' "

The dualism between students' in-school and out-of-school writing that Rhonda newly recognizes provides a glimpse into the way discourses framing at-risk youth are themselves part of the heteroglossic fabric in which teachers operate. As discourses are always overlapping and multiple, rather than clearly defined by boundaries, there are multiple discourses of at-risk youth operating at once. Describing this as students' ability to be "two things at once" points to one instance where Rhonda begins to produce a counterstory (Yosso, 2006), reorienting her actions toward a future teacherly self: a future teacherly self that she imagines can intervene and work productively in the lives of the students at Mettle Street.

In crafting this counterstory, Rhonda's journal entries begin to express what we see as a "rhetoric of the future," or a rhetoric of creating possible, future teacherly selves who will work in earnest to influence students' lives. Rhonda wrote,

> This is where the system has failed the students at Mettle Street. These "problem kids" need a different type of instruction, an educational system that supports their lives and includes them in the materials, not one that shuns them and puts labels on them. I've seen both sides at Mettle Street.

In a study of teacher identity with primary literacy teachers in Australia, McDougall (2010) found that her participants also responded to the changing demands of the present and the future. McDougall grounds this analysis in new times by offering three perspectives to which teachers identified: traditionalism, survival, or futures. Study participants who identified with traditionalism expressed "preference for traditional teaching priorities" (McDougall, 2010, p. 683), and these included 'basic' reading and writing skills. These participants also rejected the inclusion of new literacies. Participants who were in survival mode also rejected expanding definitions of literacy but embraced this stance because they felt unable/unqualified to teach new literacies. Finally, participants who saw themselves through a futures oriented perspective saw new literacies and expanded definitions of literacy as opportunities for personal growth. These teachers also saw the potential that such literacies would motivate students in new and exciting ways in the classroom. Rhonda's rhetoric of the future projects future possibilities, and looking back on her experiences in her final journal reflection, Rhonda confessed that she has made a conceptual change in thinking about the relevance of her placement at Mettle Street School:

> To be honest, when I started working at Mettle Street School, I didn't expect much of it. I'm getting my degree in elementary education, have no plans on working in a city school district, and I hadn't had much experience working with underprivileged kids. I went to a school with very little diversity, and frankly, I didn't expect the students at Mettle Street to want to listen to me, or take me serious. The only thing I thought would be relevant was the fact that I was getting a license in middle school English. Boy, was I wrong!
>
> Needless to say, my experience at Mettle Street has been a transformational one. I've found a new teaching passion that I never thought I would . . . I may not have influenced the students at Mettle Street much at all, but seeing their struggles sure has influenced me, and given me the kind of hope for my educational career that I may not have found otherwise.

Although Rhonda didn't see teaching urban at-risk students in her future, her placement at Mettle Street School challenged her to think about her own assumptions and then move to rethink larger, institutionalized assumptions. Rhonda's final journal entry recognized the many voices—the heteroglossia—present in her own conversation about working with youth at Mettle Street School. She recognized the Rhonda who wanted to keep the status quo and go back to the rural elementary classrooms in which she grew up, and this Rhonda was able to speak with the Rhonda who was discovering a teaching purpose within an urban writing center. As the semester closed, Rhonda began to reflect on and internalize a dialogue with larger educational issues of differentiated curriculum and standardization. Through her work at Mettle Street School, Rhonda began to see that she could also be a part of a very different school setting and that 'different' was not necessarily problematic.

KELLY'S TEXTS: UPLOADING THE 'VOICE OF THE FATHER'

As we have discussed, Bakhtin understood that individuals are persuaded by conversants who have authority—whether these authorities are in the form of another individual or the larger society. Welch (1993) describes Bakhtin's concept of authoritative discourse as being "the word of the father, of distant and inflexible authorities, and significantly, of teachers" (p. 498), noting that there is a gap between "the authoritative word (religious, political, moral, the word of the father, of adults and of teachers, etc.)" and one's internally persuasive discourses" (Bakhtin, 1981, p. 342). Authoritative discourse, working alongside internally persuasive discourse, produces a dialogic and dialectical struggle between these two categories. Grappling with these two forces, there is a shared sense of discourse between individual and conversant. Bakhtin (1981) notes,

> The word in language is half someone else's. It becomes "one's own" only when the speaker populates it with one's own intentions, his own accent, when he appropriates the word, adapting it to his own semantic and expressive intention. (p. 293)

Understanding teaching as a dialogic process between self and other was a new concept for many of the prospective teachers with whom we worked, and Kelly Leponte was not an exception. Kelly Laponte, a quiet and easygoing elementary education major, came to teaching with the idea that teaching was a profession that was atheoretical and that 'standards' were universal truths that dictated the quality of education that one receives. Kelly reiterates the 'voice of the father' through her subscription to authoritative discourse.

In one of her journals, Kelly wrote that she "realized how different the standards were at this school [Mettle Street School] versus where [she] went to high school" and later reflects that "many of these students [students at Mettle Street School] probably would not graduate if they were at any other school." As Vagle (2012) notes, "it is perhaps difficult to imagine a curriculum that does not center on standards" (p. 29), or what he terms 'sameness'

(p. 29). Standards, as a tool for producing 'sameness,' "limit as much as they make possible" (Vagle, 2012, p. 29). Rather than ask questions of standards such as "Who writes standards?" and "Who decides what is rigorous?" Kelly is more comfortable asserting that standards create and uphold possibilities for students. We did not necessarily find this surprising but thought about how we could assist students such as Kelly in thinking more deeply about standards and their meaning in the classroom.

Looking back at her experiences of schooling, Kelly, like Rhonda, initially expressed reservations about her placement at Mettle Street School. Following is an excerpt from her first journal entry:

> I was really nervous going into this school. I wasn't really sure even what grade level I would be working with. I only knew this was a school for students with behavioral problems or because they fell behind in regular public school. I was pleasantly surprised. Everyone I came in contact with staff-wise was very friendly and helpful . . . I feel like I am not adequate to help them and they would not want help.

Instead of worrying about the relevance of her placement, however, Kelly describes feelings of inadequacy and considers where and if she will fit in to the space of the school. Her written reflections attempt to write herself into the space. At this early point in her placement, she cannot yet find where she will fit at Mettle Street. The staff and teachers seem welcoming, but she asks, "Will my presence be adequate for students' needs? Will my presence be welcomed into the students' spaces?"

Kelly's view of teaching before her experience at Mettle Street most closely resembled a view of teaching that sought conformity with social conventions about what it means to be a teacher. Conformity, as Britzman, (1991) describes it in relation to teacher education, is more than "the uniformity of thought and the standardization of activity. As a measure for being, conformity diminishes prospects of becoming something other than what has been previously established" (p. 29). In this regard, Kelly was unsure what conventions and conformities she might upload and what ones she might challenge. As a result, Kelly worked to create a present-oriented teacherly self and future-oriented teacherly self. She looked back in time and reminded us of her nervousness. After this, she moved us forward in her writing and prompted us to consider how her present-oriented teacherly self was negotiating uncharted terrain. There was a persistence in Kelly's writing that argued that her life was changing; therefore, she must move forward in finding out what teaching is about and how she will inhabit the profession. Kelly wrote,

> The context of my service learning had a great impact on my experience. I was helping students in a 'recovery' school where their home life and background is often very difficult and that has affected their learning. This is different from how I grew up which posed a challenge for me to

> relate to the students and gain their respect. It was a unique opportunity because if I had been anywhere else, I might have been facing honors students who were better writers than I was. The fact that my Mettle Street students were not as advanced gave me a passionate reason to help them and insert myself into their writing and lives in general.

Because the students at Mettle Street were somehow 'below expectations,' Kelly believed that there was a space for her to "insert" herself into their learning experiences. She reflected on her own insecurities and on how they affected the ways she felt she could work with students. Kelly's writing, perhaps more affirming of her position as a teacher than Rhonda's, offers a framing of self that is consistent with writing as imagining a future-oriented teacherly self that will possess the possibility of 'inserting' herself into students' lives. In this way, Kelly was beginning to embrace the idea that the work of teaching could be a dialogue between teacher and student.

Kelly recognizes that her ability to dialogue with students is not only dependent on her actions, as her understanding of a teacher's role as inserting oneself into students' lives became more complicated when Kelly started to question what a teacher's role was with students at Mettle Street. She struggled, over the course of her entire experience, to resolve the idea of standards in education with her experience at Mettle Street and wrote about standards as a normalizing force in students' educational experience:

> It is hard for me to gauge where normal high school seniors should be, but I know it must be higher than where these students are. I know that their teachers care about them and care if they graduate, but do they truly care that these students grow to their full potential?

Over the course of the semester, Kelly's reiteration of the role of both standards and teachers in bringing students to what she deems to be a certain level of competence constrains her view of teaching and schooling. The force of standards, for her, becomes the voice of authority that fails to intersect with other discourses that shape adolescence, schooling, and opportunity. We continually asked ourselves how we might disrupt Kelly's "voice of the father" and whether she would be receptive to this. We offer some thoughts about this later in the chapter, when we connect teachers' writing to reflective practice in teacher education. As we remembered Bakhtin's comments that authoritative discourse will push up against an individual's own thoughts and give rise to internally persuasive discourse, we seemed not to see evidence of this being realized in Kelly's case. Throughout her experience at Mettle Street, Kelly was still seeking to validate dominant discourses that framed the teaching profession, such as the discourse of standards. We saw this as a sign that prospective teachers need guidance in negotiating authoritative discourse, and believe that writing can be a tool to help them with this work.

KATHERINE'S TEXTS: EMPHASIZING ANSWERABILITY

Katherine Sternmeister, a nontraditional student in her thirties, worried about the students she came in contact with at Mettle Street School. Over time, Katherine was able to see how her presence, even for a short time, made a difference to students. For the duration of her field experience, Katherine was very concerned about the boundaries between teachers and students and mentioned coming in contact with a former student at the grocery store. This occurrence, although ordinary, reinforced the negotiation of boundaries between teacher and students. Over the course of the semester, Katherine reflected on the relationship that had developed with this same student and viewed this relationship as almost unequal to the relationships she was developing with other students. She asked, "How might my experience now be different than in my future classroom where I will be responsible for larger numbers of students?"

Katherine looked to others for constructive feedback about her teaching and sought to understand her place at Mettle Street School. Instead of judging herself as inadequate, she searched out feedback from other teachers and staff members at the school. Although she began her teaching at Mettle Street with worry for the students, over time she was able to move from being worried about the kids at Mettle Street to creating close and caring relationships with two of the kids—one relationship that she hopes will continue, at least, on an acquaintance basis. Her belief that relationships need time and through time all relationships could grow to be fulfilling, Katherine hinged her success with students on time:

> Many of the students in the school appeared 'rough.' This is a charter school where, if you don't make the grade, you're kicked out . . . I only spent a total of about 20 hours . . . and even less time than that with each student. Although Dr. Cleary said she knew that what I was doing and saying to the students was helping them, I felt like I could have done so much more with more time.

Through her reflections, Katherine's concern for the ethical dimension of teaching was evident. When she wrote about her work at Mettle Street, she emphasized the relationships she was building with students and how these relationships shaped teaching and learning.

As we sought to characterize Katherine's emphasis on relationships with students as part of the teaching act, we looked to Juzwik's (2004) *ethics of answerability*. In outlining a theory of what she refers to as "moral personhood," Juzwik seeks to capitalize on Bakhtin's work to not only elaborate a dialogic responsiveness through texts but also to situate texts as vehicles that allow speakers to develop their sense of moral personhood. Juzwik argues that this area of moral personhood has been generally neglected in sociocultural literacy research; we would agree with this claim, and see

Katherine's case as a way to particularize the idea of moral agency within dialogic response. Juzwik notes that, although the idea of dialogism has helped to overturn problematic notions in literacy studies (for summary, see Ewald, 1993/1998, pp. 227–230), many studies have not adequately theorized what we can think about as 'agency.' In outlining an ethics of answerability, Juzwik looks to the work of Hicks (2000), who wrote that "the responses of individuated subjects are flexible and answerable in ways that can embrace, resist, or redefine what is 'given' historically or culturally" (p. 231). In this way, Hicks (2000) looks to selves as possessing answerability in the event-of-being.

Katherine continually looked for her agency as a teacher as emergent through the event-of-being. That is, she positioned herself as responsive to students' needs within the moment during her time at Mettle Street. More than many other beginning teachers, Katherine pursued ways to connect with and encourage students. Unlike others who delineated a present-oriented and future-oriented self, Katherine desired to be and become a teacher to students 'in the moment.' In one journal entry, she wrote,

> During 5th hour, I got an opportunity to talk to the girl [a student previously mentioned in her journal] about college. I had heard from Emily that she was interested in nursing and pediatrics, so I engaged her in a conversation about that. I also told her about the option of starting out at a community college and how that would be a much cheaper option. I shared with her my experience with community college and the option to even take many classes online. She visited the community college's website for a while and seemed interested. I told her if she ever had any questions or wanted any more information that I would be happy to help her.

In the preceding journal entry, Katherine clearly positioned herself in a relationship with the student, seeking to provide her with guidance and encouragement. The active engagement Katherine seeks forces us to recognize her as 'active' in representing her teacherly self, as opposed to being 'passive,' as we might characterize Kelly. Offering important questions that we, as researchers, might ask about answerability in the classroom, Juzwik outlines a series of questions that we may ask in order to discern the agency that our participants possess. One such question is, To what extent do students actively respond (so binding themselves to others) rather than passively shut down within classroom interaction? (Juzwik, 2004, p. 559). We see Katherine as seeking this active engagement, thereby creating a moral imperative with others. We see the ethical dimension of dialogism as offering insight on why and when prospective teachers assert agency. The ethical dimension of dialogism, Juzwik (2004) notes, reminds us that

> social analyses, however powerful, are never enough: the particularity of individuals embedded within morally obligating relationships must

also be examined in order to understand the intricacies of literacy teaching and learning as they emerge in "answerable" classroom practice. Answerability suggests that language and literacy be considered within contexts of students and teachers and researchers acting to position themselves, through literacy practices, as more or less responsive and responsible to others. (p. 562)

Being responsive and responsible, through writing, led us to emphasize the role of writing in prospective teachers' community-based fieldwork. We now turn to discuss how tenets of dialogism might frame reflection in teacher education, thereby continually emphasizing both the responsive and responsible sides of Bakhtin's work.

REFLECTION IN TEACHER EDUCATION AS DIALOGIC

For the remainder of this chapter, we explore how reflection in teacher education, like writing, might embody a dialogic stance. Because there has been much written about reflective practice, and therefore, much confusion in educational contexts about what constitutes meaningful reflection (Fendler, 2003; Kinsella, 2007), beginning teachers may need to consider the ways that reflection, or what we prefer to see as reflexive pedagogy, leads to revision in their teaching practice.

Reflective practice through written reflection is something that has almost become cliché in education programs, yet the act of reflecting on one's teaching can lead to a 'reflexive pedagogy,' or a teaching practice that values using language to question, evaluate, and change one's practice. As Danielewicz (2001) notes, the acts of being reflective and being reflexive are not often differentiated, and reflection in teacher education may connote contemplation and moments of looking back at one's practice devoid of any necessary critical evaluation or change (p. 156). Reflexivity, on the other hand, aims to connect an intentional means to an end and involves goals of critique and revision for the purpose of changing thought or behavior. Danielewicz writes that reflexivity "entails thinking that turns back on itself, a reexamination or revisiting of a project or an activity, and a questioning of motives, frameworks, assumptions, working strategies, conclusions, beliefs, and actions" (2001, p. 156). We see reflexivity as intimately connected to the concept of dialogism, as both are concerned with how language and social interaction are present in meaning making, and view both as tools that teacher educators must draw on to assist students in articulating the value of a teaching stance grounded in inquiry.

Fendler's (2003) discussion of reflective practice in teacher education theorizes and historicizes the practice of reflection. Through her contribution and others, teacher educators and researchers have understood that although reflective practice has been almost universally conceived of as beneficial to teachers' professional behavior and development (Schön, 1983,

1987; Zeichner & Liston, 1990), it has oftentimes suffered marginalization, as a practice, due to its connotation with various modes of thinking and writing as well as loosely defined goals. Reflection has also been based primarily on beginning teachers' memories and constructions of classroom events (as opposed to 'evidence' from classrooms); this has contributed to reflection's marginal status. Despite work throughout the past two decades that has outlined the 'how to' in reflective practice (e.g., Korthagen & Kessels, 1999) as well as work that has offered classifications of different types of reflection practiced by teachers and teacher educators (e.g., Carr & Kemmis, 1986; Gore, 1993; Zeichner & Tabachnick, 1991), reflective practice in teacher education still vacillates between associations with the personal and the pedagogical. Researchers (e.g., Hatton & Smith, 1995) have recognized that there are, indeed, different 'types' and 'stages' of reflection, ranging from attitudes of technical rationality to critical reflection, but these classifications still lean toward categorizing reflective practice as separate from its context of use, thereby promoting a process/product divide.

Genre, in a rhetorical sense, becomes a key tool in attending to reflection's local-level influences. Genre refers to not just the forms of texts, but the work these texts actually *do* in discourse communities, thereby disposing of a notion of genre as merely form and text type and, instead, embracing a new conception of genre—a newness that Devitt (1993) calls the "dynamic patterning of human experience" (p. 573). This conception of genre shifts, then, from a focus on the formal features of a text to the sources of those features. Text and textual meaning are no longer objective and static but formed based on the interaction between speaker/writer, text, and audience. Furthermore, viewing genre as only form of text divorces form and content, and a rhetorical framing of genre adheres to Bakhtin's (1981) description of genre as a space where "form and content in discourse are one" (p. 259). Genre unites process and product and becomes what Bakhtin (1986) calls "the whole of the utterance" (p. 60).

Genre, however, is malleable and is subject to change by speakers/writers. As teachers, for example, reflect on their practice in writing, their reflections become populated with many voices—voices of others, the institutions in which they work, and the jargon of teacher education itself. This heteroglossic fabric was explored in Rhonda's journal entries. When Fendler (2003) asserts the influence of "conservative, radical, feminist, and Deweyan" (p. 17) viewpoints within teacher reflection, she calls attention to reflection's heteroglossic quality.

Fendler interrogates the notion that reflection is 'natural' and, instead, posits that reflection is never neutral but always a product of historical influences. A Bakhtinian inquiry complements Fendler's (2003) genealogical analysis yet works on a local level, through genre, to highlight the ways in which individual teachers' reflections are in dialogue with both history and a local-level context. Particularly, a dialogic view of reflection permits the idea that the local context in which a reflection situated and produced is paramount to the way a particular reflection is analyzed. While a genealogical approach such as Fendler's aims to illuminate the broad, historical influences on teacher reflection, a Bakhtinian analysis focused on dialogism enables researchers to attend to the local-level influences on individual teachers' reflections.

After exploring how Rhonda, Kelly, and Katherine were able to use writing as a process for thinking and for articulating a dialogic stance as well as a stance of moral personhood, we begin with seeing writing itself through a stance of inquiry. Richardson's (2000) stance that writing is, indeed, part of the process of making meaning is unveiled through her claim that "writing is not just a mopping-up activity at the end . . . Writing is also a way of 'knowing'—a method of discovery and analysis" (p. 923). Richardson's assertion fits squarely with scholars in composition, like Emig (1977), who turned the tide to view writing as a process inside oneself, containing both utterance and answer.

Teacher Reflection as Genre: Responsive, Fluid, and Contextual

As we looked across the journal entries written by Rhonda, Kelly, and Katherine, we noticed a desire to use writing to shift initial perceptions of students at Mettle Street School. We noticed the way that all three prospective teachers approached journal writing in ways that attended to the influences of an intended other—in this case, Heidi and Melanie, teacher educators. Throughout the study, we were aware that the ways in which we framed community-based fieldwork in our methods courses would influence how beginning teachers wrote about the value of this work. When examining beginning teachers' writing, we looked to the mechanism by which this shift occurred and saw genre as this mechanism. As stated previously, genre refers not simply to text form as some have conceived of it in a literary sense. Genre, at its core, is concerned with function and purpose within a text and with how writers draw on genres in order to accomplish intended purposes.

In the previous section, we discussed Kelly's reluctance to become a teacher who could shed the authoritative voice as a way to allow an internally persuasive discourse emerge. We saw her grapple with the presence of standards throughout her experience and her journal entries developed as genres devoted to deliberating the presence of standards in the classroom. We believe that Kelly had internalized a rational approach to reflection—reflection as being a site of 'solving' problems. Because it was a repeated theme throughout her writing, we knew that Kelly wished to confront, and possibly challenge, her views about standards.

Throughout the semester, Melanie, who was the teacher educator who worked with Kelly, urged Kelly to think about her perception of her work at Mettle Street School. Melanie offered Kelly the encouragement to see her journal entries as responses to the context of Mettle Street School and the students. She prompted Kelly to focus on what she saw occurring within the school and what she thought about that. When Kelly began the journal entries, she believed that she would resolve her perceptions of standards and the students with whom she worked. She saw writing as a tool only for solution rather than a site for learning.

This dilemma echoes the conflict that prospective teachers often feel when responding simultaneously to Dewey's (1933) and Schön's (1983, 1987) conceptions of teacher reflection. Dewey's conception of reflection, as concerned with 'intelligent action' underscores the concept of a journey—one that is continuously related to ongoing progress and discovery. However, the premise of reflection, according to Schön (1983, 1987), is intuitive uncertainty, and is therefore a rejection of sorts of an ongoing quest for progress. This bind, Fendler (2003) notes, puts teachers in a position where they are expected to meet both goals—goals that are indeed difficult to meet simultaneously (p. 18).

We see that teachers, like Kelly, need a solution to residing in this bind and situate this solution through genre. We encourage teacher educators to discuss how the genre of reflection can shift, depending on the nature of the question at hand. Kelly, for example, began to understand that she was able to shift her journal's focus, or shift genre, when writing about standards at Mettle Street. She eventually came to reside in both a place where a present-oriented teacherly self and a future-oriented teacherly self could reside. By shifting genres, prospective teachers, like Kelly, reinforce teacher reflection as responsive, fluid, and contextual, therefore making genre shifts when appropriate to meet the dual goals of Deweyan 'intelligent action' and Schönian intuitive uncertainty.

IMPLEMENTING DIALOGIC REFLECTION IN TEACHER EDUCATION

A Bakhtinian conceptual framework can assist teacher educators and researchers in more fully recognizing the qualities inherent in teachers' reflective practice. Yet, what does a shift in the way teacher educators consider reflection as dialogic offer the field? First, using Bakhtinian tools allows for the acknowledgment of an explicit connection between the local-level influences on teachers' reflective practices and larger, historical influences. Sometimes referred to as a push–pull relationship between the speaker and the intended other, recognizing that this quality of heteroglossia as an inherent feature of language and language use removes the expectation that reflective practice in teacher education must be tidy. In fact, the heteroglossic quality of language underscores all text as in relation with an intended other, and therefore, is, at times, messy. Holquist (1990) references Bakhtin's notion about using language to achieve understanding and writes that "all meaning is achieved by struggle" (p. 39).

Second, an approach to teacher reflection as dialogic moves us to a next step: exploring what such a framework may offer beginning teachers, supervisors, or teacher educators. For example, with an explicit framing of teacher reflection as dialogic, might beginning teachers be moved to alter or improve their reflection? Does recognition of these dialogic features of reflection enhance, alter, or develop the very process of teacher reflection? Seeking to move reflection to be seen more as reflexive practice, we see that these questions may lead to a fruitful investigation with beginning teachers.

Bahktinian tools (Bhaktin, 1981, 1986) articulate an epistemology by way of articulating a theory of language. Teacher educators and researchers taking up a Bakhtinian conceptual framework as a way to understand reflective practice are able to better understand teachers' rhetorical moves in their thinking and reflective practice as purposeful. Viewing reflection as both process and product urges teachers and those interested in studying reflection to view reflection as intimately connected to the choices teachers make. Furthermore, understanding teacher reflection through a dialogic approach untangles the myth that teacher reflection is purely about growth as a teacher. In contrast, teacher reflection is often directed by other intentions: receiving a high grade on an assignment or finding 'resolution' to long-held questions. As Rhonda, Kelly, and Katherine illustrate, the genre of reflection is shaped in local-level ways through how knowledge is framed and experiences are structured. A dialogic approach to reflective practice in teacher reflection bridges the process/product divide and views all reflection as response to an intended other. All reflection is indeed action, and thereby urges teachers and teacher educators to consistently question and deliberate the intent of teachers' reflective practice.

REFERENCES

Bakhtin, M. (1981). *The dialogic imagination: Four essays* (M. Holquist. Ed.). Austin: University of Texas Press.
Bakhtin, M. (1986). *Speech genres and other late essays* (C. Emerson & M. Holquist, Eds.) Austin: University of Texas.
Bakhtin, M. (1993). *Toward a philosophy of the act* (V. Liapunov & M. Holquist, Eds). Austin: University of Texas Press.
Britzman, D.P. (1991). *Practice makes practice: A critical study of learning to teach.* Albany: State University of New York Press.
Carr, W., & Kemmis, S. (1986). *Becoming critical: Education, knowledge, and action research.* Basingstoke, England: Falmer.
Danielewicz, J. (2001). *Teaching selves: Identity, pedagogy, and teacher education.* Albany: State University of New York Press.
Devitt, A.J. (1993). Generalizing about genre: New conceptions of an old concept. *College Composition and Communication,* 44(4), 573–586. doi:10.2307/358391
Dewey, J. (1933). *How we think: A restatement of the relation of reflective thinking in the educative process.* New York, NY: D.C. Heath and Company.
Emig, J. (1977) Writing as a mode of learning. *College Composition and Communication,* 28(2), 122–128. doi:10.2307/356095
Eward, H. (1998). Waiting for answerability: Bakhtin and composition studies. In F. Farmer (Ed.), *Landmark essays on Bakhtin, rhetoric, and writing* (pp. 225–241). Mahwah, NJ: Erlbaum. (Original work published 1993)

Fendler, L. (2003). Teacher reflection in a hall of mirrors: Historical influences and political reverberations. *Educational Researcher, 32*(3), 16–25. Retrieved from www.jstor.org.www2.lib.ku.edu/stable/3699830

Gore, J. M. (1993). *The struggle for pedagogies: Critical and feminist discourses as regimes of truth.* New York, NY: Routledge.

Graue, M. E., Kroeger, J., & Prager, D. (2001). A Bakhtinian analysis of particular home-school relations. *American Educational Research Journal, 38,* 467–498. doi:10.3102/00028312038003467

Hatton, N., & Smith, D. (1995). Reflection in teacher education: Towards definition and implementation. *Teaching and Teacher Education, 11*(1), 33–49.

Heath, S. B. (1982). *Ways with words: Language, life, and work in communities and classrooms.* Cambridge, England: Cambridge University Press.

Hicks, D. (2000). Self and other in Bakhtin's early philosophical essays: Prelude to a theory of prose consciousness. *Mind, Culture, and Activity, 7,* 227–242. doi:10.1207/S15327884MCA0703_10 55

Holquist, M. (1990). *Dialogism.* New York, NY: Routledge.

Juzwik, M. (2004). Toward an ethics of answerability: *College Composition and Communication, 55*(3), 536–567. doi:10.2307/4140698

Kinsella, E. (2007). Embodied reflection and the epistemology of reflective practice. *Journal of Philosophy of Education, 41*(3), 395–409. doi:10.1111/j.1467-9752.2007.00574.x

Korthagen, F. A. J., & Kessels, J. P. A. M. (1999). Linking theory and practice: Changing the pedagogy of teacher education. *Educational Researcher, 28*(4), 4–17. doi:10.3102/0013189X028004004

McDougall, J. (2010). A crisis in professional identity: How primary teachers are coming to terms with changing views of literacy. *Teaching and Teacher Education, 26*(3), 679–687. doi:10.1016/j.tate.2009.10.003

Richardson, L. (2000). Writing: A method of inquiry. In N. K. Denzin & Y. S. Lincoln (Eds.), *Handbook of qualitative research: Context and method* (pp. 923–948). Thousand Oaks, CA: Sage.

Schön, D. (1983). *The reflective practitioner.* New York, NY: Basic Books.

Schön, D. (1987). *Educating the reflective practitioner.* San Francisco, CA: Jossey-Bass.

Todorov, T. (1984). *Mikhail Bakhtin: The dialogical principle* (Wlad Godzich, Trans.). Minneapolis: University of Minnesota Press.

Vagle, M. (2012). The anchor essay: Trying to poke holes in Teflon: Developmentalism; young adolescence; and contingent, recursive growth and change. In M. Vagle (Ed.), *Not a stage! A critical re-conception of young adolescent education* (pp. 11–38). New York, NY: Peter Lang.

Welch, N. (1993). One student's many voices: Reading, writing, and responding with Bakhtin. *Journal of Advanced Composition, 13*(2), 493–502. Retrieved from www.jstor.org/stable/20865929

Yosso, T. (2006). *Critical race counterstories along the Chicana/Chicano educational pipeline.* New York, NY: Routledge.

Zeichner, K. M., & Liston, D. (1990). Traditions of reform in U.S. teacher education. *Journal of Teacher Education, 34*(2), 3–20. doi:10.1177/002248719004100202

Zeichner, K. M., & Tabachnick, B. R. (1991). Reflections on reflective teaching. In B. R. Tabachnick & K. M. Zeichner (Eds.), *Issues and practices in inquiry-oriented teacher education* (pp. 1–21). New York, NY: Falmer.

4 Questioning Teaching
Disrupting a Teaching Mythology

We recognized how Rhonda, Kelly, and Katherine began to view the interactions they had with students as comprising part of the teaching act. Yet, as we have noted, the paradigm of "teacher as authority" was still held, by many prospective teachers, as the dominant model of classroom teaching (Portes & Smagorinsky, 2010). Thonus (2001), similarly, reflects that the dominant model for socializing writing tutors is one that differentiates tutor and teacher, with a tutor's role being distinct and different from a teacher's. Thonus notes that this is, indeed, a *tutoring mythology*—a mythology that constrains the tutor's role, limiting it to "issues of personality and strategies of interpersonal interaction" (2001, p. 61). We feel, similarly, that the paradigm of 'teacher as authority' bolsters a *teaching mythology* that constrains beginning teachers' views of an appropriate teacher's role. In an entry on Anne Chisholm's life graph, featured in Appendix D, we witnessed the pervasiveness of the teacher as authority paradigm in shaping beginning teachers' perceptions of the teaching act. Anne wrote,

> Mostly I feel that I'm practicing the role of being a tutor while I'm at Family Partnership. It has been rare that I'm really teaching the students something and it is more likely that I'll be working with them on their homework. I'm fine with that but I know I'm itching to get into an English classroom and really practice developing that teacher presence.

Anne's comments, and especially her lukewarm evaluation of her role through her expression "I'm fine with that" suggests that she looked on the experience at Family Partnership as distinctly not teaching. Through such a view, Anne subscribed to a teaching mythology. Other prospective teachers were also bound to a teaching mythology, and because of this perspective, they identified ways in which they felt stymied in their field site. Sarah Emerson wrote,

> I've been in limbo this semester. I feel that I have learned things at Family Partnership but I have not really learned about what it takes to be a teacher in a classroom. I see the role more as a tutor or a mentor and

not really a teacher. I've done a lot of tutoring and mentoring so I feel that I'm already good at those things. Family Partnership did teach me about the reality of homeless kids' lives.

Surely, reading such comments made us feel somewhat discouraged, and we often needed to think more carefully about how community fieldwork was presented to our students, as well as how we discussed the experience in our methods courses as it unfolded throughout the semester. As we saw in the previous chapter, beginning teachers at Mettle Street School, including Rhonda, Kelly, and Katherine, saw their agency limited as a result of teachers (most often the full-time, subject area teachers at the school) who possessed the specialized knowledge that allowed them authority and autonomy in the classroom. Juxtaposition between teacher and tutor was a focal point in many prospective teachers' narratives.

Other prospective teachers in our study described what they viewed as the 'transitional state' of identity they assumed while engaged in community fieldwork. Through their experience, they reflected on their positions of authority and on how such positions influenced the relationships they had with students. Because community fieldwork often required close relationships through one-on-one tutoring, beginning teachers sometimes lamented the fact that they were not positioned in a traditional teacher role, standing in front of a (passive) class and extolling information. They viewed the position they inhabited through their 'transitional state' as positioning them closer to the students with whom they worked yet further from curriculum. They viewed their role as not creating curriculum but, rather, as working through another teacher's curriculum with the students they tutored.

Sarah, earlier, displays this sentiment in claiming that she was already good at the roles of tutor and mentor. In setting up a mentor/tutor to teacher hierarchy, Sarah yearned for a teaching role that she felt she did not yet have. In the cases of Sarah and others, we acknowledged that prospective teachers felt as though they were missing the experience of inhabiting the role of teacher as authority and saw that they looked forward to this role despite our prompts that they challenge it.

Even though we guided prospective teachers toward challenging the role of teacher (see discussion questions featured later in this chapter, as well as examples featured in Chapter 7), we witnessed the role that developmentalism played in learning to teach. Developmentalism, as understood in education, presumes a linear progression of children's development. Children, through a developmental lens, tend to be seen as exhibiting tendencies due to their age, rather than due to other factors, such as disposition or sociocultural location. Devleopmentalism contributed to beginning teachers' desire to teach particular grade levels, because they often assumed children at particular life stages would have particular characteristics and learn in ways typical for their age.

Beginning teachers' affinity for learning to teach in a content area classroom with middle or high school youth did not lessen during their experience in community-based sites. Although prospective teachers wished to work with the age group they were being certified to teach, throughout our study we asked whether future secondary teachers might benefit from working with younger children, as well as whether future elementary teachers might benefit from experiences teaching older students, and we acknowledged that this has been a discussion generally absent from U.S. teacher education. Although we often heard prospective secondary teachers express that they wished to better understand the context of early and elementary education, we did not find evidence that this desire was addressed in most teacher education programs. It was rare that future middle/secondary teachers experienced teaching young children as part of their course work or fieldwork. And, we came to see that the preoccupation with developmentalism was part of upholding a teaching mythology. Developmentalism's certainty supported that a teaching mythology remain firmly rooted in beginning teachers' minds. Although our intention is not to dispute developmentalism altogether, we believe that allowing beginning teachers the space to challenge assumptions and mythologies can yield productive results.

Many prospective teachers viewed the new perspectives they were gaining through participation in community fieldwork as complementing their desire to inhabit a traditional teacher's role. We often saw that beginning teachers sought both experiences—one that was in a traditional field site and one in a community field site—and we encouraged this. Our hope is that teacher education programs can work in ways that offer inclusion of both community fieldwork and traditional fieldwork. At both of our institutions, we have been able to successfully integrate both experiences. As our book focuses on the inclusion of community fieldwork, we turn now to highlight how beginning teachers' perceptions on the role of tutor and teacher, and delineate how these roles emerged. We also discuss, in this chapter, productive ways that teacher educators might challenge presumptions about what fieldwork *is* and what its place is within programs.

To frame our discussion of these topics and issues, this chapter features two prospective teachers who challenged a teaching mythology in unique ways. Both teachers stood out among their peers in their respective cohorts, and both were committed to developing a teaching practice that would reach a wide spectrum of students. Henry Taylor, a preservice English teacher in his early 20s, questioned his role as teacher and how such a role might have bearing on his future work as a classroom English teacher. We maintained contact with Henry for 3 years following his work at Family Partnership and spoke with him about how perceived that his prior work with homeless students influenced his career choices as his career unfolded. Through reading Henry's reflections and engaging him in conversation, we explore how Henry's stories became important windows for identifying his understanding of himself as a future teacher, as well as his relationship with students.

The other teacher featured in this chapter is Anne Chisholm. Anne was a nontraditional student who came to teaching after spending more than a decade raising her family and relocating several times as a military spouse. Anne had always dreamed of becoming a teacher and her place in GSU's English education program led her to inhabit a role as a leader within her cohort; other, traditional-age college students looked to Anne for advice and guidance, and she accepted the maternal role she was given by members of the cohort with aplomb. Because Anne had grown up in Cedar Creek, the familiarity she had with the community context gave her confidence that her perceptions of middle and high school students growing up in Cedar Creek were accurate.

In each of these cases, we noticed an undercurrent running through the narratives that Henry and Anne told. This undercurrent was influenced by the history of the role of teacher, as well as the frameworks that dictated how gender was intertwined with teaching. In attending to Henry's and Anne's stories, we came face-to-face with developmentalism's influence on teaching, as most of the teachers with whom we worked encountered young children in community-based field sites when they were being trained to eventually teach students in middle and secondary schools. We saw how teacher education in the U.S. did not have an answer for explaining how beginning teachers' working with young children would prepare them for work with older students, and this led to our interest in articulating how the prevalence of developmentalism has constrained teachers' work. We move, through this chapter, to question and expand the role of the teacher today and to further examine how teaching, rooted in both gendered assumptions and developmental frameworks, influences prospective teachers' mythologies of teaching.

A BRIEF HISTORY OF THE ROLE OF TEACHER

Of the groups of beginning teachers involved in our study, those who worked at Family Partnership expressed the widest range of perceptions about their role as teachers while participating in community fieldwork. Some beginning teachers found that youth at Family Partnership recognized students from GSU as 'teachers' within the context of the Family Partnership organization. Sometimes, however, GSU students were acknowledged as 'volunteers.' Whereas some teachers believed that they could make certain moves with their students because they were not positioned as teachers, other prospective teachers equalized the roles of teacher, tutor, and volunteer in their written reflections. Although this equalizing view of a teacher's role was distinctly different from many others' views that endorsed the view of teacher as authority, this perspective, nonetheless, affirmed the idea that prospective teachers' identity-building process resided on a continuum that was affected by certain experiences with students. The continuum subtly carried a progress narrative, one that told preservice teachers that they would increasingly gain more knowledge over time and move from a role of student, to a role of tutor, and, eventually, to a role of teacher. This narrative of 'progress' of the teacher mirrors, in many ways, the manner in which Popkewitz (1998) references the way "personal salvation and redemption [are] tied to personal development and 'fulfillment,' words that signaled religious motifs but placed them in secular discourses of science and rational progress" (p. 24). Prospective teachers' construction of progress narratives became a way for them to seek authority while covertly maintaining the teacher as authority trope.

Historically, the teaching profession has been primarily a female occupation (Warren, 1989) that has carried the stigma of attracting lower and middle-class individuals—individuals who are sometimes more weakly prepared academically than their peers. For men, teaching has been seen as a transitory career, because men tend to choose advancement related to administrative options. Alsup (2006) notes that the rise of the mother figure in teaching arose after the industrial age, when the increase of factories and the rise of mechanization led more men to work away from home. As a result, women came to be seen as the ideal teacher, due to their believed biological nature to nurture and their role as mothers (Schell, 1997). This trend became firmly established in the mid-20th century, with three quarters of the American teachers in 1950 being female (Rury, 1989). Women also viewed teaching as a compromise between joining the workforce and staying in the home, and through the early 20th century, women's salaries were much lower than their male counterparts' were. Yet, women often viewed teaching as a way to improve their social standing through a respected occupation. In African American communities, the role of the teacher was perhaps not as gendered as within white communities, as the honorable position of "teacher" was seen as a way to 'uplift' the African American race (Perkins, 1989, p. 345).

The cultural script—briefly overviewed earlier—of the teacher has been fairly consistent over the past century. Lortie's (1975) ethnography of teachers working in a school in the Boston area revealed the way that conservative cultural scripts of teaching constrained teachers' work. And, as it has been iterated many times, in no other profession do individuals enter the profession with "12-plus years of experience interacting with and watching teachers on a daily basis" (Alsup, 2006, p. 33). Recently, there has been interest in theorizing and critiquing how media portrays teachers. Media scripts that have depicted the idealized teacher not only exhibit many of the consistencies found in the history of the teacher but also create new, more glamourized versions of who the teacher is and can be. In such media scripts, teachers often adhere to dominant cultural scripts that depict them as keepers of faith, cultivators of knowledge, or igniters of fire (see Carter, 2009). Thus, the cultural scripts tend to position teachers as 'miracle workers' and set unrealistic expectations for the inhabitance of the role of teacher.

In tandem with dominant cultural scripts setting forth a role for the teacher, Popkewitz (1998) argues that modern schooling has embarked on an almost religious commitment of "saving the soul to the problem of constructing the 'New Person' " (p. 59). Noting an emphasis on individuality by the end of the 19th century, schooling is now viewed as a way to 'rescue' the child from moral and economic evils and to nurture the child. A redemptive discourse in teaching has responded to the child by framing what is possible within the urban and rural landscape in the U.S.

The redemptive discourse in teaching is manifested in beginning teachers' responses to community-based fieldwork. Even when beginning teachers intended to refute or challenge the mentality that framed such a point of view, they often subscribed to it. It was the rare beginning teacher who was able to challenge this viewpoint, but Henry Taylor, who grew up in what he called a disadvantaged home, questioned whether teachers ought to frame their practice through redemptive themes.

Henry was quick to question whether making teaching a mission was appropriate. Henry said,

> I think it is normal to want to be a teacher who helps kids. You want to be there and be a role model for them. But, what I see is that many times this work is actually about the teacher. They [teachers] may say it is about students, but I don't exactly buy that. A lot of times it is about bolstering their role as a great teacher helping disadvantaged kids. And, especially when working in places like Family Partnership, teachers get a rise out of this.

Henry's comment that teachers "get a rise" out of working with disadvantaged kids helped us to consider how prospective teachers take up discourses of teaching, and especially discourses of teaching youth who are homeless. As we pursued our study, we recognized the need to present many of these ideas to beginning teachers as lenses from which to encourage a focus on both teacher and student. In our methods courses, discussion of fieldwork was not constrained to discussions of how fieldwork was operationalized; instead, the questions we pursued in discussion with future teachers asked prospective teachers to describe and elaborate on the role they took in their field site. The questions included in one such discussion about Family Partnership within the context of the methods class included the following:

- What have been your initial impressions of the work you are doing at Family Partnership?
- What themes that were pertinent in the training are arising in your work at Family Partnership?
- Describe the youth who you are working with at Family Partnership. What do you see as their strengths? In what ways are you working with them on activities related to literacy learning?

- Youth at Family Partnership can be considered 'at-risk' of school failure because of homelessness. What are your thoughts about the at-risk status and how you perceive the students with whom you work?
- How might you define your role as a 'teacher,' 'tutor,' or 'mentor' with youth at Family Partnership?
- Are there aspects of your work that have surprised? In what ways is the experience different than you may have anticipated?

Through discussion of the preceding questions, we encouraged beginning teachers to articulate their understanding of their work as teachers, the process of students' learning, and the perceptions they held of the students with whom they worked. We encouraged them to think more carefully about the purposes of teaching and learning, and urged them to define their role as teachers at the same time as they pivoted to the other side of the teaching act—a view of the students. We now turn to explore the role of teacher within the context of Henry's and Anne's work at Family Partnership.

PROBLEMATIZING SOCIETAL EXPECTATIONS: THE CASE OF HENRY TAYLOR

When Henry met the students that he would be working with at Family Partnership, he realized these students were not the secondary students he was expecting to tutor. He noted that the youth at the day center were primarily preschool- and elementary-age children. Reflecting on his work at Family Partnership, Henry's first comment in his journal asked questions about 'learning' and 'curricula':

> I found myself asking questions like, "How should I work with these kids so we are making the most of our time together?" and "Is playing a game together learning?" Or, "Should I try to manufacture a school-like activity so I can prove that the kids learned something?"

Henry recognized, through his questions, that learning and curricula were often fluid concepts and undefined concepts, perhaps even more so in the context of work at Family Partnership. While working at the day center, Henry was not situated as the subject area expert in English, and was not expected to be the traditional English teacher who organizes instruction and directs the literacy experiences of students. Instead, like Rhonda, Kelly, and Katherine, whom we featured in the previous chapter, Henry grappled with his role as teacher through the writing he did throughout the semester. Henry kept a reflective journal during his time working at Family Partnership and at the conclusion of the experience also completed what we called a life graph (Burke, 2007). The purpose of the life graph was to define pivotal moments within an experience and present those on a continuum of the semester. In Henry's life graph (see Appendix C), Henry defined moments at Family Partnership that stood out in his mind as significant.

From the very beginning of the semester, Henry was forthcoming about his questions and conflicts concerning not only his identity as a teacher but also how these conflicts fit within the realm of education. Much of the teacher identity that Henry articulated at the beginning of the semester was framed as responsive to society's expectations of gender roles and teaching. Henry described his students at Family Partnership as preschool- and elementary-age kids and noted that he "really enjoyed working with younger kids, prompting [him] to question whether societal expectations made [him] choose high schoolers over elementary schoolers." Later, in his journal, Henry expanded on this assertion, claiming that he felt controlled by the societal expectations, and these expectations limited and defined his teaching identity from the start. Even though he was only still a student in education classes and was just beginning fieldwork within his teacher education program, he was already considering and adjusting his identity as a secondary English teacher. Although he was articulating a view of teacher identity he anticipated while working within the context of Family Partnership, he was still making decisions and viewing himself as a teacher with the assumption that he would seamlessly become a teacher of secondary English language arts. Henry wrote,

> I've always gotten along with very young kids—I sometimes wonder if I'd be as certain about wanting to teach high school if I felt elementary school were a "real" option. There's a level of suspicion males have to deal with in elementary school settings that I think has built a barrier in my mind that keeps me from having even given elementary schoolers a chance . . . male teachers in the high school setting have had other pop culture niches carved for us.

Henry uses the reference to a pop culture niche much as Kelly, who was featured in the previous chapter, used the discourse of standards; Henry and Kelly subscribe, through these references, to an authoritative discourse that frames possibilities for the self as a future teacher. Henry's gender is clearly an important consideration in becoming a teacher. As in most teacher education classes, he was one of a handful of male students surrounded by mainly White, middle-class, female students. Part of Henry's path in becoming a teacher asked him to consider his gender and how it defined who he was in relation to society, and he drew on views of what it means to be male. Henry was able to reflect on these issues while working within Family Partnership. Because he worked outside the normal delineations of a high school, he was able to see more clearly how those norms demarcated who he was becoming, and was able to question whether he wanted to simply embody those norms or struggle against them. Henry also debated whether he wanted to be a teacher at all and noted that perhaps his first choice would be to become a teacher of young children. Yet, he continually reasserted his desire to be a secondary English teacher. He saw the identity of English teacher as less problematic than that of elementary teacher, yet he still struggled against his internalized notions of societal expectations of teachers and whether this role was one he could fully embrace. Henry wrote about how gender limited possibilities for men who wanted to be teachers:

> [W]e carry these things in our heads. The majority of my male peers seem to fall into one of categories—we all think we're going to be laid-back football coaches or self-important trouble-makers. It's a silly sort of vanity either way, but I think it demonstrates an honest reflection of our values.

Henry wrote that thinking about fitting into one of two categories was "an honest reflection of our values," and we saw this as Henry's projection of society's expectations of masculinity. As a future English teacher, Henry saw two possible identities: a coach or a troublemaker. Both of these roles were traditional, masculine roles.

When Henry was not in the traditional context of secondary English teaching and was, instead, working with young children at Family Partnership, he was more easily able to identify these predetermined roles and see them as contrasting with the one he enacted in a community-based site. In his writing, Henry considered what it meant to be an elementary teacher in our society. What did it mean to be a man who works with young children and what assumptions will be made about a male's identity if he chose to make a career of teaching young children? Although Henry was negotiating what he believed to be a less problematic role, that of a secondary English teacher, he still acknowledged social identity markers that he may not want to embody.

The space of Family Partnership allowed Henry to think about what it meant to even desire to become a teacher. He wrote,

> We hear all the time that teaching isn't really worth the effort, and we've each individually decided that that's bullshit, even though the evidence totally supports that conclusion . . . as an education student it's natural to wonder whether I'm actually going to have the balls to go through with this, or if I'm going to spend the next two and a half years getting a degree for a job that will destroy me and send me running back to the safe arms of . . . academia? Art?

Henry's response remains gendered as he asks whether he "will have the balls" to do the job. He claimed that society's expectations are 'bullshit' but a fear of emasculation also resided in Henry's commentary. He worried about being too serious and too set on becoming a teacher. At this point, we worried that he would retreat after he completed his degree and rethink his aspirations.

Although early on in American education, teachers were predominantly male, as girls began to be admitted to schools as students, advocates for girls' schooling such as Catherine Beecher and Horace Mann argued for female teachers, saying that education would not counteract traditional roles but would rather reinforce them by preparing women for the traditional sphere as caretakers of children. So here, the teacher became a motherly and nurturing figure. Sargent's (2000) study of contemporary male elementary school teachers showed that this feminization of teaching is still with us, as his participants reported gendered boundaries between students and teachers. Contact between students and their male teachers represented a threat and perversion while contact between students and their female teachers represented nurturing and protection. This is one example portraying how the 'feminine aspects' we expect of teachers becomes suspect when shown by men. Men who exude these feminine aspects of teaching are alleged of being either dangerous or homosexual.

Scholars who frame their work using masculinity theory have noted that hegemonic masculinity is often focused on opposition to feminine roles (Weaver-Hightower, 2003). In our time with Henry, we saw that he was able to acknowledge what he was choosing and what was affecting his choice of becoming a teacher, and this meant he could critique his teacher identity as it was forming. This critique was important, and by working outside of the traditional context for secondary English teaching, Henry was given a certain kind of control over his identity formation that perhaps would not have occurred within a traditional context. Henry was able to control the formation of 'teacher' instead of merely, and unknowingly, allowing outside formulations to create and drive his teacherly becoming. Through work in a community context, Henry was not able to bypass the step of acknowledging how he was being socialized into teaching. Teacher education programs, in socializing beginning teachers into field sites through what Lortie (1975) calls an "apprenticeship of observation," often bypass beginning teachers' inquiry into the role of teacher. The role of teacher, after all, is fairly solidified in school classrooms and prospective teachers are often eager to assume this solidified role, only undertaking scrutiny of it long after assuming a classroom teaching position.

On his life graph (see Appendix C), Henry reflected on his questions about teacher identity and authority and aimed to see how these questions spilled over into his course work at GSU. Henry described watching his classmates give presentations in their university classes and noted how they pondered and depicted their authority. He wrote about his peers' identities as college students as they are being made into teachers. Henry wrote,

> I marveled at how quickly people I knew as generally shiftless suddenly seem to grow up when given the authority. I began to think of maturity as situational.

The situational nature of how Henry saw the teacher identity assumed by many of his peers reaffirmed Henry's view of teachers as shape-shifters (Gee, 2004), or the act of teaching being 'put on,' much like someone might don a cloak when performing magic tricks. Henry refused to tie up his experience at the end of the semester and offered both a dose of reality as well as a nod toward hope. Writing that "the overarching problem brought to light by the experience at Family Partnership seems to be how we construct solutions where we have imperfect knowledge, and imperfect knowledge might exacerbate problems" (see Henry's life graph in Appendix C) seemed to suggest to us that Henry saw that Family Partnership, like everyone, was struggling to do the best it could as an organization and sometimes the best solutions might not be enough. Yet, Henry's final time at Family Partnership, discussed on his life graph, became a time that he expressed empowerment and hope. Henry wrote, "It seems clear, looking back, that the only solution to responsibility is courage."

We thought that a vision of "courage" positioned Henry to face future conflicts head on. As we considered what courage in community fieldwork meant, we were reminded of Flower, Long, and Higgins's (2000) assertion that studying issues in the context of service-learning teaches students that there may be a "troubling sense of contradiction telling [them] there [is] a more complex reality to grasp" (p. 188). Flower et al. understand that contemplating these contradictions is essential to the work of service in one's community. Henry's assertion that it is courage that will lead him to continually question the teacherly roles that he assumes provides hope that, despite his and others socialization into the promise and myth of teacher as authority, opportunities such as the one at Family Partnership provide a questioning ground for thinking about the role of teacher.

CONFRONTING DEVELOPMENTALISM: THE CASE OF ANNE CHISHOLM

At the time of our study, Anne Chisholm was realizing the plan of pursuing a long-held dream of becoming a teacher. Anne, in her early 40s, presented a different story to us than did Henry, because Anne's story was not only based on her experiences as a student and her desire to become a teacher but also on her experiences as a parent of three teenagers. Being the only nontraditional student and only parent among her cohort of 22 English education students, Anne was often placed in an advisory role to her peers. Through our relationship with Anne, we came to see how her teaching mythology was laced with the influence of her experiences as both a student and a parent.

From the beginning of her time at Family Partnership, Anne's writing became a space where she made sense of the youth with whom she worked. Deliberating about the role of teacher seemed less overt, but it was in discussion of the students with whom Anne worked that we saw Anne's perspective of teaching emerge. Anne frequently depicted the students at Family Partnership in comparison to other youth or to her own children. After her second week at Family Partnership, Anne wrote,

> Some of the kids I am working with seem to be either too mature or not mature enough for their age. I think it is because they've either had to be adults too soon and face responsibilities not typical for their age. Or, they've been sheltered from having different kinds of experiences—like being involved in extracurriculars and being around other kids their age.

Anne used her own circumstance to gauge what she viewed as 'normal' and a life-span development framed many of the comments she made. She wrote,

> After a few weeks of tutoring I feel like I am getting into the rhythm with things and I'm feeling more comfortable with students and families. Sometimes the families don't identify me as a college student because I am older. I just explain to them that this is my second career and that I had my first one raising my kids. They seem to respect this and give me some credit for having a life.

In both excerpts from Anne's writing, featured earlier, we saw the role that developmentalism played in Anne's consideration of the path in becoming a teacher. We witnessed the way Anne relied on both her own age/development and students' age/development to predict 'normal' behavior. To put some of Anne's comments in perspective, we suspected that Anne lived each day as a GSU student with the continual reminder of developmentalism's grasp on education. Because she was the only non-traditional student in her cohort, and was approximately 20 years older than the students she took her university education classes with, a reminder of age was omnipresent in Anne's experience. The reminder of age was often joked about in class, and Anne often joked with her peers when they discussed their lives, asking them, "Now what would your mom think of that?"

We noticed, throughout her fieldwork, that Anne sought to understand the youth with whom she worked by comparing these students to students who she constructed as 'normal' or 'typically developing.' Her comments about the youth at Family Partnership were lined with empathy but often lamented what Anne perceived of as lack of proper parenting by the parents of youth at Family Partnership. Because of Anne's role as a parent, she felt comfortable commenting on the parents at the Family Partnership and wrote,

> Problems started to come up at this point in the semester when I began to see more of how parents treat their kids. I do not want to judge but I am still troubled by their beliefs and parenting practices. I know it is

not my place to step in and act as a corrective force. In teaching, I know I'll have to cooperate with parents that I will not agree with.

Holistically, we saw that Anne's narratives from her journals and life graph (see Appendix D) were saturated with stage developmentalism, or the notion that specific stages of emotional and cognitive development frame the child and progress sequentially as the child matures. Stage developmentalism, as articulated by educational organizations committed to educating particular groups of students (see National Middle School Association, 2010) remains the dominant paradigm from which children are constructed in a Western understanding of children. In challenging the dominance of stage developmentalism, Vagle (2012) notes that "young adolescence [ages 10–15] as a developmental stage seems to have been treated more like a discovery of the 'natural' progressive order of growth and change, rather than a social construction imbued with politics, power, and struggle" (p. 12). Vagle's claim contends that developmentalism's status has been elevated to be construed as 'fact' or 'the given,' thereby constructing an understanding of youth through assumptions of developmental appropriateness.

Although not disregarding all aspects of developmentalism, we remain concerned with a strict adherence to it. Recent critiques of developmentalism, particularly by feminist scholars (e.g., Spatig, 2005), have discussed the ways in which psychological models of development have often neglected to consider the relationship between girls'/women's development and their lived experiences. Rather than replacing a metanarrative of human development, we might seek to present a more accurate story by including the lives of women and girls. A parallel could be made with the way that both elementary and secondary teachers in the United States are trained. Instead of assuming that one learns to teach by discerning developmental appropriateness, it might be prudent to place developmentalism against the lived experiences of students. In connecting developmentalism to the work of teaching, teachers view that adolescents who fit into a clearer vision of how the 'normal' adolescent is constituted are tied to a trajectory that moves them seamlessly from child to adult; therefore, they are also presumed to engage easily with developmentally appropriate curriculum. Adolescents, such as youth at Family Partnership, the Lodges, and Mettle Street School, are viewed as different from their peers who have 'normally' progressed, and therefore, they are frequently viewed as developmentally behind their normally developing peers.

We urge teacher educators to challenge developmentalism's grasp on teacher education today. As teacher educators, we have observed that teachers who are training to become middle/secondary teachers are reticent to participate in teaching young children. Secondary school in the U.S. has typically meant high school—and that sometimes this has included middle school; therefore, beginning teachers who will eventually work with middle and high school aged youth prefer that most, if not all, of their fieldwork within teacher preparation focuses on working with students of this age. As we have alluded to in previous chapters, secondary teachers are often eager to emulate the teaching practices of successful educators they have known, and it is often only after they have become teachers that they begin to question what occurs with students before they arrive in the secondary school context.

Stage developmentalism bolsters the belief that middle/secondary teaching is distinctly different from teaching young children. Burns and Hall (2012) characterize the influence of developmentalism through the following observation:

> Research on secondary English education conducted over the last fifty years, studies using principles of developmental psychology have been both prominent and productive. Such work has used theories of human development to study, describe, and even quantify general characteristics of individuals as classified by age groups and grade levels . . . the precepts of stage developmentalism have helped us address some needs of young adolescents, but they have done so at a cost . . . they have failed to account for important nuances and critiques from critical theory related to issues of power and identity. (p. 176)

Ignoring the variable nature of human development risks reaffirming a teaching mythology solidified in the promise that teaching can be atheoretical and apolitical career. Through adherence to a single paradigm of human development, we see future teachers, like Anne, running the risk of single-handedly silencing the questions that other beginning teachers may ask about youth's in-school and out-of-school participation in the world. Instead, we follow Burns and Hall's lead and endorse "systematically and continuously collecting, assessing, and revising data about students' identities and knowledge from their everyday live to contextualize academic content as an extension of students' particular experiences supplants traditional curricula based on developmental discourses of adolescence and learning" (2012, p. 186).

Anne's experience as a parent gave her a different platform from which to speak about youth, and she used her children's lives as a reference point from which to speak about development. She commented,

> My three teenagers would be resistant to spending their after-school hours at the day center. They really would. They are used to after-school activities, like sports, music practices, etc., and I've worked hard to give them that. It makes me sad to think how much the kids at Family Partnership are really missing out.

At the same time that Anne exclaims her sadness for the opportunities that youth at Family Partnership are "missing out" on, she normalizes students' access and participation to enrichment activities and privileges her role in the attainment of these opportunities.

In working with Anne over the course of the semester, we urged her to rely on her experience as a parent but to shift the focus to be on the students with whom she worked. Instead of using her role as a parent for confirmation of her own success and her children's success, we prompted Anne to rely on her experience as a lens from which to continually reflect and reframe the experience of teaching students at Family Partnership. In responding to one of our class discussion questions, "What are your thoughts about the at-risk status [of youth at Family Partnership], and how you perceive the students with whom you work?" Anne responded,

> I know the students at Family Partnership have had different lives than my kids and often that makes me really sad. But I would say that I have learned a lot from these kids, and honestly have been pretty amazed that they are as smart and resilient as they are after all that has gone on in their lives. I think I've seen a new side of Cedar Creek and I thought I knew everything about this town, having grown up here . . . but, I would say that I've really been amazed by the students I've worked with.

Anne's amazement with youth at Family Partnership convinced us that she was also amazed by her own ability to see the youth at Family Partnership in different ways at the end of the semester than the ways she viewed them at the beginning of the semester. As Burns and Hall (2012) note, "the result of gap discourses based on stage developmentalism is that any adolescents whose identities fall outside of the norms of traditional schooling renders those students as 'struggling' and in need of remediation so that they conform to supposedly universal expectations" (p. 187). Anne started in a place of believing in the promise of stage developmentalism but increasing moved to a position that reconfigured youth. Through her experience at Family Partnership, Anne was able to give credence to a more refined, more nuanced portrait of youth.

HENRY AND ANNE, CODA

We spoke with Henry Taylor 3 years after his experience with Family Partnership. After the semester, Henry had continued his work at the Family Partnership day center throughout the following spring. The director of Family Partnership commented on Henry's ability to build strong relationships with the youth at the center, and he was, as a result, a person who the youth looked forward to seeing. The youth at Family Partnership had looked forward to seeing Henry consistently over the course of 1 year.

Three years later, when we visited with Henry, he was on the brink of finishing his master's degree in gifted education. He had been taking graduate-level classes and had been working as a substitute teacher for 3 years after finishing his undergraduate degree. In our conversation, Henry noted that working with young children was still not an option for him, because he felt he would not be able to "get away with it" without suspicion from others of being a child predator. As a male, he told us that even his father had said that his working with young children, as a male, remained a suspicious enterprise. Henry said,

> I wouldn't have enough faith in myself that I could go to college and pursue this [teaching young children]. I would feel like I would be a spectacle. And, I've always been a big person with a loud voice so I've always had a problem fitting in. So, I don't think I'd want to purposely become a spectacle. I think I'd almost be distracted from the real work of teaching if I was also positioned as a spectacle.

A few weeks after our conversation with Henry, we learned that he had been offered and had accepted a position as a para-educator in the Marshall City School District. This position would allow him to work one-on-one with students and would emphasize the relationship-building aspect of teaching (as opposed to the management aspects of teaching). Henry was excited about assuming this position and did not mind assuming a position in a school that was not that of an English teacher.

Anne Chisholm, 2 years after her work at Family Partnership, was beginning her first year of teaching at a high school in a state where her family had relocated. Anne noted that her dream of becoming a teacher had finally come true, and she could not wait set up her classroom. The affluent suburb where she would now be teaching offered many enrichment opportunities, and Anne would serve as an advisor one or more clubs at the school. Anne was almost relieved to be finished with the program at GSU, and Heidi received an occasional e-mail from Anne, who seemed very at home in her new position.

The trajectories that Henry and Anne took after they graduated from GSU's program seemed to fit some of our initial expectations of both students. At times, we questioned what impact community-based field experiences had on these two individuals. Knowing both Henry's and Anne's outcomes gave us a way to 'finish' the stories of Henry and Anne yet did not provide the resolution that we thought they might. In thinking through this, we realized that it was perhaps more important, in both cases, to capture the nuances of the contexts in which both learned to teach. The semesters that Henry and Anne spent at Family Partnership allowed us to understand the relational dynamics between teacher and students—the moment-to-moment interactions that chronicled the relationship between future teachers and youth. In such moments, we were able to observe how interactions are intertwined with what Holland and Lave (2001) call *history-in-person*. Holland and Lave note that histories of social inequality operate within the present and within individuals' engagements in cultural practices. They write that the "energy of enduring struggles . . . [are] realized in local practice" (Holland & Lave, 2001, p. 13). The histories, then, of prospective teachers and students intersect in these local contexts—contexts like Family Partnership—and teachers and students make sense of each other within these contexts.

It is for this reason that we believe teacher education programs should urge prospective teachers to disrupt the frameworks we have explored in this chapter. In so doing, teacher educators endorse a critical stance that urges prospective teachers to question dominant discourses and the position they maintain within them. In questioning his desire to teach secondary students, Henry reflected on how his biases as a future teacher may affect his future perceptions of students, as well as his potential ability to extend himself beyond these initial perceptions. Henry discovered that, through his own experience and his experience at Family Partnership, he had constructed a counterstory that helped keep him cognizant of his role as a teacher and of what implications that had for students. Henry wrote,

> These experiences [i.e., Family Partnership] keep us in-check. You know, they keep us from being too full of ourselves. I never want to feel so important that I can't change. You know, like my ego is so big that I can't see anything else. I saw a lot at Family Partnership and maybe didn't expect that. I learned a lot about just what a huge job it is to be a parent and to parent your kids when the chips are down. I saw that every time I was there. I know that I didn't expect that.

This gives us affirmation that prospective teachers' experiences within teacher education programs can disrupt the normative. The counterstory that Henry articulates, saying, "These experiences [kept] us in-check," references the need for teacher education to continually stretch beginning teachers' perceptions and understandings, and to do so through a deliberate engagement with what *is* and what can be. As prospective teachers bring their own histories, normalized behaviors and expectations into fieldwork, we must strive for an opening of these cultural scripts to emerge in practice. From there, we might urge prospective teachers, like Anne and Henry, to produce and critique their counterstories, aiming for the promotion of a more defined critical stance in the education of future teachers.

REFERENCES

Alsup, J. (2006). *Teacher identity discourses: Negotiating personal and professional discourses.* Mahwah, NJ: Erlbaum.

Burns, L.D., & Hall, L.A. (2012). Using students' funds of knowledge to enhance middle grades education: Responding to adolescents. In M. Vagle (Ed.), *Not a stage! A critical re-conception of young adolescent education.* (pp. 175–189). New York, NY: Peter Lang.

Burke, J. (2007). *The English teacher's companion* (3rd ed.). Portsmouth, NH: Heinemann.
Carter, C. (2009). Priest, prostitute, plumber? The construction of teachers as saints. *English Education* 42(1), 61–90. Retrieved from www.jstor.org.www2.lib.ku.edu/stable/40607917 Higher Education Press.
Flower, L., Long, E., & Higgins, L. (2000). *Learning to rival: A literate practice for intercultural inquiry.* Mahwah, NJ: Erlbaum.
Gee, J. P. (2004). *Situated language and learning: A critique of traditional schooling.* London, England: Routledge.
Holland, D., & Lave, J. (Eds.). (2001). *History in person: Enduring struggles, contentious practice, and intimate identities.* Santa Fe, NM: School of American Research Press.
Lortie, D. (1975). *Schoolteacher: A sociological study.* Chicago, IL: University of Chicago Press.
National Middle School Association. (2010). *This we believe: Keys to educating young adolescents.* Westerville, OH: National Middle School Association. Retrieved from: www.amle.org/AboutAMLE/ThisWeBelieve/tabid/121/Default.aspx
Perkins, L. M. (1989). The history of blacks in teaching: Growth and decline within the profession. In D. Warren (Ed.). *American teachers: Histories of a profession at work* (pp. 344–369). New York, NY: Macmillan.
Popkewitz, T. S. (1998). *Struggling for the soul: The politics of schooling and the construction of the teacher.* New York, NY: Teachers College Press.
Portes, P. R., & Smagorinsky, P. (2010). Static structures, changing demographics: Educating teachers for shifting populations in stable schools. *English Education,* 42(3), 236–247. Retrieved from www.jstor.org/stable/40607989
Rury, J. (1989). Who became teachers? The social characteristics of teachers in American history. In D. Warren (Ed.), *American teachers: History of a profession at work* (pp. 9–48). New York, NY: Macmillan.
Sargent, P. (2000). Real men or real teachers? Contradictions in the lives of men elementary teachers. *Men and Masculinities,* 4, 410–433. doi:10.1177/1097184X00002004003
Schell, E. E. (1997). *Gypsy academics and mother-teachers: Gender, contingent labor, and writing instruction.* Portsmouth, NH: Boynton Cook.
Spatig, L. (2005). Feminist critique of developmentalism: What's in it for teachers? *Theory and Research in Education,* 3(3), 299–326. doi:10.1177/1477878505057431
Thonus, T. (2001). Triangulation in the writing center: Tutor, tutee, and instructor perceptions of the tutor's role. *Writing Center Journal,* 22(1), 59–82.
Vagle, M. (2012). The anchor essay: Trying to poke holes in Teflon: Developmentalism; young adolescence; and contingent, recursive growth and change. In M. Vagle (Ed.), *Not a stage! A critical re-conception of young adolescent education* (pp. 11–38). New York, NY: Peter Lang.
Warren, D. (Ed.). (1989). *American teachers: Histories of a profession at work.* New York: Macmillan.
Weaver-Hightower, M. (2003). The "boy turn" in research on gender and education. *Review of Educational Research,* 73(4), 471–498. doi:10.3102/00346543073004471

5 Questioning Curriculum
Reenvisioning Assumptions about Curricular Control and Expectations

Henry Taylor and Anne Chisholm questioned the role of teacher, in part, because of an adherence to a *teaching mythology*. A teaching mythology constrains beginning teachers' view of an appropriate teacher's role (Hallman & Burdick, 2011) and, generally, adheres to the 'teacher as authority' paradigm (Portes & Smagorinsky, 2010). Yet, a teaching mythology also deals intimately with what we know as *curriculum*. Often unstated and implied, the relationship between teacher and curriculum is paramount to the work of teaching. However, what role does curriculum play in the act of teaching?

The word *curriculum* connotes a myriad of visions. When thinking about curriculum in relationship to the field of English language arts, some may think of the canon of English literature while others may think of recitation of vocabulary and mastery of grammar rules. The acquisition of knowledge that is fixed and extant in the world has been viewed by many as the purpose of learning, and a diverse range of scholars (e.g., Eisner, 1982) have discussed how classrooms have traditionally been conceptualized as spaces where the teacher is positioned as a provider of knowledge, dispensing it for students to obtain. This view of curriculum has stressed a knowledge that stands apart from the learner.

In contrast to this view, a conception of teaching, learning, and curriculum as dialogic—that is, teaching, learning, and curriculum built around students' and teachers' interactions and interpretations of topics presented in the classroom—has been proposed as a framework designed to engage students as inquirers (Applebee, 1996; Nystrand, Gamoran, Kachur, & Prendergast, 1997; Stock, 1995), therefore promoting a design of active learning. These vastly different conceptions of curriculum have prompted us to consider the nature of teaching, learning, and curriculum in the community-based spaces of Family Partnership, the Lodges, and Mettle Street School. In this chapter, we consider different conceptions of curriculum and how beginning teachers negotiate multiple curricular traditions.

Some scholars have cited that the dominant curricular models guiding the field have produced, over time, a nexus of theoretically competing curricular paradigms. Bickmore, Smagorinsky, and O'Donnell-Allen (2005) call this nexus a "tension between traditions" and emphasize the difficulty of beginning teachers' apprenticeship into such a model, writing that each of the traditions

> require[s] different orientations to the subject matter and suggest different ways to arrange class, relate to students, organize student activity, conceive of assessment, regard and encourage knowledge, consider the meaning of meaning, and otherwise orchestrate students' experiences in relation to the curriculum. (p. 25)

Tensions between curricular traditions often come from the various sources of power that exert control on teaching and curriculum within a schooled space. Furthermore, the conflicts that teachers may feel come from curricular tension but also from tension within the contexts in which teachers work. Bickmore et al. give an example of this contextual tension when they write:

> A school system, for instance, might emphasize personal attention to students and their individual needs and trajectories, but at the same time require students to satisfy external, uniform standards for performance such as those measured on standardized tests. Schools thus often produce for teachers a double bind; that is, they impose conflicting demands that make a consistent response difficult. (2005, p. 25)

Later in the article, Bickmore et al. admit that calling these situations a "double bind" is perhaps an overly simplistic description of such tensions. Most teachers, indeed, feel the impact of many stakeholders' demands on their classroom work. When we then place prospective teachers within these contexts for field experiences, they, too, will unknowingly be apprenticed into their supervising teachers' contexts and conflicts and will most likely uncritically conform to the orientations of that classroom teacher. For this reason, we look to the ways prospective teachers orient themselves to curricular models in nonschooled spaces where fewer curricular tensions exist—or, at least, different tensions exist. We feel that prospective teachers' understanding of curriculum within nontraditional contexts will produce critical touchstones for future teaching.

Despite existing tensions, the models guiding curriculum in English language arts have established approaches to curriculum that remain salient today. This history has influenced the education of prospective English teachers and methods classes in the subject area of English language arts; for example, methods courses have generally continued to frame curriculum through these curricular models (see Smagorinsky, 2008, for a discussion). Furthermore, professional materials available to teachers of English continue to resonate with these models. The dilemma that Bickmore et al. (2005) name as the "tension between traditions" continues to shape beginning teachers' entrance into the field.

Matters of curriculum in the teaching of English language arts, as in all disciplines, are inherently tied to matters of instruction (Applebee, 1996). Applebee (1996) states that curriculum is what "provides domains for conversation, and the conversations that take place within those domains are the primary means of teaching and learning" (p. 37). Curriculum and instruction, then, are always intertwined, and instruction, at its core, is driven by curricular theory. The decisions that teachers make in their day-to-day instruction are always undergirded by curricular theories.

In subscribing to a conceptualization of curriculum that is in dialogue with instructional practices, acknowledgment of the tension between traditions is important in order to gain a sense of one's purpose in teaching. Although the three curricular models (see Squire, 2003, for this discussion) that have framed the discipline of English language arts—the *skills* model, the *cultural heritage* model, and the *personal experience* model—are often linked to various manifestations of teaching and learning (e.g., the *cultural heritage* model is often linked to core knowledge curricula), it is beginning teachers' processes of learning to recognize the overlap, tension, and symmetry among the models that can lead to interrogation and questioning of dominant paradigms that shape the field.

ENGAGING IN RECIPROCAL TRANSFORMATION: CURRICULUM IN NONSCHOOL SPACES

What has been referred to as the 'social turn' in the field of composition and rhetoric has allowed professors of college writing to take their teaching outside the classroom doors, both figuratively and literally. The social turn in Composition Studies is committed to finding authentic audiences and writing contexts that were not defined by artificial classroom exercises (see Mathieu, 2005, for this discussion). Instructors of composition saw that often the writing done in college classrooms was too far removed from the actual writing that students would need to be able to do in the disciplines, the workforce, and in the community. Traditional composition classrooms focused on assignments and activities that imagined an audience, although the audience was truly only the teacher who would be assigning a grade. Students were asked to imagine an audience at the university, in the community, or in a future job position and were then asked to conjure up contexts within which most had very little experience. These assignments and imaginings, therefore, were judged by some composition scholars (e.g., Gere, 1994) to be deficient and inauthentic. The social turn encouraged students to begin to see themselves as a part of a discourse community that was beyond the classroom, allowing students to experience crossing intellectual boundaries, in turn interacting with perspectives and needs outside the walls of the academy. We can place service-learning and writing in the community movements in college writing curriculum alongside the social turn.

Deans, Roswell, and Wurr (2010) explains the ways that community engagement through service-learning has enhanced English studies, saying,

> Thus, service-learning is not volunteerism or community service; nor is it simply an academic internship or field placement. While service learning may draw on these practices, it is at heart a pedagogy of action and reflection, one that centers on a dialectic between community outreach and academic inquiry. (pp. 97–98)

Others have argued that writing in the community benefits college writing students by providing an opportunity for gaining a social awareness and critical stance that may not be possible through the limited classroom work of isolated textual analysis and production (Cushman, 1999; Goldblatt, 2007; Herzberg, 2010; Higgins, Long, & Flower, 2010).

In similar ways, we believe that allowing prospective teachers to write about teaching experiences in out-of-school spaces will provide them with a way to critique and become conscious of curricular choices that are imperceptible within a traditional classroom space. In these unschooled spaces, there is more curricular freedom, fewer stakeholders, and looser, more undefined relationships between teacher and students. These areas of flexibility provide a space for prospective teachers to interact in more actively reflective and critical ways.

A key addition to how we understand teaching English language arts looks to a facet of teaching that has often been left out of curriculum guides: the value of the relationship between teacher and students. Throughout our work, we have become aware of the fact that adults' construction of youth and the maintenance of relationships with youth are often not problematized by the adults who seek to become teachers. Teachers and students must seek a relationship with one another in order to engage in any learning of content. As Nukkula (2003) notes, "transformational learning occurs when students sense that they too have moved their teachers, through their efforts and accomplishments and through their deep engagement in the learning process" (pp. 15–16). Thus, a *reciprocal transformation* occurs. This reciprocal transformation is an overarching umbrella to effectively teaching youth in the 21st century.

To understand what this practice looks like in nonschool spaces, we turn to the experience of how several prospective teachers understood their emerging practice while working at the Lodges, a collection of group homes for adolescents who have become wards of the state. These teachers, Sharon Burns, Geneen Sandovar, and Jacob Downing, provide insight into how curriculum and instruction as well as teachers' characterizations of young people must shift in tandem in order for beginning teachers to be successful in the act of teaching. Through looking on these teachers' dedication to both content and to students' learning, we illustrate how these three prospective teachers were able to question dominant curricular paradigms within the

112 Questioning Curriculum

field, as well as employ an understanding of a reciprocal transformation to the role of teacher and student.

The three prospective teachers that we feature in this chapter put forth a sophisticated analysis of the intertwining of relationships with teaching. They understand that, in order to draw on any curricular model of teaching English language arts in an effective manner, teachers must use the relationships they have with students as pivotal aspects of teaching practice—seeking to make ties with students yet providing them with the learning opportunities they need for their futures. As Genishi and Dyson (2009) state, "in the early 21st century we seem stuck in a time warp in which children who embody certain kinds of diversity have become the problem, and standardization has become the 'fix,' though not a quick or workable one" (p. 10). Sharon, Geneen, and Jacob see the value of including a reciprocal transformation as part of understanding curriculum, thereby seeking to include the spectrum of student diversity within considerations of curriculum.

RETHINKING MODELS OF ENGLISH LANGUAGE ARTS CURRICULUM

As previously noted, curriculum in English language arts has often been equated with the preconceived subject matter of a particular domain of knowledge, thereby stressing knowledge that stands apart from the learner. In English language arts, the 'great books' of Western culture have been a typical starting point for how curricular subject matter is understood. In the present, it is possible to recognize that there was never just one canon of great literature but to what extent have researchers, teachers, and teacher educators considered how the vision of curriculum that English studies has produced affects secondary English classrooms today?

When thinking about the issue of the English language arts curriculum, many today still look to the 1966 Dartmouth Seminar to lead the way. Although much time has passed since 1966, Squire (2003) writes that the models of the secondary English language arts curriculum discussed at the Dartmouth Seminar, the skills model, the cultural heritage model, and the personal experience model—sometimes called process model—have remained salient. The skills model, stressing 'functional' literacy, has been criticized for focusing too much on the acquisition of 'correct' grammar, vocabulary, and spelling, and in so doing, ignores other possible dimensions of the English curriculum. The cultural heritage model, stressing the need for a culturally unifying English curricular content and intended to fill a void left by the skills model, does not ultimately fill this void for it takes culture as a 'given.' The personal experience model allows for student voice and incorporates students' lived experiences as essential to curriculum.

We see these three models as manifesting themselves in English classrooms today. The skills model is present in the Common Core State Standards, stressing preparation for future workplaces. The cultural heritage model remains present in the teaching of 'classic' texts, and the personal experience model is often drawn on in the classroom through journaling and reflective activities. The concept of the relationship between teachers and students as being integral to curriculum in English language arts is not captured through adherence to any one of these models. Yet, the personal experience model, the model that Dixon (1967) most closely aligned himself with, offers a nod to the importance of the lives of students and teachers. We show how the personal experience model has often been highlighted among the three models of curriculum by depicting its significance in Figure 5.1. We now turn to look at prospective teachers' experiences with curriculum and highlight how they expressed the power in using personal experience and relationships as a catalyst for teaching English.

RELATIONSHIPS AS INTEGRAL TO CURRICULUM

Within the skills and cultural heritage models, students are expected to see the teacher as the authority over content. These models are fully dependent on a particular power dynamic between teachers and students—one in which the teacher has authority and control over the learning relationship. This echoes the traditional relationship between adults and adolescents, a relationship in which adolescents are inherently distinct and at odds with each other in ways that demand adult dominance and adolescent compliance.

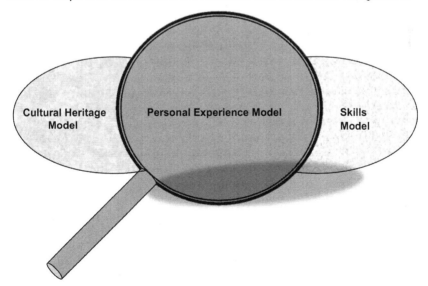

Figure 5.1 Models of English language arts curriculum

Note: Personal experience becomes the lens through which teachers must view other models of instruction. The personal experience model becomes the 'catalyst for teaching adolescents.'

Prospective teachers were able to create relationships with kids at the Lodges in a way they never could have in a traditional school setting. They worked in a small-group setting, and on the kids' 'home base.' The space was not configured by the students and was not theirs in the way a child's home or bedroom might be. Also, this space was not overseen by the prospective teachers in the same way that a teacher's classroom is overseen by a teacher's authority. Rather, prospective teachers maintained authority over the curriculum, but had little authority over the space.

In a classroom setting, kids from the Lodges would be labeled as 'problem students,' and this was a label that the teachers, other students, and especially the kids themselves would know. They would be seen as the outsiders within the configured space because of their reliance on the state, because of their backgrounds, and because of the place where they lived. In the setting of the creative writing workshop, however, the kids from the Lodges were the norm. Instead, the prospective teachers were the outsiders who were uncertain about their position within the space, and who were curious and anxious about who the students were. Jacob, a prospective teacher and an employee at the Lodges, described the kids who resided at the Lodges in this way:

> I think that a lot of people who are unfamiliar with The Lodges come into the homes expecting the youth to be engaged, participate, and somewhat interested that you are there; in reality, most are the complete opposite. These teenagers have been bounced from foster home to foster home or have been in and out of jail . . . It took my wife and I well over six months to finally start building rapport with them, to really connect with them, and for them to take an interest in us where there was some level of respect. . . . They [the kids] are extremely creative and they kept us on our toes on what they were going to write next . . . Anyone who went to the Lodges would feel like an outsider. These youth have very little reason to trust anyone and for anyone to walk in and think they can control them is naïve. Trust is certainly something earned, not given.

So, while the kids in the creative writing workshops provided by Melanie's prospective teachers participated voluntarily, they were still reticent and did not participate in the ways that they might have in a traditional classroom. The respect a student gives to a teacher's authority is not a given within the space of the Lodges. As Jacob said, any trust (and therefore respect) must be earned. Relationships of power and control that are taken for granted within the confines of a classroom space were overturned within this space.

The issues of power, control, and authority were clear to Jacob because of his history at the Lodges. Sharon and Geneen, although newcomers to the site, were also aware of these issues and wrote about them in their journals. Sharon described in her very first journal entry that there were issues of trust and she saw that in order to teach the students, she would need to find ways to make them comfortable:

> It was clear that they were a little unsure of us, and it was probably clear to them that we were a little unsure of what we were doing as well ... We all wrote a piece about our names ... so it didn't feel like we were just telling them what to do ... My goal for the next week [is to think about] some topics that the kids will feel like writing about. I hope that if I share more writing with them and get to know them, they will become more comfortable around me and begin to write what they really want to say.

Sharon noted that the activity of writing about names, a bit of very personal writing, was one that they did together; therefore, it created more connection and equality within the group. Sharon showed careful reflection throughout her journal entries regarding what assignments might interest the kids, and she assumed that sharing her writing would be motivating to the students. Sharon never commented in her journal about what she thought the students needed to know or what skills or concepts she should focus on in future workshops. Instead, her commentary within her journal focused on how to connect to the students, how to feel more secure, and instead of "just telling them what to do," Sharon sought to find ways to motivate the students to share their ideas in writing.

Geneen also discussed issues of authority, especially as she learned to negotiate this over time within the space of the Lodges. She wrote:

> My peers and I have been provided a unique opportunity because we are working with these kids in the comfort of their own living quarters and they have volunteered to be there ... I have been impacted by their [kids at the Lodges] maturity and have seen that teachers can make a difference by simply showing students they care about them and respect them. A teacher can do this in little ways every day and this is where I think they have the most control ... I am progressively getting more comfortable helping these students learn to improve their writing skills. It is much easier for me to be authoritative now than it was just a few weeks ago. I am starting to understand what it feels like to be in charge.

Geneen sees that being in charge comes through the little things teachers do, by "showing students they care about them and respect them." The authority that Geneen begins to claim is a very different one that is often subscribed to by classroom teachers. The classroom teacher's authority is often merely claimed and assumed by both teachers and students. Because of the unusual space of the Lodges, Geneen has learned that a truer and more authentic authority can come from mutual respect, care, and trust.

Her work at the Lodges allowed her to experience how she could establish this very different sort of authority.

RELATIONSHIPS AND SHARED AUTHORITY

At the Lodges, Geneen, Sharon, and Jacob worked collaboratively to create weekly lessons. Because their writing workshop was a new program at the Lodges, and the three prospective teachers had free reign in creating the curriculum, there were no standards that had to be met. There were no guidelines handed to them regarding what they could or could not teach. The three teachers decided they would focus on creative writing instead of academic writing, and from there they created writing activities that they felt would engage the students. From the very first session, the three teachers wrote with the students, and this practice was carried throughout the sixteen weeks of the workshop. From the very beginning, then, through the act of writing with the students, these prospective teachers were aware that the roles of authority were very different from classroom expectations. About midway through the placement, Sharon reflected on what she did to have "control" within the writing workshops at the Lodges:

> In the situation I am in, I am very lucky in matters of freedom and control. We . . . have a say in what we want to do each time we meet. We don't have much control over attendance, but we do have the ability to adapt to what we want to do with the students we have. Because we basically teach what we want, we are really concerned about what the students want to learn or find interesting . . . our lesson from one week can influence the next week's lesson.

Jacob had a history of experiences with the kids at the Lodges, but when he reflected in his journal, he also described a new understanding of teaching, authority, and relationships with students:

> This experience, and tutoring students at the Lodges, in general, has shed light on a whole different realm of what I thought teaching was going to be like. It quickly busted my bubble that students were engaged, ready, and willing to learn what I had to say. This project has helped me realize it is quite the opposite . . . The youth and the Lodges are all about challenging authority. Even once a rapport is established with them and they somewhat have respect towards you, they will continue to push the authority and to see what they can get away with. They are constantly challenging what I am teaching and my motives . . . the biggest thing I learned from this project was simply that *what* you teach is just as important as *how* you teach.

Because Jacob and his peers were able to choose *what* they taught, they were able to think even more carefully about *how* they taught. They also began to see that the *what* and the *how* sometimes intertwined. The curricular decisions they made were often focused on student motivation. Their teaching goals seemed to center on building trust and inviting students to participate in writing activities that would spark their interest and motivate them to share their ideas on paper. The writing assignments ranged from pieces about their names to interviewing and writing about each other. Sharon, Jacob, Geneen, and the students also wrote about music, and the prospective teachers brought in a variety of music clips, choosing from popular genres as well as what they assumed to be the kids' culturally specific music choices (rap, Latino).

When we considered the curriculum that the teachers built, we saw that the curriculum did not focus on skill building and only focused some on cultural heritage. Jacob described the curriculum in one of his later journals through the following characterization:

> We allowed the students to focus on creativity rather than on writing structure. This gave them the opportunity to just write without having to worry about conventions and format—which was something we discovered our students were very appreciative of. Many of them stated that it was nice to have an opportunity to write without being graded on how they write.

Jacob, Geneen, and Sharon elected to let students participate in writing activities where students could obtain fluency and express themselves on paper. Their goals in the writing workshop were not for students to create formal, academic texts. Nor were they interested in teaching grammar and mechanics. Instead, they 'discovered' that their students appreciated being able to write and be listened to without the threat of an authority figure stepping in and telling them what they had done wrong. When students shared their writing, the prospective teachers modeled and encouraged feedback that focused on the students' ideas and content. Usually the writing was read aloud instead of being assessed on the page, so mechanical errors were not noticeable. As Sharon stated, "We share ideas this way and make writing truly a social process."

In her final paper, Sharon reflected on her experience as a whole and considered how different her future work as a classroom teacher might be:

> I know when I walk into my classroom, I won't have near as much say in what I get to teach. I will have a curriculum I need to get through. Part of me is comforted by this because it is difficult to connect objectives and lesson plans on your own. One of our concerns at our site is moving from one topic to the next too quickly. Sometimes I am afraid

we do this. I have noticed when we transition from one topic to another smoothly, the students are more open to participating and writing freely.

Sharon voices an interesting point: that for some teachers, complete curricular freedom can be just as uncomfortable as the tensions among traditions that many teachers feel. Especially for a beginning teacher, both freedom and tension can be overwhelming. At the same time, in her reflection, we see that Sharon begins to think carefully about curricular design. Issues such as 'objectives,' 'coverage,' and 'transitions' have become more than just theoretical concepts to her. She is considering how these concepts work with real students and how they fit into the relationships and trust she has created within the context of her curriculum.

When we considered what bearing this had on curricular models, we felt the need to include teachers and students within the representation of the curricular models. We sought to depict teachers and students as active within curriculum. Figure 5.2 presents a visual that depicts shared authority between teachers and students, while at the same time depicting the overlap of curricular models still present in English language arts.

Through merging curriculum with the presence of teachers and students in Figure 5.2, we aim to ask prospective teachers to view curriculum, teaching, and learning in a more holistic manner.

Teacher and Students in English Language Arts Curricular Models

An interesting part of studying the history of curriculum in English language arts alongside what is happening in classrooms today is uncovering how different curricular models are sometimes designated for different groups of students. Because the three curricular models have different goals and philosophies, they are often deemed appropriate for different kinds of students. For example, adolescents who fit into a clearer vision of the 'normal' adolescent are tied to a trajectory that moves them seamlessly from child to adult; therefore, they also are presumed to move easily from a curriculum founded on skills or cultural heritage. Yet, we see such differentiations as a myth. As we have discussed in the previous chapter, we think that all adolescents must be 'reimagined' so they can take part in various models of curriculum.

A recognition of 'reimagining' adolescents prompts us to turn back to look at our curricular models and argue for a new framing that includes teacher and students. When making a critique of the skills and cultural heritage models, John Dixon, who described English language arts curricular models in his 1967 book *Growth Through English*, aligned himself with the personal experience model, a model he viewed as concerned with students' process in the English classroom versus the teaching of a defined content. Later, Dixon (2003) noted that members of the Dartmouth Seminar "moved

Questioning Curriculum 119

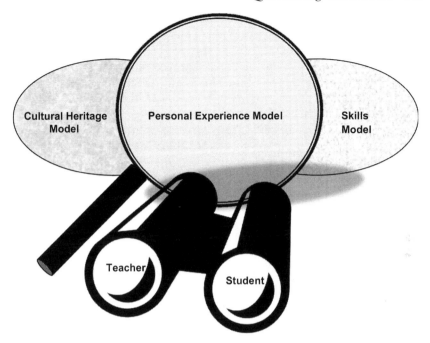

Figure 5.2 The concept of Reciprocal Transformation

from an attempt to define '*What* English is'—a question that throws the emphasis on nouns like *skills* and *proficiencies*, set *books*, and *heritage*—to a definition by *process*, a description of the activities we engage in through language" (p. 7, italics in original). In so doing, Dixon advocated for the process model in the form of the personal experience agenda by stressing that language is learned through the process of *doing*—it is learned through action. By encouraging students to share their life's experiences, the personal experience model, according to Dixon allows students to "build [their] own representational world[s] and work to make this fit reality as [they] experience it" (2003, p. 13).

We would argue that Dixon's focus on *doing* is our goal, yet may not be enough. As we seek to connect the discipline of English language arts to a changing youth population—one in which adult-to-adolescent progression is often not a neat and linear progression—we see that the relationship between teacher and student must be integrated throughout the curricular models the discipline draws upon. As depicted in Figure 5.2, we see that the student and the teacher must be present within curricular models and a reciprocal transformation between teacher and students must somehow be accounted for in curriculum. We see that this potential for reciprocal transformation must frame all three models of curriculum, as this concept stresses a "sense of shared responsibility or commitment toward learning from each other" (Quijada Cerecer, 2011, p. 179).

By the end of the experience at the Lodges, Sharon wrote in her journal in a subtly different way. Her writing illustrated a breakthrough in her thinking about herself, the students, and the curriculum. When she began her work at the site, she used singular pronouns such as *I*, *he*, and *she* to refer to herself and students at the Lodges. She also used *they* or *them* to refer to kids from the Lodges as a group. Toward the end of her experience, however, Sharon began using plural pronouns such as *we* and *our*, showing that she had mentally integrated herself within a group of people at the Lodges. Sharon wrote, "Today helped me see writing as more of a social process. We spent so much time because every time we got stuck, we would talk about our ideas. When someone mentioned something, it would spur new ideas and keep us moving on descriptions." Here, Sharon does not distinguish between student and teacher. The students (*they*) did not get stuck or talk about their ideas. *We* got stuck. *We* talked about *our* ideas. When new ideas came up, this kept *us* moving. The teacher and student identities are intertwined within the process of writing and finding ideas about writing. The relationship between teacher and student grew to become woven into one and, as a result, portrayed the reciprocal transformation (Nukkula, 2003) that encompassed learning with and from one another.

Given our understandings as teacher educators and our work with prospective teachers placed at the Lodges, we seek to move toward representing curriculum in English language arts as not neutral, but as laden with the relationships that must be fostered between teacher and students. Unlike the spheres of curricular models shown in Figure 5.1, we see the importance that teacher and students move into a different learning relationship with one another, one in which a reciprocal transformation has roots. In order to do this, we must reconceptualize models of curriculum to include the relationship between the teacher and the students.

CURRICULUM, A CAVEAT

Applebee (1996) elaborates on the way curriculum is indeed something more than merely content matter, citing a need to reframe curriculum through what he refers to as "domains for conversation." As we seek to further integrate the relationship aspect of teaching into curricular models, we maintain concern for the relegation of types of curriculum for particular populations of students. Stressing the need for students to experience a curriculum that includes personal experience as a platform for knowledge creation continues to work against a 'basic skills' model of education (Knapp & Turnball, 1990) so frequently assumed as appropriate for students such as the population of students at the Lodges. Deemed behind academically and at-risk, students at the Lodges were often labeled as those who were already permanently behind—and, therefore, their (lack of) progress, to some, appeared irreversible. The term *basic skills*—and even the term *skills*—kept learning and teaching with students such as those at the Lodges isolated to a space that undervalued the transactions students have with curricular content. A 'basic skills,' or 'skills,' approach to curriculum aims to remediate at-risk individuals through skills-driven teaching and learning techniques rather than through meaningful engagement with material or other learners. As researchers who have studied classroom discourse have shown (Gamoran, Nystrand, Berends, & LaPore, 1995), students who are tracked into 'low-ability' or 'struggling' categories tend to have instruction that relies more heavily on skills-based, or remedial-based, instruction than do 'high-achieving' students. The targeting of skills tends to weaken the link between learning new material and students' prior experiences.

Students at the Lodges, because of their status as students at-risk of school failure, have been schooled using a basic skills curriculum more often than students attending mainstream schools (Gamoran et al., 1995). To combat these characterizations, we stress providing a portrait of teaching and learning for students at the Lodges as founded on curriculum that invites students to interact and engage with texts and other learners. The experiences of Sharon, Geneen, and Jacob contribute to this aim. Teacher educators play an important role in assisting prospective teachers in understanding how curricular characterizations and the 'tension between traditions' affects the teaching and learning of diverse populations of students, and teacher educators can powerfully transform dominant views of curriculum through a more integrated, more relationship-centered understanding of curriculum.

REFERENCES

Applebee, A. (1996). *Curriculum as conversation*. Chicago, IL: University of Chicago Press.

Bickmore, S., Smagorinsky, P., & O'Donnell-Allen, C. (2005). Tensions between traditions: The role of contexts in learning to teach. *English Education, 38*(1), 23–52. Retrieved from www.jstor.org.www2.lib.ku.edu/stable/40173210

Cushman, E. (1999). The public intellectual, service learning, and activist research. *College English, 61*(3), 328–336. Retrieved from www.jstor.org.www2.lib.ku.edu/stable/379072

Deans, T., Roswell, B. S., & Wurr, A. J. (Eds.). (2010). *Writing and community engagement: A critical sourcebook*. Boston, MA: Bedford-St. Martin's.

Dixon, J. (1967). *Growth through English*. Champaign, IL: National Council of Teachers of English.

Dixon, J. (2003). Historical considerations: An international perspective. In J. Flood, D. Lapp, J. R. Squire, & J. Jensen (Eds.), *Handbook of research on teaching the English language arts* (pp. 18–23). Mahwah, NJ: Erlbuam.

Eisner, E. (1982). *Cognition and curriculum: A basis for deciding what to teach and how to evaluate*. New York, NY: Longman.

Gamoran, A., Nystrand, M., Berends, M., & LePore, P. C. (1995). An organizational analysis of the effects of ability grouping. *American Educational Research Journal, 32*, 687–715. http://dx.doi.org/10.3102/00028312032004687

Genishi, C., & Dyson, A. H. (2009). *Children, language, and literacy: Diverse learners in diverse times.* New York, NY: Teachers College Press.

Gere, A. R. (1994). Kitchen tables and rented rooms: The extracurriculum of composition. *College Composition and Communication, 45*(1), 75–92. doi:10.2307/358588

Goldblatt, E. (2007). *Because we live here: Sponsoring literacy beyond the college curriculum.* Cresskill, NJ: Hampton Press.

Hallman, H. L., & Burdick, M. N. (2011). Service learning and the preparation of English teachers. *English Education, 43*(4), 341–368. Retrieved from http://search.proquest.com.www2.lib.ku.edu/docview/874324979?accountid=14556

Herzberg, B. (2010). Community service and critical teaching. In T. Deans, B. S. Rowsell, & A. J. Wurr (Eds.), *Writing and community engagement: A critical sourcebook* (pp. 138–148). Boston, MA: Bedford-St. Martin's.

Higgins, L., Long, E., & Flower, L. (2010). Community literacy: A rhetorical model for personal and public inquiry. In T. Deans, B. S. Rowsell, & A. J. Wurr (Eds.) *Writing and community engagement: A critical sourcebook* (pp. 167–201). Boston, MA: Bedford-St. Martin's.

Knapp, M., & Turnball, B. (1990). *Better schooling for children of poverty: Alternatives to conventional wisdom.* Washington, DC: U.S. Department of Education.

Mathieu, P. (2005). *Tactics of hope: The public turn in English composition.* Portsmouth, NH: Boynton/Cook.

Nukkula, M. J. (2003). Identity and possibility: Adolescent development and the potential of schools. In M. Sadowski (Ed.), *Adolescents at school: Perspectives on youth, identity, and education* (pp. 7–18). Cambridge, MA: Harvard Education Press.

Nystrand, M., Gamoran, A., Kachur, R., & Prendergast, C. (1997). *Opening dialogue: Understanding the dynamics of language and learning in the English classroom.* New York, NY: Teachers College Press.

Portes, P. R., & Smagorinsky, P. (2010). Static structures, changing demographics: Educating teachers for shifting populations in stable schools. *English Education, 42*(3), 236–247. Retrieved from www.jstor.org/stable/40607989

Quijada Cerecer, P. D. (2011). Power in community building: Learning from indigenous youth how to strengthen adult-youth relationships in school settings. In A. Ball & C. Tyson (Eds.), *Studying diversity in teacher education* (pp. 171–182). New York, NY: Rowman & Littlefield.

Smagorinsky, P. (2008). *Teaching English by design: How to create and carry out instructional units.* Portsmouth, NH: Heinemann.

Squire, J. R. (2003). The history of the profession. In J. Flood, D. Lapp, J. R. Squire, & J. Jensen (Eds.), *Handbook of research on the teaching the English Language Arts* (pp. 3–17). Mahwah, NJ: Erlbaum.

Stock, P. L. (1995). *The dialogic curriculum: Teaching and learning in a multicultural society.* Portsmouth, NH: Boynton/Cook.

6 Questioning Normal
Composing Ethical Representations of At-Risk Youth

As education researchers, ethical representation of our participants—particularly those who are most stigmatized through labels such as being at-risk of school failure—demands that we consider how participants' enact *agency*. To understand participants' agency, we must first think about identity, as Hall (2000) writes, as "not already 'there'; [but] rather . . . a production, emergent in process. It [identity] is situational—it shifts from context to context" (p. xi). Like prospective teachers, identity as students labeled at-risk of school failure is not fixed but is continually reshaped. Although societal discourses about at-risk populations of students certainly have influence on perceptions of who the at-risk students are, it is important to recognize the agency that individuals possess. Agency is often made visible through the stories that participants tell, and Gordon, McKibbin, Vasudevan, and Vinz (2007) remind us that stories are the sites where researchers can explore territories filled with conflicts, tensions, and competing forces. The territories that we explore in this book are spaces of tensions and they exist as boundary spaces, allowing for movement and change.

In order to best explore these spaces, we urge researchers to explore the ethical dimensions of participants' movement and change. Movement and change can often take place over time through participants' interactions and relationships, and to represent this movement in participants themselves, we must attend to constructing an ethical representation of our participants. We must also look at our own relationship with our participants. For example, Luttrell's (2003) stance as a critical ethnographer does not aim to make the emotional facets of her inquiry invisible. Instead, Luttrell claims that it is these difficult sites of emotional knowing that can facilitate the creation of multiple truths. Luttrell's ability to "ethnographically know," in fact, relies on her emotional ties to her research and to her participants, and she identifies her work as a "person-centered" approach to ethnography, claiming this as an "experience-near way of describing and knowing" her participants (2003, p. 6). Experience-near knowing promotes the goal of engaging people in talking about and reflecting on their subjective experiences.

CHALLENGING THE REPRESENTATION OF OUR PARTICIPANTS

Like Juzwik (2004), Lachuk and Gomez (2013) highlight the need for researchers to understand the ethical nature of researchers' relationships with their participants and draw on Bakhtin's (1993) answerability as a way to emphasize the importance of researchers' relationships with participants. As we discussed in Chapter 3, answerability can be considered an ethical response called for by lived experience where "all of [the individual's] constituent moments must not only fit next to each other in the temporal sequence of his life, but must also interpenetrate each other in the unity of . . . answerability" (Bakhtin, 1990, p. 2). Answerability is a double-voiced concept, meaning that it entails researchers' call to be both ethically responsible and responsive to participants.

Throughout their work in community-based spaces, many prospective teachers highlighted how they became answerable to students by challenging how students were constructed by others. As we illustrated in Chapter 4, both gender and developmental discourses operate mainly through binaries: male/female and adolescent/adult. These binaries proved to be sites where prospective teachers advocated for students' identities. As prospective teachers began to question and work within the binaries, they began to see how a more nuanced portrait of youth might be possible.

Henry Taylor, during his work at Family Partnership, felt especially like an advocate for the teens who were involved in the program. During his time at Family Partnership, Henry developed a relationship with two teen brothers, Michael and Damian. Both teens attended the local high school and had interests in sports and video games. Yet, Henry saw how the space of Family Partnership did not necessarily have the space for Michael and Damian to develop these interests, as it had far more young children in the program. Henry wrote,

> It's generally unfair that these two young men are lumped in with the little kids because they really are almost adults. The day center just can't provide video games or a basketball court like it provides board books and board games. Michael and Damian probably wish they could try out for the basketball team but that's just not going to happen for lots of reasons. They are just kind of stuck, emerging as men but still positioned like little kids.

In fairness, Family Partnership needed to make some delineation between children and adults, and because Michael and Damian were children, they were often grouped with young children who required supervision at all times. Henry, however, saw how Michael and Damian were often bored and restless at the day center, yearning to play basketball or stay after school at the high school to be with other kids their age. On a few occasions, Henry was able to take the two boys to a park nearby and play basketball. Henry commented,

> It was just going to a park and shooting hoops . . . nothing special and nothing that cost anything. But it made me see that these two [Michael and Damian] are just under constant supervision and are pretty bored. I may not be the coolest 22-year old, but they made me feel like I was.

Henry challenged the way Michael and Damian were labeled as 'children' and knew that they had different needs than many of the other young children in the Family Partnership program. Yet, Michael and Damian were not considered 'normal' adolescents either. As we explored in the previous chapter, at-risk youth, and teenagers, more generally, are constructed through normalized discourse and common characterizations of the period known as 'adolescence' (Lesko, 2001). Lesko notes that the terms *adolescent* and *adolescence* are connected to the "rise to a modern nation-state" (2001, p. 9) and therefore position the 'normal' adolescent as someone who transitions into good and responsible citizenship. The 'abnormal' adolescent, then, is someone who engages in behaviors considered deviant and threatening to his or her transition to 'normal' adulthood. The tracing of adolescence also reveals a focus on White, middle-class, male youth whose positive characterization relies on the characterization of other adolescent youth (e.g., 'at-risk' youth). A consideration, then, of the term *adolescent* as a cultural construction is important in reflecting on how at-risk youth are portrayed by prospective teachers, as (a) a cultural construction of adolescence recognizes how the production of 'deviant' adolescents is possible only against 'normal' adolescents and (b) a cultural consideration of adolescence questions the assumption that progress is always made throughout history and asks a fundamental question of whether it is advantageous to construct a period of development between childhood and adulthood called adolescence.

In affirming Michael and Damian, Henry needed to understand how they were constructed as adolescents, as well as what possibilities existed for them to be 'normal' in the day-to-day. Because of their status as at-risk students and homeless teens, Henry saw many doors close for them. He knew that trying out for the basketball team at school was not an option for the boys, as this would require an adult be available to transport the boys to and from practice. Even if an alternate arrangement were made, Henry knew that the boys were not seen as 'normal' youth with a family who could provide the logistical supports that were in place for many other kids. Henry commented that these "little things" signaled abnormality to others and wrote,

> Before being at Family Partnership, I thought of homelessness as one thing: not having a home. But now I can see how all the little things

surrounding homelessness produce challenges. So, it is not just that Michael and Damian don't have a home, but it is that they don't have a parent with a reliable car who could pick them up after practice. And, even if they could get a ride home after practice, would someone really want to drop them off at the congregation they are sleeping at for the night? That's not just a little thing, but a big signal that these kids' lives are different from other kids' lives . . . homelessness is really about all the little things that put your life out of the range of 'normal.'

CHARACTERIZATIONS OF ADOLESCENCE

One of the traditional spaces where adolescents can be judged as 'normal' is in the high school classroom. Here, students are trained to become educated and complete adults. Another space of articulating 'normal' is within the middle-class family home where adolescents are taught values and responsibilities within an intact family unit (see Lareau, 2003, for a discussion). Most secondary English teachers experience success within the traditional high school and middle-class family spaces, and it is clear what *normal* means within these contexts. Yet, beginning teachers may still have little understanding of how nontraditional spaces or nontraditional families may construct assumptions of 'deviant' adolescence to others. When working with students who are successful in traditional spaces, 'normal' becomes reinforced.

Although Henry identified Michael and Damian as 'normal' teens with typical teen interests, he learned over the course of the semester that both boys were struggling in school. Henry wrote about how he perceived their struggle in a journal entry after first-quarter grades had come out:

> Today I found out that Michael and Damian had both failed two classes. I don't know if they were both the same classes, but I know that report cards came out and both will need to repeat classes if they don't get their grades up by the end of the semester. I really was shocked because when I asked Michael and Damian about school, they just shrug and tell me 'fine.' But I guess I don't see them at school and, now, thinking about it, I've rarely seen either of them do homework. I hate to be one of those teachers who question whether these kids are failing because they are homeless, but I can imagine these two don't have parents who ask them about their homework.

Here, Henry struggles to articulate how he views both boys as normal and abnormal at once. Petrone and Lewis (2012) discuss that common characterizations of the time labeled as adolescence often justify teachers' thinking about their students as well as dictate the respective roles that they play as teachers to such students. In examining how secondary English teachers think about their prospective students, Petrone and Lewis denaturalize normalized ways of thinking about adolescents—ways of thinking that "position young people in powerful, predictable, and oftentimes problematic ways" (2012, p. 256). One of the problematic ways that adolescents are characterized is through a lens of being 'incomplete people.' In their study, one preservice teacher explained that adolescents, by nature, are incomplete in both a cognitive and emotional manner. This teacher noted, " 'I believe the mind is very 'plastic' at this time—almost like a baby's, except that the brain now has the ability to process big ideas and think abstractly' " (Petrone & Lewis, 2012, p. 267). Several other preservice teachers echoed such statements, which led them to reason that the appropriate role of a teacher was to be a therapist and counselor to their future students (Petrone & Lewis, 2012, p. 272). We see Henry begin to express skepticism about labeling Michael and Damian as abnormal, preferring to remain on the outside of the situation. Yet, we also see him struggle to explain the boys' failing grades.

Other education researchers (e.g., Collin, 2012; Dutro, 2010; Kelly, 2000) have approached thinking about the construction of adolescence through considering the role that discourse plays in composing portraits of youth. Kelly (2000), who has written about the construction of pregnant and parenting teens, highlights the relationship that the teens with whom she worked have with the discourses in which they operate, describing this relationship through the dichotomous construct of teen mothers as victims/teen mothers as free agents. Recognizing that viewing teen mothers as victims neglects giving girls personal agency and, conversely, viewing teen mothers as free agents neglects the recognition of discourses that influence and shape teen mothers' subjectivities. To avoid these poles of discourse determinism, Kelly emphasizes a critical stance. A critical stance attends to both the "agency and the lived experiences of the research participants (especially the most vulnerable); the extra-local context of research sites, including the various asymmetrical power relations; and the documentation of oppressive ideologies and practices with an eye toward envisioning more emancipatory alternatives" (Kelly, 2000, pp. 8–9). This complex understanding of a critical stance leads Kelly to an understanding that "ethnographers will collude in unequal relations of power despite our political goals to challenge and transform them" (2000, p. 203).

Henry, in his writing about Michael and Damian, positions himself as a critical ethnographer and grapples with his ability to change or even influence the trajectory of Michael and Damian's school success. Yet, he feels tangled within a web in which he struggles to articulate the agency that both he and the boys both possess; Henry recognizes, however, that he does, indeed, have some influence on the boys' lives.

OUR OWN COLLUSION

Our own "collusion," as Kelly (2000) calls it, in pursuing an ethical representation of our participants calls us, as researchers, to continually grapple with the relationship between 'researcher' and 'researched.' Henry's collusion starts to bother him, and he asks himself what participation he has had in the situation. Recognizing that he rarely—if ever—saw the boys do homework, Henry wants to more clearly see his part within the story. Henry begins to ask, "What is the story that he would tell about Michael and Damian and how might it be different from the boys' story?" In pursuing the representation of his own story and the stories of participants, individuals such as Henry aim to capture the local technologies that play a part in shaping and producing discourses while also recognizing the tensions, problems, and collusion that scholars (e.g., Wolcott, 2002) have faced when doing such work.

Michael and Damian's story is a story that presents a portrait of two young men who have experienced periods of homelessness throughout their lives. Now living with their father and three younger siblings in the Family Partnership program, Michael and Damian have faced more challenges than many adolescents their age have. They have witnessed their mother's incarceration and have changed schools multiple times throughout their years of schooling; they were now facing the challenge of graduating from high school soon with grades that were putting this attainment in jeopardy, and, at the same time, they were preparing to think about life as adults. Michael and Damian were seen, for these reasons, as at-risk youth. Although it has been argued that drawing attention to the narratives of at-risk teens may make these young people even more "hypervisible" (Pillow, 2004), several scholars (e.g., Gomez, 2007; Ladson-Billings, 2002) have used narrative methods and participants' stories to understand and document the experiences of underrepresented or marginalized groups. Participants' stories, instead of being 'fixed,' are adherent to a notion of identity that is "negotiated, open, shifting, and ambiguous" (Kondo, 1990). As Watson (2006) notes, participants' stories often reject "discourse determinism" (p. 511) and instead seek to draw on the resources available to construct an identity.

For example, in contemplating Luttrell's (2003) work with pregnant and parenting students, we can see that the aim of her work is not to create a single story from the stories she tells about her participants; rather, Luttrell recognizes that all researchers assume a normative or universal relation to truth when speaking about research participants (Carspecken, 1996). This references what Behar and Gordon (1995) have called the "double crisis of representation." The double crisis of representation has two roots: one in the postmodern turn and the other in the critique of the White, middle-class feminist version of women's experiences. The double crisis of representation has implications for the possibilities that researchers will be able to depict the lives and experiences of their research participants. To illustrate this, Luttrell points out that she had been told, throughout her ffieldwork, that she, as a White scholar, "had no business re-representing the lives of black youth" (2003, p. 168). Luttrell disagreed with this claim, while also clearly understanding that she could not break free from the social and racialized world in which she operated. Not only was it her responsibility to debunk myths and stereotypes about pregnant and parenting teens, but it was also her duty to create alternative visions of at-risk youth. It is through these alternative visions, Luttrell argues, that the process of becoming and being made can be explored.

Henry Taylor worked to represent the lives of Michael and Damian more fully. Although he acknowledged the challenges both boys had faced and were currently facing, he aimed to try to understand how the context of the boys' lives had influenced the possibilities that existed for them. He wished to understand the boys' experience as both a product of individual and familial circumstance but also as an outcome of the broader social and historical context. Henry was able to understand that, in constructing the at-risk student, both 'micro'- and 'macro'-level processes must be taken into account. Individual and social dynamics, as well as past and present day circumstances, must be contemplated in order to understand the 'real.' Henry wrote about this in his final journal entry:

> This experience [at Family Partnership] showed me that it is never just one thing that impacts a kid's life. It is not just their family life or how their parents treat them. It is never just the opportunities (or lack thereof) that they have while growing up. It is all of these things and more. It actually has as much to do with what society tells you you are as what you think you are.

Henry's reference to "what society tells you you are" reminds us of Hacking's (1996/2002) insistence of "dynamic normalism," or the idea that "numerous kinds of human beings come into being hand in hand with our invention of the ways to name them" (p. 113). Naming others is something that Henry views as a powerful way to shape people and as something he recognizes as limiting agency. Prospective teachers who worked with students at Family Partnership and the Lodges contemplated, throughout their experience, the possibility of an ethical response to the youth with whom they worked and how they might open up spaces within society for more varied ways of seeing youth.

Ming Nguyen was one prospective teacher who began to reflect on her notion of self-as-teacher yet also thought increasingly more about how she constructed the homeless students with whom she worked with over the time of her experience at Family Partnership. In Chapter 2, we discussed Ming's work with Penny, a middle school student who was in the Family Partnership program and who had recently been identified to participate in the school's gifted and talented program. Prospective teachers used Penny's status as a gifted and talented student to challenge the construction of the 'homeless adolescent,' and Penny's status as a homeless student who was also labeled 'gifted and talented' provided a concrete context from which to discuss preconceived notions of students and how teachers react to these preconceptions.

Another prospective teacher who worked at Family Partnership, Rebecca Avery, initially characterized the view she had of at-risk adolescents' knowledge through positioning out-of-school knowledge as informal and residing outside of the academic space of school. Because she contrasted the space of school with the community-based space of Family Partnership, Rebecca continued to question the direct relevance that her work in community-based sites had to her work as a future classroom teacher. Rebecca wrote in her journal:

> At Family Partnership, I can work one-on-one with students and can get to know their interests and strengths. I know this is important in teaching also, but it seems more possible in an out of school space such as the one we are working in. When working with Jason [an adolescent at Family Partnership], I've been able to ask him about what he is good at and how this matches up with what he studies at school. There seems to be a space for me to interact with him and a way to use his strengths to help him with school knowledge. I don't know if I could do this in the classroom.

Rebecca recognized a quality of the out-of-school space and questioned how this would be the same or different in a classroom. She alluded to a bridge metaphor between Jason's out-of-school interests and the academic learning that she knew he would undertake in a school context. In her comments about her experience working with adolescents at Family Partnership, Rebecca imagined what she believed to be the "pedagogical third space" (Kirkland, 2008, 2010). Kirkland (2008, 2010) calls for a "pedagogical third space" in teaching that synthesizes traditional school literacies with students' lived literacies. Like other scholars have noted (e.g., Hull & Schulz, 2002; Kinloch, 2012), asking how out-of-school knowledge intersects with in-school knowledge can be a useful way for prospective teachers to challenge dominant discourses that shape literacy learning and what counts as knowledge.

Throughout her experience working with Jason, Rebecca saw that a potential learning space resided between Jason's out-of-school knowledge and his in-school knowledge yet still contemplated whether a recognition of this space was possible within a school context. However, a key facet of Rebecca's experience at Family Partnership was that she viewed the possibility that at-risk students could reside in such spaces. In her journal, Rebecca wrote about the particulars of the space, both geographical and curricular, that resided outside of school. Rebecca wrote,

> Jason is really knowledgeable about cars and is always reading magazines about cars and other vehicles when I'm at Family Partnership (until I ask him if he has any homework). I know nothing about cars and many times I have asked him questions about why he is into cars.

> I've learned that he has actually worked on cars, fixed his uncle's car, and just has a lot of knowledge about cars, in general. I wouldn't necessarily think that this translates directly to school, but I've found that through our conversations that Jason is able to tell me quite a bit of detailed information about cars. I think this has made him feel more comfortable with me, and when we worked on an essay for English class, I think he was more open to describing things and writing about them because of our many conversations about cars.

Rebecca was able to recognize how Jason's out-of-school knowledge constructed him as a particular type of adolescent. She was also able to see that, for students who are labeled at-risk of school failure, 'mismatches' between out-of-school and in-school learning can assist in solidifying teachers' visions of at-risk youth as far from the profiles that 'normal' adolescents inhabit. Rebecca's realization of this helped her see how Jason's knowledge might assist him in particular ways with school tasks. Yet, this recognition deconstructs the normal–abnormal binary of the adolescent, as she learns to recognize the complex construction of knowledge in-context and how this knowledge is continually reshaped. She wrote in her journal,

> I have been amazed by Jason because he has taught me a lot about myself. I guess I'd hate to admit this, but I didn't think that Jason's knowledge about the things he is interested in (like cars) had anything to do with his school success. I realized that it does and his knowledge can contribute to his school learning. But Jason also showed me that I was close-minded in thinking about who he was. Because I didn't label him immediately as an academically-able student, I think I didn't hold as high of expectations for him as I should have.

Rebecca, Ming, and Henry illustrate how the community-based field experience at Family Partnership challenged prospective teachers' dichotomous understandings of normal–abnormal and alternative–traditional. Initially, the experience at Family Partnership was perceived of by teachers as being 'alternative' and therefore standing in contrast with a traditional field placement in a classroom within a school. Many prospective teachers who were involved with tutoring youth at Family Partnership were previously unaware of the presence of homeless students in the schools they had attended. The unfamiliarity that the teachers expressed with the issue of homelessness resonated with the research literature, as homelessness is often described as an invisible aspect of students' lives in the classroom (see Barton, 1998).

At the beginning of their experience at Family Partnership, prospective teachers viewed 'normal' in contrast to the homeless students at Family Partnership. In the initial meetings before embarking on the field experience, teachers expressed surprise that schools within the community of Cedar Creek enrolled students who were homeless. Rebecca noted that the community, as a whole, had a high level of education among its population; therefore, parents who were educated would not be experiencing homelessness. This correlation between more education and less homelessness in the community was based on the perception that homelessness was an entrenched issue in the lives of the people experiencing it; as Rebecca later found out, some of the families she worked with at Family Partnership were only recently experiencing homelessness due to job loss or other, more temporary circumstances. Another prospective teacher, Anne Chisholm, featured in Chapter 4, believed that homelessness was not present in the community of Cedar Creek because the community did not have many resources for homeless families. As she later found out, Family Partnership was just one service out of several that served the homeless population in the community.

The prospective teachers who experienced a field placement at the Lodges also found themselves reconstructing their idea of 'normal' students. They reconsidered what normal students looked like in terms of motivation and openness when working with students living in a group home overseen by the state. Because students from the Lodges attended regular public schools, the field placement occurred at the Lodges campus on the weekends, during the students' free time. Geneen Sandovar was a prospective secondary social studies teacher who worked at the Lodges with a group of four other prospective teachers during the course of a semester. Geneen and her classmates organized and oversaw a creative writing workshop held for 2 hours on Sunday afternoons that was open to any of the students at the Lodges. When she began, Geneen voiced reservations regarding working with students who lived at the Lodges, especially regarding how welcoming they would be to her and her classmates. She asked a lot of questions such as "Why are the kids there? What will they be like? What are they interested in?" Because Geneen was a college junior and secondary education major, she had participated in numerous observation hours in area high schools, yet she still felt that she would not know what to expect from the students at the Lodges because they seemed to be 'different' from the kids she saw and worked with in local school settings.

When Geneen participated in the debriefing interview at the end of her time at the Lodges, she shared candidly how she felt when she started her field placement:

> At the beginning I was pretty nervous and apprehensive because I didn't know what to expect . . . I kind of thought the kids were going to be really resistant and not excited to be there and have bad attitudes, and I also didn't know how much authority I would have.

Geneen described her expectations of the students at the Lodges as "resistant and not excited . . . [with] bad attitudes," and in the same sentence, she expressed uncertainty about her own authority. Geneen's expectations of the students at the Lodges were deeply linked to her expectations of the traditional teacher/student relationship. As a college junior, she already embraced the 'normal' dichotomy of authoritarian teacher and passive student, and her fears stemmed from an expectation that students at the Lodges would not fit into that 'normal' dichotomy. Geneen also assumed that students at the Lodges would reveal a certain agency that students in a classroom might not. She questioned whether students would be resistant or what might happen if they did not submit to her authority. Such questions created an uncomfortable and nontraditional curricular space that invited Geneen to rethink issues of authority, agency, and relationship and of how these fit into the 'normal' or the 'expected.'

Over time, however, prospective teachers built relationships with students at the Lodges, and as they did, Geneen and her peers began to see these students differently. They described the students in their journals with less anxiety and more empathy. One breakthrough came during a Sunday creative writing interview activity. Geneen spent time talking one-on-one with a student who lived at the Lodges named Sam. She described their conversation in her journal:

> He said that most of the teenagers who live there have been kicked out of their homes by their parents/guardian, had run away from home, or had gotten in trouble with the law and had been sent there (usually drug use was involved). I was expecting the kids who lived there to be rough, unapproachable and angry—but those I have encountered are the opposite. They appear laid back, yet insecure like most teenagers I have been around. They flirt with each other, act silly and immature, tell us how boring school is—they have all the behaviors of so-called 'normal' teenagers who live with their families at home.

When Geneen was able to talk to Sam and listen to his point of view, she no longer saw him or the other residents of the Lodges as frightening or unusual, even though Sam described the unusual circumstances that placed students in the group homes. While interacting with a student from the Lodges outside the confines of concretely defined classroom roles, the teacher/student dichotomy was transposed. Sam took on the role of teacher and explained to Geneen what life was like at the Lodges, why students became residents there, how it felt to live there. Geneen described how she began to see students at the Lodges as having "all the behaviors of so-called 'normal' teenagers"—far different from the "rough, unapproachable and angry" students she expected to meet. By allowing herself to be taught by Sam, she was able to connect with him in a unique way and began to see him and other students at the Lodges as normal.

As the field placement went on, Geneen continued to reflect on the teacher/student dichotomy and on the question of her authority as well as the normalcy of her students:

> After a while, I got a feel for how they [the students] reacted and they were pretty receptive and enjoyed being there. They listened really well, and at that point I got a feel for the authority I had. I would say it's not like a normal teacher-student relationship at all. It was more on an equal plane; they [the students] became more comfortable with me and my peers, kind of opened up a little bit more and were a little bit more relaxed.

Geneen understood that the situation in which she taught was an unusual one and commented that "my peers and I have been provided a unique opportunity because we are working with these kids in the comfort of their own living quarters and [these students] have volunteered to be there [participate in the activities designed by prospective teachers]." Prospective teachers were not working with students from the Lodges in a traditional classroom setting; therefore, as Geneen worked over time with the students, she found herself building relationships with them and thus began to understand the power of building relationships between teacher and student. This relationship building allowed each person to see the other as he or she really was, as set apart from the expectations normalcy or established roles that each might too easily perform in a traditional classroom. Approaching teaching as a reciprocal act, "where teachers teach student, and students teach teachers in ways that are facilitative" (Kinloch, 2012, p. 122), has been described by a way to combat unbalanced power relations between students and teacher and allow for more transformative interactions within the spaces of teaching.

Geneen described how these transformed relationships between teacher and students had an impact on all:

> They [students at the Lodges] have good attitudes and are respectful of us [prospective teachers from Wilkerson University] when we are with them. I have been impacted by their maturity and have seen that teachers can make a difference by simply showing students they care about them and respect them.

Geneen began her field placement fearfully, expecting the students to be angry and closed off. She viewed students from the Lodges as far from 'normal' high school students. Over time, however, as she was able to work closely with these students in their own living spaces, she saw that the kids at the Lodges were, in many ways, just like other teenagers. Perhaps more importantly, through this reunderstanding of who is normal she also reevaluated the role teachers play with these students. The fear she had expressed, over time, changed to respect and care, and she saw teaching as at least partially based upon the individual relationships teachers build with their students.

Harding's (2009) assertion that identities are always connected through relationship, history and culture resonated with us as we observed that

Geneen's identity as a teacher was in a process of becoming through her understanding of the relationship she had built with the students at the Lodges. Geneen was, in fact, acknowledging how her relationship with students would always be an integral aspect of her teacher identity. Because this acknowledgment took place outside the confines of a traditional school setting, both Geneen and her students at the Lodges were allowed more agency in their negotiation of relationship and identities-in-relationship. Within a traditional classroom setting, where teacher and student identities are predefined, there may be little room for this sort of negotiated agency.

THE SEARCH FOR AGENCY

Experiences working with youth at Family Partnership and the Lodges also prompted beginning teachers to recognize that adolescents, indeed, possess agency. Through awareness of a dialectical relationship between adolescents' agentive selves and the discourses in which they operate, teachers were able to account for the back and forth between self and discourse. We see this as working within the dialectic of 'both ways' of ethnographic knowing.

Dorothy Smith (1990) has been explicit in addressing 'both ways' of ethnographic knowing, and has focused on the possibility of a "dialectics of discourse and the everyday" (p. 202). Smith articulates this in reference to women's active placement in their worlds:

> It is easy to misconstrue the discourse as having an overriding power to determine the values and interpretation of women's appearances in local settings, and see this power as essentially at the disposal of the fashion industry and media. But women are active, skilled, make choices, consider, are not fooled or foolish. Within discourse there is play and interplay. (1990, p. 202)

In the preceding quotation, Smith (1990) understands that while discourse may shape possibilities, participants enact agency and have the ability to take up their agency in various ways. Prospective teachers who worked at within Family Promise and the Lodges were able to deconstruct two important binaries: the normal–abnormal binary of adolescence and the authoritative–submissive binary of a traditional teacher/student relationship. Ming Nguyen, Rebecca Avery, Henry Taylor, and Geneen Sandovar made their agency visible through the stories they told within their journals and interviews. Furthermore, they made the agency of the youth with whom they worked visible. They saw how the agency of their students complicated the idea of the 'normal' adolescent and worked to take this message out into the world.

REFERENCES

Bakhtin, M. (1990). *Art and answerability: Early philosophical essays* (M. Holquist, Ed., & V. Liapunov, Trans.). Austin: University of Texas Press.

Bakhtin, M. (1993). *Toward a philosophy of the act* (V. Liapunov & M. Holquist, Eds.). Austin: University of Texas Press.

Barton, A. C. (1998). Teaching science with homeless children: Pedagogy, representation, and identity. *Journal of Research in Science Teaching, 35*(4), 379–394. doi:10.1002/(SICI)1098-2736(199804)35:4<379::AID-TEA8>3.0CO;2-N

Behar, R., & Gordon, D. (1995). *Women writing culture.* Berkeley: University of California Press.

Carspecken, P. (1996). *Critical ethnography in educational research: A theoretical and practical guide.* New York, NY: Routledge.

Collin, R. (2012). Composing the career portfolio and the classed subject. *Research in the Teaching of English, 46*(3), 260–284. Retrieved from http://search.proquest.com.www2.lib.ku.edu/docview/922949502?accountid=14556

Dutro, E. (2010). What 'hard times' means: Mandated curricula, class-privileged assumptions, and the lives of poor children. *Research in the Teaching of English, 44*(3), 255–291. Retrieved from www.jstor.org.www2.lib.ku.edu/stable/27784362

Gomez, M. L. (2007). Seeing our lives intertwined: Teacher education for cultural inclusion. *Language Arts, 84*(4), 365–374. Retrieved from www.jstor.org.www2.lib.ku.edu/stable/41962205

Gordon, E., McKibbin, K. Vasudevan, L., & Vinz, R. (2007). Writing out of the unexpected: Narrative inquiry and the weight of small moments. *English Education, 39*(4), 326–351. Retrieved from www.jstor.org.www2.lib.ku.edu/stable/40173261

Hacking, I. (2002). Making up people. In *Historical Ontology* (pp. 99–114). Cambridge, MA: Harvard University Press. (Original work published 1996)

Hall, S. (2000). Foreword. In D. A. Yon, *Elusive culture: Schooling, race, and identity in global times* (pp. ix–xii). Albany, NY: SUNY Press.

Harding, S. (2009). A socially relevant philosophy of science? Resources from standpoint theory's controversiality. *Hypatia, 19*, 25–47. doi:10.1111/j.1527-2001.2004.tb01267.x

Hull, G., & Schultz, K. (2002). *School's out! Bridging out-of-school literacies with classroom practice.* New York, NY: Teachers College Press.

Juzwik, M. (2004). Toward an ethics of answerability. *College Composition and Communication, 55*(3), 536–567. doi:10.2307/4140698

Kelly, D. M. (2000). *Pregnant with meaning.* New York, NY: Peter Lang.

Kinloch, V. (2012). *Crossing boundaries: Teaching and learning with urban youth.* New York, NY: Teachers College Press.

Kirkland, D. (2008). "The rose that grew from concrete": Postmodern blackness and new English education. *English Journal, 97*(5), 69–75. doi:10.2307/30046887

Kirkland, D. (2010). Englishes in urban contexts: Politics, pluralism, and possibilities. *English Education, 42*(3), 293–306. Retrieved from www.jstor.org.www2.lib.ku.edu/stable/40607993

Kondo, D. K. (1990). *Crafting selves: Power, gender, and discourses of identity in a Japanese workplace.* Chicago, IL: University of Chicago Press.

Lachuk, A. J., & Gomez, M. L. (2013). Becoming answerable to our participants: A methodological essay on life history. In C. S. Rhodes & K. J. Weiss (Eds.), *Ethical issues in literacy research* (pp. 9–20). New York, NY: Routledge.

Ladson-Billings, G. (2002). I ain't writin' nuttin': Permissions to fail and demands to succeed in urban classrooms. In L. Delpit & J. K. Dowdy (Eds.), *The skin that we*

speak: Thoughts on language and culture in the classroom (pp. 107–120). New York, NY: The New Press.
Lareau, A. (2003). *Unequal childhoods: Class, race, and family life.* Oakland: University of California Press.
Lesko, N. (2001). *Act your age! A cultural construction of adolescence.* New York, NY: RoutledgeFalmer.
Luttrell, W. (2003). *Pregnant bodies, fertile minds.* New York, NY: Routledge.
Petrone, R., & Lewis, M. A. (2012). Deficits, therapists, and a desire to distance: Secondary English preservice teachers' reasoning about their future students. *English Education, 44*(3), 254–287. Retrieved from http://search.proquest.com.www2.lib.ku.edu/docview/1004728885?accountid=14556
Pillow, W. (2004). *Unfit subjects.* New York, NY: RoutledgeFalmer.
Smith, D. E. (1990). *Texts, facts, and femininity.* London, England: Routledge.
Watson, C. (2006). Narratives of practice and the construction of identity in teaching. *Teachers and Teaching: Theory and Practice, 12*(5), 509–526. doi:10.1080/13540600600832213
Wolcott, H. F. (2002). *The sneaky kid and its aftermath: Ethics and intimacy in fieldwork.* Walnut Creek, CA: AltaMira.

7 The Promise of Work at the Margins
Community Fieldwork in Teacher Education

The time that prospective teachers spent in their community-based field placements was irreplaceable. In no other field placement would they have the opportunity to see education and teaching through the lenses of marginality. Whether working with students in a day center for homeless families, a writing center at an alternative charter school, or a group home, the prospective teachers in our study were able to work closely with students in ways that they could not experience within the realms of the traditional classroom.

Kirkland (2010) encourages teacher educators to rethink the ways in which we envision and teach secondary English because in the nature of current discourses, "the pluralistic, dynamic, hybrid, and fluid nature of English swells, shifts, and is ultimately transformed in urban contexts, which are themselves complicated by linguistic legacies of survival and oppression" (p. 296). We see community-based fieldwork as an integral part of educating teachers to comprehend and then act on a new understanding of the teaching of English—especially within but not exclusive to urban/ rural settings. We have moved beyond a time where we can only teach the canon and grammar skills and expect all students to act heterogeneously within our classrooms. Because of this, we must look for nontraditional, even marginal, sites for our prospective teachers to learn to work with diverse students and through diverse curricula.

We have spent time in this book contrasting the identity work that prospective teachers may do in community-based field sites versus what possibilities exist in traditional field placements. As we have also spent time breaking down binaries, we also wish to leave readers with a sense that the placements of 'community fieldwork' and 'traditional fieldwork' need not be dichotomized. Instead, community fieldwork adds promise to teacher education programs alongside traditional fieldwork, especially as field experiences, more generally, seek to respond to a shifting demographic in U.S. schools. We frame prospective teachers' work in community-based sites as gradual movement and change throughout the discourse communities in which they operate and see Reynolds's (2004) characterization of such a space as a metaphor for community fieldwork:

And because readers and writers don't just "cross over" the margins of discrete discourse communities from alienation to acceptance, we need a sense of place—for texts and classrooms and cultures—defined by contestations and differences that extend well beyond boundary lines. Places, whether textual, material, or imaginary, are constructed and reproduced not simply by boundaries but also by practices, structures of feeling, and sedimented features of *habitus*. (p. 2)

Indeed, Reynolds highlights the significance of *habitus* in doing this work so that the concrete and lived is emphasized. The theory/practice merging of community fieldwork happens through making the opportunity for work in community field sites a reality for beginning teachers.

QUESTIONING BEFORE CONSTRICTING

Throughout *Community Fieldwork in Teacher Education: Theory and Practice*, we have aimed to explore the work that prospective teachers' undertook in nontraditional, community-based spaces for teaching and learning. We have illustrated how teachers' counterstories synthesized perceptions of their own past and therefore allowed them to assert new identities as beginning educators. Chapter 1 presented readers with the context of our work, giving readers a sense of how our work emerged from our practice as teacher educators. We debated the tenets of service-learning and questioned how these applied to our own work. We also emphasized that teachers work within what Schön (1987) refers to "swampy zones of practice" (p. 3), and artistry in teaching urges the teacher to re-shape practice while engaged in practice. From here, in the second chapter, we aimed to frame teachers' work in community-based sites as identity work, stressing that through practice, all teachers engage in a process of composing themselves as teachers. We explored how a Bakhtinian framework stressed reciprocity between the self and other, and how teachers' understandings of this relationship became more nuanced as they recognized how dominant discourses shaped possible selves. In Chapter 3, we looked further into how teachers operationalized their identity making within their writing, and how writing became a forum in which, as Emig (1977) notes, presented "a unique form of feedback" (p. 125) to teachers through their continual response and revision. We extended a focus on writing in Chapter 4 by showing how teachers debated a subscription to a teaching mythology within their own practice. Finally, in Chapters 5 and 6, we debated how community-based fieldwork presented teachers with new considerations of curriculum and of students themselves, thereby highlighting the potential that such work has in reshaping perceptions of what it means to 'do school' and which students are capable of 'doing school.' Each of the prospective teachers in our study went through transitions of thinking throughout the weeks of their field placement. Their assumptions of teaching, teacher identity, adolescence, at-risk students, authority, and curriculum were all brought into question. In questioning these assumptions, it was important for them to see the multiplicity that existed within the spaces of schools, and how traditional schooling, through standardization, tends to overly simplify the variances within the spaces of school.

In *Writing, Reading, and Research*, Veit, Gould, and Gould (2013) recommend that writing instructors help 'open up' a student's writing (pp. 41–42). By this, the authors claim that when instructors open up a student's draft, they allow students to be in charge of their own revision process. Students are no longer dependent upon the teacher to understand what can be done to improve the text. Instead, the ways that teachers allow a student to open up a draft is through questioning the student to think more carefully about the goals of the draft and providing feedback that helps students see different possibilities in a text.

Similarly, community field placements help prospective teachers 'open up' drafts of their practice. Because their teaching work is outside the confined space of a traditional classroom, they are not as dependent on the constrictions of those spaces. At the Lodges, prospective teachers did not have the constriction of curriculum mandates, so they were able to open up their practice by experimenting with content and methodology. This opening up allowed prospective teachers to reconsider how instruction affects motivation and how trust and relationships enhance literacy education. At Mettle Street School, prospective teachers did not have the constriction of teacher identity as it is typically seen against the 'teacher as authority' image. Because they were placed in a nonclassroom space, and worked with students one-on-one, the assumption of teacher authority and student/teacher relationships was opened up to new possibilities. This opening up allowed prospective teachers at Mettle Street School to see the students differently than how the community defined the students. Through this, they were able to revise the ways they saw at-risk students and relationships between teachers and students. At Family Partnership, prospective teachers opened up a contemplation of developmentalism as it relates to teaching and questioned the ways they viewed possibilities for themselves as dictated through prescribed understandings of children's development. It was through the opening up of their 'texts of practice' that these prospective teachers experienced new opportunities to reconsider their identities as teachers, and their identities within contexts and relationships.

Teacher educators (e.g., Cochran-Smith, 1995; Coffey, 2010; Gay, 2003) have asserted that what is needed in teacher education programs is space and opportunity for prospective teachers to undertake such identity work. Prospective teachers must be presented with contexts for broadening their belief systems and constructing more sophisticated understandings of students as learners. As Henry Taylor described, prior beliefs can be influenced through community-based, nonschool teaching experiences. As the field of teacher education reiterates a commitment to prepare teachers to teach

The Promise of Work at the Margins 141

diverse groups of students, it is important that this move beyond rhetoric and into the spatial and temporal contexts in which we live. Creating spaces within teacher education programs where beginning teachers can question the assumed binaries in concrete ways is a worthwhile endeavor and a move toward embracing programmatic features committed to beginning teachers' growth during the preservice years.

A NEW NORMALCY: PALIMPSEST KNOWING

Often found in ancient writings, the term palimpsest refers to a document that has layers of writing within one document. Often, the original text has been erased so a new text can be inscribed, yet the original markings are still somewhat visible. Reynolds (2004) describes studying a writer as a palimpsest:

> Like a parchment used for writing where other symbols remain visible—a never-quite clean slate . . . Studying writing/composing as a palimpsest means acknowledging the vague or faint traces left by homeplaces, changes in the landscape, mental maps, or spatial memory. (p. 139)

The experiences of prospective teachers behave as these marks of parchment. These are marks that their own texts of practice will be written and rewritten over, but will still be visible and a part of the complete document. The prospective teachers in this study were imprinted through the community sites where they experienced a different sort of teacher training. The inscription of community placements will certainly be written over by future experiences: their student teaching placements, their first teaching jobs, and their veteran teaching years. However, this inscription will still be visible in their future teaching but will be layered on over time.

As we worked through our discussion of prospective teachers' work in community-based sites, we emphasized the power of both the dialogic and the local. The dialogic stressed responsiveness on the part of teachers and the local stressed how context intimately affects the act of teaching. An adjacent discussion to these emphasized concepts, however, is the reality of the 'doubleness' (Marshall, Smagorinsky, & Moore, 1995) that exists in the world of education. Marshall et al. (1995) specifically linked the concept of doubleness to the perplexities of practice that teachers might find themselves in with regard to matters of curriculum (specifically in reference to the teaching of literature). For example, Marshall et al. describe that, at the same time that teachers advocate for student-centered instruction, they may exhibit teacher-directed evaluative strategies, noting that often these teachers are not aware that their stated beliefs were different from the beliefs enacted in the classroom.

We see that the concept of doubleness can be extended to the world of education writ large. At the same time that teachers are taught the power of dialogue and response, they may step into a classroom and experience the world of standardization. At the same time teachers seek to question and reframe understandings of at-risk learners, they may enter schools that reinscribe these definitions. Doubleness can appear at every turn. Whereas some (e.g., Smagorinsky, 2002) have suggested that a conceptually coherent teacher education program—a conceptual home base—is the best way to "provide the critical faculties for recognizing the disparity between the traditions and enabling both recognition and critique of their differences" (Bickmore, Smagorinsky, & O-Donnell-Allen, 2005, p. 48), we also see that a strong base of conceptual tools may not be enough if it is not paired with practice that prompts beginning teachers to rethink assumptions and dominant paradigms. Teachers still must choose how to operate within the doubleness. Although conceptually coherent programs may provide beginning teachers with more aptitude to critique, and perhaps more confidence in doing so, they still do not necessarily confront the issue of doubleness head on. We, by asking beginning teachers to live the doubleness, trust that theory and practice can more artfully merge. If urged to reside within the doubleness, we see that a conceptually coherent teacher education program can build upon we what see as the asset of marginality—helping prospective teachers articulate the double binds that they face.

QUESTIONING FORWARD: CURRICULAR IMPLICATIONS AND FUTURE INQUIRIES

We hope that other teacher education programs will embrace nontraditional, community-based field placements as valuable experiences for beginning teachers. Although the student-teaching experience and many classroom observation experiences are already the norm in teacher training, the community-based field placement is one that will allow prospective teachers to grow exponentially. This experience teaches prospective teachers to question their previous assumptions and reflect on their identities, curriculum, and relationships within the education system. From this, a thinking practice can emerge that will continue when they have their own classrooms, and can certainly pave the way for furthering reflective teaching and teacher leadership.

For future discussions, we hope that other teacher educators and researchers are able to enact community field placements that expand the work we have presented in this book. We believe there are many opportunities for teacher education programs to reach out to the community, and we know there are multiple possibilities for prospective teachers to learn from community members and organizations. Teacher education programs can view these partnerships as reciprocal relationships where beginning teachers and community programs are receiving as much as they are giving. Eby (1998) speaks to the importance of a reciprocal relationship in community-based learning by describes how community-based learning can be transformational in the best of circumstances. Yet, when created in hierarchical ways, these programs can actually harm individuals and communities. We take this as a lesson in emphasizing the dialogic throughout our work and including answerability as a layer within the dialogic. Being answerable to others urges us to foreground responsiveness and responsibility.

Over the last 5 years, as we supported prospective teachers who worked and learned within community-based field placements, we ourselves have learned more about incorporating this into our course work, especially how writing can deepen the learning that occurs.

Curricular Concerns in Education

In connecting community fieldwork to teacher education, prospective teachers will need assistance understanding that the work they will be doing will be closer to what is thought of traditionally as 'tutoring,' rather than 'teaching.' Although we have spent time in this book deconstructing terminology, beginning teachers' views of tutoring and teaching may be solidified before they are given the opportunity to think more broadly about these terms. Sharing articles and allowing beginning teachers to discuss their understandings of the differences between tutoring and teaching may be a helpful way to introduce work in community field sites.

When designing a methods course in English/Language Arts education that incorporates community fieldwork, there are particular strategies that Heidi learned through several years teaching of the course *Curriculum and Instruction in Middle/Secondary English Language Arts Classrooms*. These strategies included the following:

- **Emphasizing that students' education happens in school and out of school**

  This includes investigating definitions of literacy, how young people become literate, as well as how and why young people use literacy. In class, as beginning teachers begin to develop philosophies of literacy education, they will learn to take into account the histories of learners.

- **Understanding that curriculum is not a concept that means one size fits all**

  Rather, curriculum is constructed through content and interaction. Students and teachers are active participants in constructing curriculum; therefore, curriculum can be individualized.

- **Incorporating multicultural education principles of social justice and equity into the English/Language Arts curriculum**

  Through an incorporation of these principles, teachers can create lessons with high expectations for all students. Such lessons honor students' lifeworlds and personal literacies and support their achievement.

- Alongside prospective teachers, critically examining research, theories, and practices in English education

  Through emphasizing that research in English education can explore the social, cultural, and political implications of literacy education will help beginning teachers see that knowledge they are gaining in community fieldwork has implications for research in the field.

Through incorporating the preceding principles into a methods course that includes community fieldwork, prospective teachers will see that tenets undergirding teaching and learning are not just specific to the community field site but can also be infused in practice as a way to operationalize these principles.

Curricular Concerns in Composition

In connecting community fieldwork to composition course work, fieldwork becomes a focus or a topic for writing. The field site becomes a site for reflection and exploration and expression and a place where students can analyze and synthesize, through writing, the theory they have read with the realities they experience. The writing tasks become more authentic and therefore combine personal, social, and academic forms. When including community field placements within a composition course for prospective teachers, the curricular effect in composition is layered and complex. College students are working to become better writers, while learning writing pedagogy and theory, and working with student writers outside the contexts of traditional paradigms. College students may stumble and succeed at their own writing as they work through ways to help younger students at community sites learn to overcome their own stumbling blocks and see success. College students, while reading theory, also then see what actually holds true in the sites where they work with students who are considered marginal or at-risk.

When designing a composition course that incorporates community fieldwork, there are particular strategies that Melanie learned through several years teaching of the course *Advanced Composition—Teaching Emphasis*. These strategies included the following:

- **Explaining, modeling, and assigning reflective journal writing**

  Prospective teachers can often summarize and describe their fieldwork experiences quite successfully, but it becomes challenging to them to analyze the experiences and critically comment on what they had seen and done at the site. Modeling this kind of critical analysis is important.

- **Discussing and debriefing experiences while in class**

  Through discussion and debriefing, students can see similarities and differences in their classmates' experiences and how these may either disrupt notions of what community fieldwork must be like. Discussion and debriefing can also allow students to draw more general conclusions that span their varied experiences.

- When discussing class assignments, drawing on students' community fieldwork experiences can be helpful reference points

   In drawing on their experiences, students are able to reference what they have seen and done at their community fieldwork site. For example, when Melanie's class discussed a chapter by Gee titled, "Literacy, Discourse, and Linguistics: Introduction and What Is Literacy?" (2001), Melanie moved discussion her students to use what they saw in their fieldwork as evidence to illustrate Gee's terminology. Another example that Melanie used was when students were working in response groups. When students were working in groups, Melanie asked them to think about what type of response was constructive. Then she asked them to think about how they could use this understanding of response when they returned to their field placements.

- Assigning a longer research paper can help students use their journals and experiences in their field placements as evidence and research to support a thesis.

   Assigning a research paper that connects to fieldwork allows students to synthesize their understanding of their fieldwork while also allowing them to see, as writers, how support can come from a variety of sources. This type of research paper can be a precursor into teaching action research or ethnographical research in a more advanced writing course.

MOVING FORWARD: PAIRING COMMUNITY FIELDWORK WITH REFLECTIVE PRACTICE

For instructors who would like to integrate community fieldwork into their own classrooms, we want to especially emphasize the importance of reflection in the form of reflective writing and reflective class discussions. Reflective writing and reflective discussions become more than just spaces to pursue a passive reporting of experience. They also become more than empty expressive practices of emotional response. When modeled, prompted, and then responded to by instructors and peers, reflective writing and reflective discussion become a tool for thinking, and therefore become the platform for reflexive pedagogy (Danielewicz, 2001). Reflective writing and reflective discussion become the space where dialogic response is made concrete. As a result, these responses can then be revisited, considered, and analyzed. Prospective teachers can see and more thoroughly comprehend their learning as it takes place, and they can synthesize information from multiple sources. The act of written reflection, when paired with the experience of the community field placement, has the tremendous value of being able to interrupt predicted teaching chronologies (Britzman, 1991). Through this interruption, prospective teachers become more active in their own visions of the teaching act and more aware of their becoming. In all, prospective teachers enact "reflection-in-action" (Schön, 1987) through reflective writing assignments, and this encourages them to critically read their future teaching experiences.

Specifically, we found that the following writing and discussion prompts were helpful for student reflection in both courses. These prompts were used in both written reflection and in class discussion. Prompt 1 is useful before beginning teachers enter the field, and they can contemplate their expectations before they begin working in their site. Reflecting on expectations allows beginning teachers to consciously account for the stories they may have heard or the informal knowledge they have that could affect their interactions at the site. Prompts 2 through 6 are useful to share with beginning teachers as reflective journal prompts throughout their fieldwork experience. Finally, Prompt 7 allows students the possibility of creasing a dialogic expression with their earlier selves. This is an important prompt to help students synthesize their experiences and look forward.

1. Reflecting on Expectations

Before beginning your community fieldwork, please describe how you see the site and the students at the site. Where do you think your expectations come from? Have you had any past experiences with the site or students at the site? Have you learned about the site in other ways than your firsthand experience? What do you expect your work there will entail? What role do you think you will play? What challenges do you think you might face? What do you hope to share? What do you hope to learn?

2. Reflecting on Context

Describe the geographical space of the community fieldwork site. Where is it located in the community, and what does the surrounding landscape look like? Describe the architectural space; what is the building like, what is the room you are in like, and what are the spaces like where you and the students work together? Describe the social spaces: Where do students have more or less freedom? Where do adults have more or less freedom? What groups or individuals seem to have authority over the different spaces?

3. Reflecting on Students

Who are the students you work with? Can you describe them as a group? As individuals? How do these students fit into your understanding of adolescents? Of learners? How would you describe the students' relationships with each other? With you? With other adults at the site? What have they shared with you about their lives in and out of school?

4. Reflecting on Other Adults

What adults are present at your field placement? What roles do they play? What are their interactions like with you? With students? With each other? Who seems to hold authority in this site? Are there various levels of authority? How do you know? How do you see the adults affecting the students or vice versa?

5. Reflecting on Curriculum

What do you know about the curriculum at the site? Is there a clearly defined curriculum with which you are involved? If not, why? If not, how do you proceed with regard to curriculum? How do you teach or tutor without a specific curriculum? If there is a clearly defined curriculum, how would you describe it? What is valued and what is included or excluded? Who is responsible for creating and on implementing the curriculum? What part do you have in affecting the curriculum? How do you see students' understanding of and interaction with what they are expected to learn?

6. Reflection on Theory

How does what you are seeing in your fieldwork compare to what we have read and discussed in class? Does the theory we have read complicate, confirm, or conflict with what you have seen in your community site? What explanation do you have for any inconsistencies you see between theory and practice? What understandings have come from the theories that have helped you in your work at the field placement?

7. Speaking Back to Expectations

Now that you have completed your community fieldwork experience, look back on your reflection on early expectations (Prompt 1). How do these expectations compare to the reality of your experience? Were your early expectations of students, adults, and the site itself accurate? Did your anticipated challenges, contributions, and learning come to fruition? Did you encounter challenges, possibilities, and lessons that you hadn't expected to learn?

    As we encouraged our students to reflect on their experiences in community-based field sites, throughout the process we, ourselves, have also reflected upon the implications of our study. We see great promise in community field placements for the training of English language arts teachers, so it follows that we also see implications that will reach into secondary students' lives and farther into their communities. We see that this could be the beginning of a unique understanding and a more conscious response of community impact through teacher education. Teacher educators already understand that a school is only a piece of a larger community, and future teachers must be sensitive to community influences on student learning. Therefore, we need to explore multiple invitations for prospective teachers and communities to intermingle and learn from each other. Community fieldwork can be one important invitation, and we have seen, through our own research and reflection, that this invitation has great impact on our future teachers. We encourage other teacher educators to share similar invitations with prospective teachers.

Theoretically, we see that, throughout our book, we have worked between two discourses: the 'normative' and the 'dialogic.' Like Britzman (1991), we have often sought to challenge the normative through adherence to the dialogic, as we see that "dialogic discourses can offer different ways to reconceptualize practice and, most significantly, attend to the complex vulnerabilities of lived experience in ways that move beyond essentializing the self and thus abstracting the individual from the social world" (p. 239). In some ways, through a more purposeful focus on local, community-based sites, we have hoped to magnify the possibilities of the dialogic, presenting prospective teachers with an invitation to articulate the normative and the dialogic in their everyday world. We have also emphasized the promise in working at the margins, for it is at the margins where prospective teachers may more readily 'open up' their practice, seeking new possibilities and understandings.

REFERENCES

Bickmore, S., Smagorinsky, P., & O'Donnell-Allen, C. (2005). Tensions between traditions: The role of contexts in learning to teach. *English Education, 38*(1), 23–52. Retrieved from www.jstor.org.www2.lib.ku.edu/stable/40173210

Britzman, D. P. (1991). *Practice makes practice: A critical study of learning to teach.* Albany: State University of New York Press.

Cochran-Smith, M. (1995). Color blindness and basket making are not the answers: Confronting the dilemmas of race, culture, and language diversity in teacher education. *American Educational Research Journal, 32,* 493–522. Retrieved from www.jstor.org.www2.lib.ku.edu/stable/1163321

Coffey, H. (2010). "*They* taught *me*": The benefits of early community-based field experiences in teacher education. *Teaching and Teacher Education, 26,* 335–342. doi:10.1016/j.tate.2009.09.014

Danielewicz, J. (2001). *Teaching selves: Identity, pedagogy, and teacher education.* Albany: State University of New York Press.

Emig, J. (1977) Writing as a mode of learning. *College Composition and Communication, 28*(2), 122–128. doi:10.2307/356095

Eby, J. W. (1998). *Why service-learning is bad.* Retrieved from www.messiah.edu/documents/Agape/wrongsvc.pdf

Gay, G. (Ed.). (2003). *Becoming multicultural educators: Personal journeys toward professional agency.* San Francisco, CA: Jossey-Bass.
Gee, J. P. (2001). Ligeracy, discourse, and Linguistics: Introduction and what is literacy? In E. Cushman, M. Rose, B. Kroll, & E. R. Kintgen (Eds.), *Literacy: A critical sourcebook* (pp. 525–544). Boston, MA: Bedford/St. Martin's.
Kirkland, D. (2010). Englishes in urban contexts: Politics, pluralism, and possibilities. *English Education, 42*(3), 293–306. Retrieved from www.jstor.org.www2.lib.ku.edu/stable/40607993
Marshall, J. D., Smagorinsky, P., & Moore, M. W. (1995). *The language of interpretation: Patterns of discourse in discussions of literature* (NCTE Research Report No. 27). Urbana, IL: National Council of Teachers of English.
Reynolds, N. (2004). *Geographies of writing: Inhabiting places and encountering difference.* Carbondale: Southern Illinois Press.
Schön, D. (1987). *Educating the reflective practitioner.* San Francisco, CA: Jossey-Bass.
Smagorinsky, P. (2002). *Teaching English through principled practice.* Upper Saddle River, NJ: Merrill/Prentice Hall.
Veit, R., Gould, C., & Gould, K. (2013). *Writing, reading, and research.* Stamford, CT: Cengage Learning.

Appendix A

Syllabus for Curriculum and Instruction in Middle School/Secondary English Language Arts Classrooms

CURRICULUM & TEACHING 533:

Curriculum and Instruction in Middle/Secondary
English Language Arts Classrooms
3 credit hours

Instructor: Dr. Heidi Hallman

Purpose of course:

This is an English/Language Arts methods course that focuses on understanding middle and secondary students as literacy learners. In this course we will:

- Become familiar with the major concepts and approaches of English/Language Arts and literacy education, focusing on the written and oral language development of students from grades 6–12.
- Focus our inquiry on reading and writing assessment of individual students, matching instruction to assessment information, and modifying curriculum based on individual needs.
- Practice various forms of reading and writing assessments and develop instructional plans based on these assessments.
- Investigate definitions of literacy, how young adults become literate, as well as how and why young adults use literacy.
- Critically examine research, theories, and practices in English Education and explore the social, cultural, and political implications of literacy education.
- Incorporate multicultural education principles of social justice and equity into the English/Language Arts curriculum in order to create lessons with high expectations for all students. These lessons honor students' lifeworlds and personal literacies, and also support their achievement.
- Utilize and understand standards-based approaches to lesson planning.

Appendix A

REQUIRED TEXTS:

Anderson, M. T. (2004). *Feed*. Cambridge, MA: Candlewick Press.
Burke, J. (2007). *The English Teacher's Companion, 4th edition*. Portsmouth, NH: Heinemann.
Christensen, L. (2000). *Reading, writing, and rising up: Teaching about social justice and the power of the written word*. Milwaukee, WI: Rethinking Schools.
Moore, D., Alvermann, D., & Hinchman, K. (Eds). (2000). *Struggling adolescent readers: A collection of teaching strategies*. Newark, DE: International Reading Association.
Ryan, P. (2000). *Esperanza Rising*. New York, NY: Scholastic.
Smagorinsky, P. (2008). *Teaching English by Design: How to create and carry out instructional units*. Portsmouth, NH: Heinemann.
Tovani, C. (2000). *I read it, but I don't get it*. Portland, ME: Stenhouse.

REQUIRED ARTICLES:

Alsup, J., Conard-Salvo, T., & Peters, S. (2008). Tutoring is real: The benefits of the peer tutor experience for future English Educators. *Pedagogy: Critical Approaches to Teaching Literature, Language, Composition, and Culture, 8*(2), 237–347.
Black, R.W. (2005). Access and Affiliation: The literacy and composition practices of English-language learners in an online fanfiction community. *Journal of Adolescent and Adult Literacy, 49*(2), 118–128.
Brandt, D. (1998). Sponsors of literacy. *College Composition and Communication, 49*(2), 165–185.
Gee, J.P. (2001). Literacy, discourse, and linguistics: Introduction and what is literacy? In E. Cushman, M. Rose, B. Kroll, & E. R. Kingten (Eds.) *Literacy: A Critical Sourcebook* (pp. 525–544). Boston, MA: Bedford/St. Martin's.
Hairston, M. (1982). The winds of change: Thomas Kuhn and the revolution of the teaching of writing. *College Composition and Communication, 33*(1), 76–88.
Hallman, H.L. (2007). Negotiating teacher identity: Exploring the use of electronic teaching portfolios with preservice English teachers. *Journal of Adolescent and Adult Literacy, 50*(6), 474–485.
Sommers, N. (1980). Revision strategies of student writers and experienced adult writers. *College Composition and Communication, 31*(4), 378–388.
Weaver, C. (1996). Teaching grammar in the context of writing. *English Journal, 85*(7), 15–24.

Requirements

1. Literacy History

2. Discussion Leader

Lead the day's discussion in which you share your understandings of the week's required readings related to the session's topic.

3. Tovani Reading Strategy Presentation

In groups of 2–3, demonstrate how to conduct a comprehension reading strategy with a small, large, or whole group.

4. Field Experience Journal

You will have the option of completing fieldwork in (1) a middle/high school English classroom, or (2) completing fieldwork in a community-based site, a program for homeless families. You may also choose to complete both field experiences. In both options for fieldwork, you will be given questions to guide your observations/interactions, which should be recorded as field notes in a journal format.

You will also be required to teach at least one lesson at your field site. The lesson can be one of any length. Some ideas for lesson formats include teaching an introductory lesson to a novel or unit; teaching a mini-lesson related to the teaching of writing; facilitating a discussion with small or large groups of students. The idea of teaching a lesson in the community-based site will be slightly different than teaching in a classroom. We will be discussing the concept of students' "out-of-school" literacies. Your lesson plan should reflect this and conversations in class will give you ideas for how you might frame such lessons. Community-based fieldwork will take the form of working with homeless youth in the after-school or evening hours. The organization that we are partnering with serves homeless families. The youth in the program are school-aged and will benefit greatly from your involvement with the program.

You will complete at least 20 hours of field experience this semester.

5. Literature Circles and Two Teaching sessions

For the literature circles, we will read two young adult novels in the course and you will prepare to participate in a literature circle to discuss each of the novels. For the teaching sessions, you will be asked to compose a lesson plan, clearly stating objectives for the lesson as well as procedures and assessments.

6. Thematic Unit

As a final requirement of the course, you will prepare a 2–4 week thematic unit. The unit should revolve around a particular theme and be prepared for a diverse student population. The unit should include but is not limited to the following:

- ✓ Narrative Overview of the Unit
- ✓ Unit Rationale
- ✓ Background Information about the Students
- ✓ Background Information about the School
- ✓ Objectives (Two of the objectives should be from the KS standards.)
- ✓ Materials
- ✓ Sampling of Activities (at least 5) for the 2–4 weeks
- ✓ Complete lesson plans for two days of the unit

7. Participation and Attendance

Come to class each week on time. (If an emergency arises and you will be late or absent, call or email me before class.) Each unexcused absence (beyond one) will result in a 2 pt. deduction from your grade.

Appendix B

Syllabus for Advanced Composition—Teaching Emphasis

ENGLISH 300:

Advanced Composition—Teaching Emphasis

3 credit hours

Instructor: Dr. Melanie Burdick

Course Objectives:

The skills and concepts taught within English 300 are designed to reinforce, supplement and extend those introduced in English 101. By the end of the semester students in English 300 will be able to . . .

1. perform complex and sustained analyses of texts
2. support and sustain logical and ethical argumentation
3. conduct sophisticated research
4. engage with and synthesize sources
5. demonstrate sustained reasoning and critical thinking
6. show an understanding of how form and language can be applied within a discipline
7. use academic writing conventions appropriate to upper-division work
8. appropriately adapt language within varied rhetorical situations

These objectives will be assessed through a final course portfolio that must include a minimum of two polished essays addressing differing rhetorical situations as well as a reflective cover letter.

Course Activities:

This section of English 300 is designed particularly for education majors, so we will be writing and also discussing the best ways to teach writing. This course is intended to help students connect discussions of educational and composition theory to classroom research and practice. In order to enhance their understanding of writing as both a process and social act, students will participate in the following learning activities:

- write in many genres and for varying purposes and audiences
- examine and reflect upon their own writing processes
- study current writing theory and research
- analyze and judge varying philosophies of writing assessment
- gain experience responding to and assessing student writing
- present a lesson on the teaching of writing
- create a research project regarding a particular challenge in the teaching of writing
- work closely with students in a school or community center, and reflect upon how course readings and assignments connect with or complicate what happens with real students in varied contexts
- create a portfolio of written work

The class is designed so students begin to see themselves not only as teachers of writing, but also as writers themselves. Students will be asked to begin the process of classroom inquiry and teacher leadership that generates both influential classroom instruction and vital educational reform. This will be a discussion-based course with a workshop atmosphere. The success of the class as a whole depends upon everyone's regular attendance and active participation. The service learning component is unique to this particular section of English 300—Teaching Emphasis and is purposefully included to give teacher candidates more hands-on experiences working with diverse students.

Textbooks:

- *Inside Out* by Kirby, Liner and Vinz
- *6+1 Traits of Writing* by Ruth Culham

REQUIRED ARTICLES:

Brandt, D. (1998). Sponsors of literacy. *College Composition and Communication*, 49(2), pp. 165–185.
Connolly, P. (1989). Writing and the ecology of learning. In Connolly, P. & Vilardi, T. (Eds.) *Writing to Learn in Mathematics and Science* (pp. 1–14). New York: Teachers College Press.
Fisher, D., Frey, N., & Elwardi, R. (2008). Powerful pens: Writing to learn with adolescents. In Fisher, D. & Frey, N. (Eds.) *Improving Adolescent Literacy: Content Area Strategies at Work* (pp. 169–187). Upper Saddle River, NJ: Pearson.
Gee, J.P. (2001). Literacy, discourse, and linguistics: Introduction and what is literacy? In Cushman, E., et al. (Eds.) *Literacy: A Critical Sourcebook* (pp. 525–544). Boston, MA: Bedford/St. Martin's.

Hairston, M. (1982). The winds of change: Thomas Kuhn and the revolution of the teaching of writing. *College Composition and Communication, 33* (1), 76–88.

Kirkland, D. (2008). The rose that grew in concrete: Postmodern blackness and new English education. *English Journal, 97* (5), 69–75.

McLeod, S.H. (1992). Defining WAC: Writing to learn and learning to write. In McLeod, S.H., & Soven, M. (Eds.) *Writing Across the Curriculum* (pp. 3–6). Newberry Park: Sage Publishers.

Spandel, V. (2006). Speaking my mind: In defense of rubrics. *English Journal*, 96 (1), pp. 19–22.

Sommers, N. (1980). Revision strategies of student writers and experienced adult writers. *College Composition and Communication.*

Weaver, C. (1996). Teaching Grammar in the Context of Writing. *English Journal*, 85(7), pp. 15–24.

Wilson, M. (2007). Why I won't be using rubrics to respond to my students' writing. *English Journal*, 96(4), pp. 62–66.

Required Course Assignments and Activities

Formal Papers:

You will be writing four formal papers this semester. Since the most essential work of any writing class is revision, you will be working with several drafts of each paper. Revision actually means re-seeing, and you will receive response from me and from your response group as you work through the revision process to help you re-see each paper.

Formal Paper Assignments:

1. *Literacy Narrative*—a story describing who you are as a reader, writer and future literacy teacher.
2. *Discussion of Writing Across the Curriculum*—Using the articles from class, write about the viability of the WAC movement in contemporary schools. You are not required to, but you may focus on the subject area and/or grade level you intend to teach.
3. *Annotated Bibliography and Article Critique*—a list and summary of sources you plan to use in your multi-genre research paper. A 2–3 page critique of a professional article from your annotated bibliography in which you explain its usefulness for a novice teacher.
4. *Multi-genre Research Paper*—a research paper that is written through multiple genres on an issue of teaching writing
5. *Analysis of your service learning*—a reflective and analytical paper in which you synthesize your service learning work with the readings activities and discussions you have experienced in class.

Discussant Role:

With one of your peers, lead a 30-minute discussion in which you share your understandings of the week's required readings.

Service-Learning and Journal:

You will have a unique component to the course that will give you experience working with elementary, middle, or high school literacy learners. A tutoring and/or teaching experience (also the service-learning component of the course) will match you with a learner/learners in the community where you can begin to make connections between theory and practice of writing instruction. You will participate in 16–20 hours over the course of the semester and document your experience in a journal. You may use the prompts given to you in class as a way to reflect on this experience. You should write at least one journal entry for each visit you make to your service-learning site. Each journal entry should be titled and dated.

In small groups in class on particular three class days (see course schedule), you will share your journals and discuss students' literacy learning in your tutoring site. On these dates, the journals will also be collected and graded. You will also write a paper about this experience in which you reflect upon your service learning and analyze how it fit into or conflicted with the ideas we have discussed in class.

Portfolio:

At the end of the semester, instead of a final exam, you will submit a final portfolio of your writing. This portfolio should present your best work, and should portray the process you went through during the semester to produce that work. Final and rough drafts of all formal papers will be required in the portfolio.

Attendance and Participation:

Since this course is student-centered and discussion-driven, your attendance and participation is essential for your success and the success of the class as a whole. Many class periods will be spent working on writing exercises and group discussions that would be impossible for you to make up on your own.

Appendix C

Henry Taylor's Life Graph

August

In August we got our first look at the syllabus. I knew I would do a field placement but didn't know that working with homeless families would be an option.

September

We had our first informational meeting. I felt apprehensive about meeting in a church but the staff quickly won me over.

My first day set a cheerful tone for the rest of the project. I discovered that I really enjoyed working with younger kids, prompting me to question whether social expectations made me choose high schoolers over elementary schoolers. This led to a deeper questioning of my decision-making process that became characteristic of my time working at the center this semester.

October

I was left completely along with the kids for about 45 minutes, in which they did their best to stretch my attention in as many directions as possible. Things got really serious when the phone range, one of the girls picked up and then, after a moment said, "Here, let me give you to a grown-up." As she handed the phone to me I realized that as far as she could tell *I* was the grown-up, and this meant having to take responsibility for things.

I had probably my most difficult day in the program. I had an excellent experience with the kids I've been working with, but while I was out of the room I overheard what might have been one of the mothers yelling very, very harshly at her baby son. I couldn't determine what had happened, whether it was a common occurrence, or what would happen if I told anyone. A few weeks later I saw the mother's face in the newspaper in a story about how the program helped her turn her life around and find a home for herself and her family. I thought about how often in education potentially serious problems manifest and often both action and inaction seem too risky to contemplate.

November

I led and witnessed multiple in-class presentations this month. I marveled at how quickly people I knew as generally shiftless suddenly seemed to grow up when given authority. I began to see authority as situational.

Due to numerous illnesses and then a few miscommunications, this was my first time with the new family. I got to work with Annie and see her brother and Tonya discuss whether or not he actually had homework. This also was my last day at the center and I wondered whether the brother felt mistrusted and whether that would make him less likely to do his homework. The overarching problem brought to light by my experience this semester seems to be how we construct solutions in situations where we have imperfect knowledge and imperfect knowledge might exacerbate problems.

December

I filled out my life graph, finally starting to piece together common themes in my notes. It seems clear that the only solution to responsibility is courage.

Appendix D

Anne Chisholm's Life Graph

Wednesday, February 29, 2012

This afternoon I went to the Day Center for training for tutoring. This "training" was not at all what I expected. First, I was given a tour of the day center and the actual "training" portion was quite short, and truly I thought it was inadequate. I was shown a short video explaining how to interact with guests. I guess I thought It would be more "hands-on" in some way.

Monday, March 5, 2012

I spent the night as an overnight host last night. It was my first time doing this and I struggled with what I saw. Kids were running wild, there was little parent involvement, and what I did see was negative. Kids were up way too late and were basically eating junk food. I didn't see a single fruit or vegetable while I was there. I can see this being somewhat acceptable for teenagers but not for little kids.

Monday, March 29, 2012

Mostly I feel that I'm practicing the role of being a tutor rather than being a teacher. It has been really rare that I actually teach anything while I'm at the day center. Mostly I'm working with kids on their homework. I'm fine with that but I know that I'm itching to get into an English classroom to develop that teacher presence.

Thursday, April 12, 2012

This evening when I arrived the families were still eating dinner. Rachelle, who is the same age as my daughter (13), said, "Hey, come sit down by me!" It reinforced to me that kids care that I'm here. I also think I've developed a relationship with Rachelle's mom because we both have 13-year old daughters. I've started to think that maybe I will feel sad when I leave at the end of the semester. Rachelle said to me tonight, "Don't leave! Stay one more hour!"

Thursday, April 26, 2012

Things are still going well. I can see the value in being flexible when being a teacher. These kids generally always tell us that they don't have homework (I'm not sure why because my own kids always have homework!) and they generally don't have a great environment to do homework in. We do what we can do in the situations we're in, and that's all that can be asked of people.

Thursday, May 3, 2012

Last visit tonight ☹ I have learned how resilient these families are.

References

Alcoff, L. (2006). *Visible identities: Race, gender and the self.* New York, NY: Oxford University Press.
Alsup, J. (2006). *Teacher identity discourses: Negotiating personal and professional discourses.* Mahwah, NJ: Erlbaum.
Amobi, F. A. (2006). Beyond the call: Preserving reflection in the preparation of "highly qualified" teachers. *Teacher Education Quarterly, 33*(2), 23–35. doi:10.1177/0888406411420887
Anderson, J., & Erickson, J. (2003). Service-learning in preservice teacher education *Academic Exchange Quarterly, 7*(2), 111–115.
Anzaldua, G. (2007). *Borderlands/La Frontera: The new mestiza* (3rd ed.). San Francisco, CA: Aunt Lute Books.
Applebee, A. (1996). *Curriculum as conversation.* Chicago, IL: University of Chicago Press.
Bacon, N. (1997) Community service writing: Problems, challenges, questions. In L. Adler-Kassner, R. Crooks, & A. Watters (Eds.), *Writing the community: Concepts and models for service-learning in composition.* (pp. 39–55). Sterling, VA: Stylus Publishing.
Bakhtin, M. (1981). *The dialogic imagination: Four essays* (M. Holquist, Ed.). Austin: University of Texas Press.
Bakhtin, M. (1986). *Speech genres and other late essays* (C. Emerson & M. Holquist, Eds.). Austin: University of Texas.
Bakhtin, M. (1990). *Art and answerability: Early philosophical essays* (M. Holquist, Ed., & V. Liapunov, Trans.). Austin: University of Texas Press.
Bakhtin, M. (1993). *Toward a philosophy of the act* (V. Liapunov & M. Holquist, Eds.). Austin: University of Texas Press.
Barone, T. (1995). Persuasive writing, vigilant readings, and reconstructed characters: The paradox of trust in educational storytelling. In J. Hatch & R. Wisniewski (Eds.), *Life history and narrative* (pp. 63–74). Washington, DC: The Falmer Press.
Barton, A. C. (2013). Crafting a future in science: Tracing middle school girls' identity work over time and space. *American Educational Research Journal, 50*(1), 37–75. doi:10.3102/0002831212458142
Barton, A. C. (1998). Teaching science with homeless children: Pedagogy, representation, and identity. *Journal of Research in Science Teaching, 35*(4), 379–394. doi:10.1002/(SICI)1098-2736(199804)35:4<379::AID-TEA8>3.0CO;2-N
Bartholomae, D. (1986). *Inventing the university.* New York, NY: Guilford.
Behar, R., & Gordon, D. (1995). *Women writing culture.* Berkeley: University of California Press.

References

Beijaard, D., Meijer, P. C., & Verloop, N. (2004). Reconsidering research on teachers' professional identity. *Teaching and Teacher Education, 20*(2), 107–128. Retrieved from https://openaccess.leidenuniv.nl/bitstream/handle/1887/11190/10_404_07.pdf?sequence=1

Bernstein, B. (1996). *Pedagogy, symbolic control and identity: Theory, research, critique*. New York, NY: Taylor & Francis.

Bickmore, S., Smagorinsky, P., & O'Donnell-Allen, C. (2005). Tensions between traditions: The role of contexts in learning to teach. *English Education, 38*(1), 23–52. Retrieved from www.jstor.org.www2.lib.ku.edu/stable/40173210

Bizzell, P. (1994)."Contact zones" and English studies. *College English, 56*(2), 163–169. Retrieved from www.jstor.org.www2.lib.ku.edu/stable/378727

Blome, W. W. (1997). What happens to foster kids: Educational experiences of a random sample of foster care youth and a matched group of non-foster care youth. *Child and Adolescent Social Work Journal, 14*(1), 41–53. Retrieved from http://link.springer.com/article/10.1023/A:1024592813809

Bloom, L. R. (1998). *Under the sign of hope: Feminist methodology and narrative interpretation*. Albany: State University of New York Press.

Boesch, E. (2007). The enigmatic other. In L. Mathias & J. Valsiner (Eds.), *Otherness in question: Labryrinths of the self* (pp. 3–9). Charlotte, NC: Information Age Publishing.

Boyle-Baise, M. (2002). *Multicultural service learning*. New York, NY: Teachers College Press.

Britzman, D. P. (1991). *Practice makes practice: A critical study of learning to teach*. Albany: State University of New York Press.

Bruffee, K. A. (1984). Collaborative learning and the 'conversation of mankind.' *College English, 46*(7), 635–652. Retrieved from www.jstor.org/stable/376924

Bruner, J. (2002). Narratives of human plight: A conversation with Jerome Bruner. In R. Charon & M. Montello (Eds.), *Stories matter: The role of narrative in medical ethics* (pp. 3–9). New York, NY: Routledge.

Bucholtz, M., & Hall, K. (2005). Identity and interaction: A sociocultural linguistic approach. *Discourse Studies, 7*, 585–614.

Burns, L. D., & Hall, L. A. Using students' funds of knowledge to enhance middle grades education: Responding to adolescents. In M. Vagle (Ed.), *Not a stage! A critical re-conception of young adolescent education* (pp. 175–189). New York, NY: Peter Lang.

Burke, J. (2007). *The English teacher's companion* (3rd ed.). Portsmouth, NH: Heinemann.

Carr, W., & Kemmis, S. (1986). *Becoming critical: Education, knowledge, and action research*. Basingstoke, England: Falmer.

Carspecken, P. (1996). *Critical ethnography in educational research: A theoretical and practical guide*. New York, NY: Routledge.

Carter, C. (2009). Priest, prostitute, plumber? The construction of teachers as saints. *English Education, 42*(1), 61–90. Retrieved from www.jstor.org.www2.lib.ku.edu/stable/40607917

Carter-Andrews, D. J. (2009). "The hardest thing to turn from": The effects of service-learning on preparing urban educators. *Equity & Excellence in Education, 42*(2), 272–293. doi:10.1080/10665680903060261

Causey, V., Thomas, C., & Armento, B. (2000). Cultural diversity is basically a foreign term to me: the challenges of diversity for preservice teacher education. *Teaching and Teacher Education, 16*, 33–45. doi:10.1016/S0742-051X(99)00039-6

Chase, S. E. (2003). Learning to listen: Narrative principles in a qualitative research methods course. In R. Josselson, A. Lieblich, & D. P. McAdams (Eds.), *Up close and personal: The teaching and learning of narrative research* (pp. 79–99). Washington, DC: American Psychological Association.

Childers, P. B., Fels, D., & Jordan, J. (2005). The secondary school writing center: A place to build confident, competent writers. *Praxis: A Writing Center Journal*, 2(1). Retrieved from http://projects.uwc.utexas.edu/praxis/?q=node/91

Christensen, L. (2000). *Reading, writing, and rising up: Teaching about social justice and the power of the written word*. Milwaukee, WI: Rethinking Schools.

Clandinin, D. J. (1985). Personal practical knowledge: A study of teachers' classroom images. *Curriculum Inquiry*, 15, 361–385. Retrieved from www.jstor.org/stable/1179683

Clandinin, D. J., & Connelly, F. M. (2000). *Narrative inquiry*. San Francisco, CA: Jossey-Bass.

Clandinin, D. J., Downey, C. A., & Huber, J. (2009). Attending to changing landscapes: Shaping the interwoven identities of teachers and teacher educators. *Asia Pacific Journal of Teacher Education*, 37(2), 141–154. doi:10.1080/13598660902806316

Cochran-Smith, M. (2001). Reforming teacher education: Competing agendas. *Journal of Teacher Education*, 52(4), 263–265. doi:10.1177/0022487101052004001

Cochran-Smith, M. (1995). Color blindness and basket making are not the answers: Confronting the dilemmas of race, culture, and language diversity in teacher education. *American Educational Research Journal*, 32, 493–522. Retrieved from www.jstor.org.www2.lib.ku.edu/stable/1163321

Coffey, H. (2010). "*They* taught *me*": The benefits of early community-based field experiences in teacher education. *Teaching and Teacher Education*, 26, 335–342. doi:10.1016/j.tate.2009.09.014

Collin, R. (2012). Composing the career portfolio and the classed subject. *Research in the Teaching of English*, 46(3), 260–284. Retrieved from http://search.proquest.com.www2.lib.ku.edu/docview/922949502?accountid=14556

Compton-Lilly, C. (2003). *Reading lives: The literate lives of urban children*. New York, NY: Teachers College Press.

Cuban, L. (1993). *How teachers taught: Constancy and change in American classrooms, 1890–1990*. New York, NY: Teachers College.

Cushman, E. (1999) The public intellectual, service learning, and activist research. *College English*, 61(3), 328–336. Retrieved from www.jstor.org.www2.lib.ku.edu/stable/379072

Danielewicz, J. (2001). *Teaching selves: Identity, pedagogy, and teacher education*. Albany: State University of New York Press.

Darling-Hammond, L. (2006). *Powerful teacher education*. San Francisco, CA: Jossey-Bass.

Darling-Hammond, L., Hammerness, K. Grossman, P., Rust, F., & Shulman, L. (2005). The design of teacher education programs. In L. Darling-Hammond & J. Bransford (Eds.), *Preparing teachers for a changing world* (pp. 390–441). San Francisco, CA: Jossey-Bass.

Deans, T., Roswell, B. S., & Wurr, A. J. (Eds.). (2010). *Writing and community engagement: A critical sourcebook*. Boston, MA: Bedford-St. Martin's.

Devitt, A. J. (1993). Generalizing about genre: New conceptions of an old concept. *College Composition and Communication*, 44(4), 573–586. doi:10.2307/358391

Dewey, J. (1933). *How we think: A restatement of the relation of reflective thinking in the educative process*. New York, NY: D.C. Heath and Company.

Diver-Stamnes, A. C. (1995). *Lives in the balance: Youth, poverty, and education in Watts*. Albany: State University of New York Press.

Dixon, J. (1967). *Growth through English*. Champaign, IL: National Council of Teachers of English.

Dixon, J. (2003). Historical considerations: An international perspective. In J. Flood, D. Lapp, J. R. Squire, & J. Jensen (Eds.), *Handbook of research on teaching the English language arts* (pp. 18–23). Mahwah, NJ: Erlbaum.

Dutro, E. (2010). What 'hard times' means: Mandated curricula, class-privileged assumptions, and the lives of poor children. *Research in the Teaching of English, 44*(3), 255–291. Retrieved from www.jstor.org.www2.lib.ku.edu/stable/27784362

Dyson, A. H., & Genishi, C. (2005). *On the case: Approaches to language and literacy research.* New York, NY: Teachers College Press.

Eby, J. W. (1998). *Why service-learning is bad.* Retrieved from www.messiah.edu/documents/Agape/wrongsvc.pdf

Eisner, E. (1982). *Cognition and curriculum: A basis for deciding what to teach and how to evaluate.* New York, NY: Longman.

Emig, J. (1977) Writing as a mode of learning. *College Composition and Communication, 28*(2), 122–128. doi:10.2307/356095

Ewald, H. (1993). "Waiting for answerability": Bakhtin and composition studies. *College Composition and Communication, 44*(3), 331–347. doi:10.2307/358987

Eyler, J., & Giles, D. E. (1999). *Where's the learning in service-learning?* San Francisco, CA: Jossey-Bass.

Family Promise. (n.d.-a). *Our work.* Retrieved from www.familypromise.org/our-work

Family Promise. (n.d.-b). *Does working work?* Retrieved from www.familypromise.org/poverty-facts-your-neighborhood-does-working-work/

Family Promise of Lawrence. (n.d.). *History timeline.* Retrieved from http://lawrencefamilypromise.org/history-timeline/

Farmer, F. (2002). Review: Community intellectuals. *College English, 65*(2), 202–210.

Feiman-Nemser, S., & Buchmann, M. (1987). When is student teaching teacher education? *Teaching and Teacher Education, 3*(4), 255–273.

Feinstein, S. (2005). *The spirit of generosity: Service learning in a pre-service teacher education program.* Retrieved from ERIC database. (ED490389)

Fels, D., & Wells, J. (2011). *The successful high school writing center: Building the best program with your students.* New York, NY: Teachers College Press.

Fendler, L. (2003). Teacher reflection in a hall of mirrors: Historical influences and political reverberations. *Educational Researcher, 32*(3), 16–25. Retrieved from www.jstor.org.www2.lib.ku.edu/stable/3699830

Flannery, M. (2008). "She discriminated against her own race": Voicing and identity in a story of discrimination. *Narrative Inquiry, 18*(1), 118–130.

Flower, L. (1997). Partners in inquiry: A logic for community outreach. In L. Adler-Kassner, R. Crooks, & A. Watters (Eds.), *Writing the community: Concepts and models for service-learning in composition* (pp. 95–117). Washington, DC: American Association for Higher Education Press.

Flower, L. (2002). Intercultural inquiry and the transformation of service. *College English, 65*(2), 181–201. doi:10.2307/3250762

Flower, L. (2008). *Community literacy and the rhetoric of public engagement.* Carbondale: Southern Illinois Press.

Flower, L., Long, E., & Higgins, L. (2000). *Learning to rival: A literate practice for intercultural inquiry.* Mahwah, NJ: Erlbaum.

Friesen, M. D., & Besley, S. C. (2013). Teacher identity development in the first year of teacher education: A developmental and social psychological perspective. *Teaching and Teacher Education, 36*, 23–32. doi:10.1016/j.tate.2013.06.005

Gallagher, C. (2002). *Radical departures: Composition and progressive pedagogy.* Urbana, IL: National Council of Teachers of English.

Gamoran, A., Nystrand, M., Berends, M., & LePore, P. C. (1995). An organizational analysis of the effects of ability grouping. *American Educational Research Journal, 32*, 687–715. http://dx.doi.org/10.3102/00028312032004687

Gay, G. (Ed.). (2003). *Becoming multicultural educators: Personal journeys toward professional agency.* San Francisco, CA: Jossey-Bass.

References

Gee, J.P. (1996). *Social linguistics and literacies: Ideology in discourses* (2nd ed.). Philadelphia, PA: Falmer Press.

Gee, J.P. (1999). *An introduction to discourse analysis: Theory and method.* New York, NY: Routledge.

Gee, J.P. (2001). Literacy, discourse, and linguistics: Introduction. In E. Cushman, M. Rose, B. Kroll, & E.R. Kintgen (Eds.), *Literacy: A critical sourcebook* (pp. 525–544). Boston, MA: Bedford/St. Martin's.

Gee, J.P. (2004). *Situated language and learning: A critique of traditional schooling.* London, England: Routledge.

Gee, J.P., Hull, G., & Lankshear, C. (1996). *The new work order.* Boulder, CO: Westview Press.

Geertz, C. (1973). Thick description: Toward an interpretive theory of culture. In *The Interpretation of Cultures: Selected essays* (pp. 3–32). New York, NY: Basic Books.

Genishi, C., & Dyson, A.H. (2009). *Children, language, and literacy: Diverse learners in diverse times.* New York, NY: Teachers College Press.

Gere, A.R. (1994). Kitchen tables and rented rooms: The extracurriculum of composition. *College Composition and Communication, 45*(1), 75–92. doi:10.2307/358588

Goldblatt, E. (2007). *Because we live here: Sponsoring literacy beyond the college curriculum.* Cresskill, NJ: Hampton Press.

Gomez, M.L. (2007). Seeing our lives intertwined: Teacher education for cultural inclusion. *Language Arts, 84*(4), 365–374. Retrieved from www.jstor.org.www2.lib.ku.edu/stable/41962205

Gomez, M.L., & White, E. (2010). Seeing one another as "other." *Teaching and Teacher Education, 26,* 1015–1022. doi:10.1016/j.tate.2009.10.044

Gomez, M.L., Black, R.W., & Allen, A. (2007). "Becoming" a teacher. *Teachers College Record, 109*(9), 2107–2135. Retrieved from www.tcrecord.org.www2.lib.ku.edu/library/Issue.asp?volyear=2007&number=9&volume=109

Gordon, E., McKibbin, K. Vasudevan, L., & Vinz, R. (2007). Writing out of the unexpected: Narrative inquiry and the weight of small moments. *English Education, 39*(4), 326–351. Retrieved from www.jstor.org.www2.lib.ku.edu/stable/40173261

Gore, J.M. (1993). *The struggle for pedagogies: Critical and feminist discourses as regimes of truth.* New York, NY: Routledge.

Graue, M.E., Kroeger, J., & Prager, D. (2001). A Bakhtinian analysis of particular home-school relations. *American Educational Research Journal, 38,* 467–498. doi:10.3102/00028312038003467

Gruenewald, D.A. (2003). The best of both worlds: A critical pedagogy of place. *Educational Researcher, 32*(4), 3–12. doi:10.3102/0013189X032004003

Hacking, I. (1986). Making up people. In T.C. Heller, M. Sonsa, & D.E. Weller (Eds.), *Reconstructing individualism* (pp. 222–236). Stanford, CA: Stanford University Press.

Hacking, I. (1990). *The taming of chance.* New York, NY: Cambridge University Press.

Hacking, I. (1995). The looping effects of human kinds. In D. Sperber, D. Premack, & A. Premack (Eds.) *Causal cognition: An interdisciplinary approach* (pp. 351–383). Oxford, England: Oxford University Press.

Hall, S. (2000). Foreword. In D.A. Yon, *Elusive culture: Schooling, race, and identity in Global times* (pp. ix–xii). Albany, NY: SUNY Press.

Hallman, H.L. (2007). Negotiating teacher identity: Exploring the use of electronic teaching portfolios with preservice English teachers. *Journal of Adolescent & Adult Literacy, 50*(6), 474–485. doi:10.1598/JAAL.50.6.5

Hallman, H.L., & Burdick, M.N. (2011). Service learning and the preparation of English teachers. *English Education, 43*(4), 341–368. Retrieved from http://search.proquest.com.www2.lib.ku.edu/docview/874324979?accountid=14556

References

Harding, S. (2009). A socially relevant philosophy of science? Resources from standpoint theory's controversiality. *Hypatia, 19*, 25–47. doi:10.1111/j.1527-2001.2004.tb01267.x

Hatton, N., & Smith, D. (1995). Reflection in teacher education: Towards definition and implementation. *Teaching and Teacher Education, 11*, 33–49.

Heath, S. B. (1982). *Ways with words: Language, life, and work in communities and classrooms.* Cambridge, England: Cambridge University Press.

Herrington, D. E., Kidd-Herrington, K., & Kritsonis, M. A. (2006). Coming to terms with No Child Left Behind: Learning to teach the invisible children. *National Forum of Special Education Journal, 18*(1), 1–7.

Herzberg, B. (2010). Community service and critical teaching. In T. Deans, B. S. Rowsell, & A. J. Wurr (Eds.), *Writing and community engagement: A critical sourcebook* (pp. 138–148). Boston, MA: Bedford-St. Martin's

Hicks, D. (2000). Self and other in Bakhtin's early philosophical essays: Prelude to a theory of prose consciousness. *Mind, Culture, and Activity, 7*, 227–242. doi:10.1207/S15327884MCA0703_10 55

Higgins, L., Long, E., & Flower, L. (2010). Community literacy: A rhetorical model for personal and public inquiry. In T. Deans, B. S. Rowsell, & A. J. Wurr (Eds.), *Writing and community engagement: A critical sourcebook* (pp. 167–201). Boston, MA: Bedford-St. Martin's.

Holland, D., & Lave, J. (Eds.). (2001). *History in person: Enduring struggles, contentious practice, and intimate identities.* Santa Fe, NM: School of American Research Press.

Holland, D., Lachicotte, W., Skinner, D., & Cain, C. (1998). *Identity and agency in cultural worlds.* Cambridge, MA: Harvard University Press.

Hollingsworth, S. (1990). Teachers as researchers: Writing to learn about ourselves—and others. *Quarterly of the National Writing Project and the Center for the Study of Writing and Literacy, 12*(4), 10–18.

Hollins, E. (2011). Teacher preparation for quality teaching. *Journal of Teacher Education, 62*(4), 395–407. doi:10.1177/0022487111409415

Holquist, M. (1990). *Dialogism.* New York, NY: Routledge.

Hong, J. Y. (2010). Pre-service and beginning teachers' professional identity and its relationship to dropping out of the profession. *Teaching and Teacher Education, 26*(8), 1530–1543. doi:10.1016/j.tate.2010.06.003

hooks, b. (1990). *Yearning: Race, gender, and cultural politics.* Boston, MA: South End Press.

hooks, b. (2000). *Feminist theory: From margin to center.* London, England: Pluto Press.

Howey, K., & Zimpher, N. (Eds.). (2006). *Boundary spanners.* Washington, DC: American Association of State Colleges and Universities.

Hull, G., & Schultz, K. (2002). *School's out! Bridging out-of-school literacies with classroom practice.* New York, NY: Teachers College Press.

Jenkins, R. (1996). *Social identity.* London, England: Routledge.

Juzwik, M. (2004). Toward an ethics of answerability: *College Composition and Communication, 55*(3), 536–567. doi:10.2307/4140698

Kaufman, J. E. (2004). Language, inquiry, and the heart of learning: Reflections in an English methods course. *English Education, 36*(3), 174–191. Retrieved from www.jstor.org.www2.lib.ku.edu/stable/40173092

Kent, R. (2006). *A guide to creating student-staffed writing centers, grades 6–12.* New York, NY: Peter Lang.

Kelly, D. M. (2000). *Pregnant with meaning.* New York, NY: Peter Lang.

Kinloch, V. (2012). *Crossing boundaries: Teaching and learning with urban youth.* New York, NY: Teachers College Press.

Kinloch, V., & Smagorinsky, P. (2014). *Service-learning in literacy education: Possibilities for teaching and learning.* Charlotte, NC: Information Age Publishing.

Kinsella, E. (2007). Embodied reflection and the epistemology of reflective practice. *Journal of Philosophy of Education, 41*(3), 395–409. doi:10.1111/j.1467-9752.2007.00574.x

Kirkland, D. (2008). "The rose that grew from concrete": Postmodern blackness and new English education. *English Journal, 97*(5), 69–75. doi:10.2307/30046887

Kirkland, D. (2010). Englishes in urban contexts: Politics, pluralism, and possibilities. *English Education, 42*(3), 293–306. Retrieved from www.jstor.org.www2.lib.ku.edu/stable/40607993

Knapp, M., & Turnball, B. (1990). *Better schooling for children of poverty: Alternatives to conventional wisdom.* Washington, DC: U.S. Department of Education.

Kondo, D. K. (1990). *Crafting selves: Power, gender, and discourses of identity in a Japanese workplace.* Chicago, IL: University of Chicago Press.

Korthagen, F. A. J., & Kessels, J. P. A. M. (1999). Linking theory and practice: Changing the pedagogy of teacher education. *Educational Researcher, 28*(4), 4–17. doi:10.3102/0013189X028004004

Lachuk, A. J., & Gomez, M. L. (2013). Becoming answerable to our participants: A methodological essay on life history. In C. S. Rhodes & K. J. Weiss (Eds.), *Ethical issues in literacy research* (pp. 9–20). New York, NY: Routledge.

Ladson-Billings, G. (2001). *Crossing over to Canaan: The journey of new teachers in diverse classrooms.* San Francisco, CA: Jossey-Bass.

Ladson-Billings, G. (2002). I ain't writin' nuttin': Permissions to fail and demands to succeed in urban classrooms. In L. Delpit & J. K. Dowdy (Eds.), *The skin that we speak: Thoughts on language and culture in the classroom* (pp. 107–120). New York, NY: The New Press.

Lareau, A. (2003). *Unequal childhoods: Class, race, and family life.* Oakland: University of California Press.

Lave, J., & Wegner, E. (1991). *Situated learning: Legitimate peripheral participation.* New York, NY: Cambridge University Press.

Lefebvre, H. (1991). *The production of space.* Malden, MA: Blackwell.

Lesko, N. (2001). *Act your age! A cultural construction of adolescence.* New York, NY: RoutledgeFalmer.

Lortie, D. (1975). *Schoolteacher: A sociological study.* Chicago, IL: University of Chicago Press.

Luke, A., & Elkins, J. (1998). Reinventing literacy in new times. *Journal of Adolescent & Adult Literacy, 42*(1), 4–7.

Luttrell, W. (2003). *Pregnant bodies, fertile minds.* New York, NY: Routledge.

Marshall, J. D., Smagorinsky, P., & Moore, M. W. (1995). *The language of interpretation: Patterns of discourse in discussions of literature* (NCTE Research Report No. 27). Urbana, IL: National Council of Teachers of English

Marx, S. (2004). Regarding whiteness: Exploring and intervening in the effects of white racism in teacher education. *Equity & Excellence in Education, 37*, 31–43. doi:10.1080/10665680490422089

Massey, D. (1999). Philosophy and politics of spatiality: some considerations. The Hettner-Lecture in Human Geography. *Geographische Zeitschrift, 87*(1), 1–12.

Mathieu, P. (2005). *Tactics of hope: The public turn in English composition.* Portsmouth, NH: Boynton/Cook.

McChesney, K. (1993). Homeless families since 1980. *Education and Urban Society, 25*, 361–379.

McDougall, J. (2010). A crisis in professional identity: How primary teachers are coming to terms with changing views of literacy. *Teaching and Teacher Education, 26*(3), 679–687. doi:10.1016/j.tate.2009.10.003

McInerney, P., Smyth, J., & Down, B. (2011). 'Coming to a place near you?' The politics and possibilities of a critical pedagogy of place-based education. *Asia-Pacific Journal of Teacher Education, 39*(1), 483–494. doi:10.1080/13598 66X.2010.540894

Merriam, S. B. (2001). *Qualitative research and case study applications in education.* San Francisco, CA: Jossey-Bass.

Mertz, J. S., Jr., & Schroerlucke, K. (1998). *Technology consulting in the community* (Carnegie Mellon Center for University Outreach Reports). Retrieved from www.cmu.edu/outreach/csinc

Mikolchak, M. (2014). Service-learning in English comp. In V. Kinloch & P. Smagorinsky (Eds.), *Service-learning in literacy education: Possibilities for teaching and learning* (pp. 211–224). Charlotte, NC: Information Age Publishing.

Miles, M. B., & Huberman, A. M. (1994). *Qualitative data analysis* (2nd ed.). Thousand Oaks, CA: Sage.

Mintz, S., & Hesser, G. (1996). Principles of good practice in service-learning. In B. Jacoby & Associates (Eds.), *Service-learning in higher education* (pp. 26–52). San Francisco, CA: Jossey-Bass.

Mishler, E. (1999). *Storylines: Craftartists' narratives of identity.* Cambridge, MA: Harvard University Press.

Moje, E. (2008). Foregrounding the disciplines in secondary literacy teaching and learning: A call for change. *Journal of Adolescent & Adult Literacy, 52*(2), 96–107. Retrieved from www.jstor.org.www2.lib.edu.ku/stable/20111747

Moore, M. (2014). Service-learning and the fields-based literacy methods course. In V. Kinloch & P. Smagorinsky (Eds.), *Service-learning in literacy education: Possibilities for teaching and learning* (pp. 105–115). Charlotte, NC: Information Age Publishing.

Moya, P. (2006). What's identity got to do with it? Mobilizing identities in the multicultural classroom. In L. M. Alcoff, M. Hames-Garcia, S. Mohanty, & P. Moya (Eds.), *Identity politics reconsidered* (pp. 96–117). New York, NY: Palgrave.

National Alliance to End Homelessness. (2014). Snapshot of homelessness. Retrieved from www.endhomelessness.org/pages/snapshot_of_homelessness

National Middle School Association. (2010). *This we believe: Keys to educating young adolescents.* Westerville, OH: Author. Retrieved from www.amle.org/AboutAMLE/ThisWeBelieve/tabid/121/Default.aspx

North, S. M. (1984). The idea of a writing center. *College English, 46*(5), 433–446.

Nukkula, M. J. (2003). Identity and possibility: Adolescent development and the potential of schools. In M. Sadowski (Ed.), *Adolescents at school: Perspectives on youth, identity, and education* (pp. 7–18). Cambridge, MA: Harvard Education Press.

Nystrand, M., Gamoran, A., Kachur, R., & Prendergast, C. (1997). *Opening dialogue: Understanding the dynamics of language and learning in the English classroom.* New York, NY: Teachers College Press.

Oakes, J., Franke, M. L., Hunter Quartz, K., & Rogers, J. (2006). Research for high quality urban teaching: Defining it, developing it, assessing it. *Journal of Teacher Education, 53*(3), 228–235. doi:10.1177/0022487102053003006

Perkins, L. M. (1989). The history of blacks in teaching: Growth and decline within the profession. In D. Warren (Ed.). *American teachers: Histories of a profession at* work (pp. 344–369). New York, NY: Macmillan.

Petrone, R., & Lewis, M. A. (2012). Deficits, therapists, and a desire to distance: Secondary English preservice teachers' reasoning about their future students. *English Education, 44*(3), 254–287. Retrieved from http://search.proquest.com.www2.lib.ku.edu/docview/1004728885?accountid=14556

Pillow, W. (2004). *Unfit subjects.* New York, NY: RoutledgeFalmer.

Popkewitz, T. S. (1998). *Struggling for the soul: The politics of schooling and the construction of the teacher.* New York, NY: Teachers College Press.
Popkewitz, T. S. (2009). Curriculum study, curriculum history, and curriculum theory: The reason of reason. *Journal of Curriculum Studies, 41*(3), 301–319. doi:10.1080/00220270902777021
Popkewitz, T. S. (2010). The limits of teacher education reform: School subjects, alchemies, and an alternative possibility. *Journal of Teacher Education, 61*(5), 413–421. doi:10.1177/0022487110375247
Portes, P. R., & Smagorinsky, P. (2010). Static structures, changing demographics: Educating teachers for shifting populations in stable schools. *English Education, 42*(3), 236–247. Retrieved from www.jstor.org/stable/40607989
Poulou, M. (2007). Student-teachers concerns about teaching practice. *European Journal of Teacher Education, 31*(1), 91–110. doi:10.1080/02619760600944993
Pratt, M. (1991). Arts of the contact zone. In *Profession '91* (pp. 33–40). New York, NY: Modern Language Association. Retrieved from www.jstor.org/stable/25595469
Quijada Cerecer, P. D. (2011). Power in community building: Learning from indigenous youth how to strengthen adult-youth relationships in school settings. In A. Ball & C. Tyson (Eds.), *Studying diversity in teacher education* (pp. 171–182). New York, NY: Rowman & Littlefield.
Quint, S. (1994). *Schooling homeless children: A working model for America's public schools.* New York, NY: Teachers College Press.
Reynolds, N. (2004). *Geographies of writing: Inhabiting places and encountering difference.* Carbondale: Southern Illinois Press.
Richardson, L. (2000). Writing: A method of inquiry. In N. K. Denzin & Y. S. Lincoln (Eds.), *Handbook of qualitative research: Context and method* (pp. 923–948). Thousand Oaks, CA: Sage.
Rich, M. F. (2000). America's diversity and growth: Signposts for the 21st century. *Population Bulletin, 55*(2), 1–43. doi:10.1598/RRQ.41.2.3
Rogers, T., Marshall, E., & Tyson, C. (2006). Dialogic narratives of literacy, teaching, and schooling: Preparing literacy teachers for diverse settings. *Reading Research Quarterly, 41*(2), 202–224.
Rose, M. (2010). Opinion: Writing for the public. *College English, 72*(3), 284–292. doi:198.252.15.206
Rury, J. (1989). Who became teachers? The social characteristics of teachers in American history. In D. Warren (Ed.), *American teachers: History of a profession at work* (pp. 9–48). New York, NY: Macmillan.
Sargent, P. (2000). Real men or real teachers? Contradictions in the lives of men elementary teachers. *Men and Masculinities, 2,* 410–433. doi: 10.1177/1097184X00002004003
Schell, E. E. (1997). *Gypsy academics and mother-teachers: Gender, contingent labor, and writing instruction.* Portsmouth, NH: Boynton Cook.
Schön, D. (1983). *The reflective practitioner.* New York, NY: Basic Books.
Schön, D. (1987). *Educating the reflective practitioner.* San Francisco, CA: Jossey-Bass.
Schutz, A., & Gere, A. R. (1998). Service learning and English studies: Rethinking "public" service. *College English, 60*(2), 129–149. doi:10.2307/378323
Sheehy, M. & Leander, K. M. (2004). Introduction. In K. Leander & M. Sheehy (Eds.), *Spatializing literacy research and practice* (pp. 1–14). New York, NY: Peter Lang.
Shor, I. (1996). *When students have power: Negotiating authority in a critical pedagogy.* Chicago, IL: University of Chicago Press.
Shrofel, S. (1991). Developing writing teachers. *English Education, 23*(3), 160–177. Retrieved from www.jstor.org/stable/40172760

Shulman, L. (2005). Pedagogies of uncertainty. *Liberal Education, 91*(2), 18–25. Retrieved from http://search.proquest.com.www2.lib.ku.edu/docview/209812613/abstract?accountid=14556

Sleeter, C. (2008). Equity, democracy, and neoliberal assaults on teacher education. *Teaching and Teacher Education, 24*(8), 1947–1957. doi:10.1016/j.tate.2008.04.003

Smagorinsky, P. (2002). *Teaching English through principled practice*. Upper Saddle River, NJ: Merrill/Prentice Hall.

Smagorinsky, P. (2008). *Teaching English by design: How to create and carry out instructional units*. Portsmouth, NH: Heinemann.

Smagorinsky, P. (2014). Service-learning in an alternative school as mediated through book club discussions. In V. Kinloch & P. Smagorinsky (Eds.), *Service-learning in literacy education: Possibilities for teaching and learning* (pp. 85–103). Charlotte, NC: Information Age Publishing.

Smith, D. E. (1990). *Texts, facts, and femininity*. London, England: Routledge.

Spatig, L. (2005). Feminist critique of developmentalism: What's in it for teachers? *Theory and Research in Education, 3*(3), 299–326. doi:10.1177/1477878505057431

Squire, J. R. (2003). The history of the profession. In J. Flood, D. Lapp, J. R. Squire, & J. Jensen (Eds.), *Handbook of research on the teaching the English Language Arts* (pp. 3–17). Mahwah, NJ: Erlbaum.

Stock, P. L. (1995). *The dialogic curriculum: Teaching and learning in a multicultural society*. Portsmouth, NH; Boynton/Cook.

Stake, R. (1995). *The art of case study research*. Thousand Oaks, CA: Sage.

Stake, R. (2000). Case studies. In N. Denzin & Y. S. Lincoln (Eds.), *Handbook of qualitative research* (2nd ed., pp. 435–454). Thousand Oaks, CA: Sage.

Strauss, A. & Corbin, J. (1998). *Basics of qualitative research: Techniques and procedures for developing grounded theory* (2nd ed.). London, England: Sage.

Tatto, T. (1996). Examining the values and beliefs about teaching diverse students: Understanding the challenges for teacher education. *Educational Evaluation and Policy Analysis, 18*, 155–180. doi:10.3102/01623737018002155

Theobald, P. (2006). A case for inserting community into public school curriculum. *American Journal of Education, 112*(3), 315–334. doi:10.1086/500711

Todorov, T. (1984). *Mikhail Bakhtin: The dialogical principle* (Wlad Godzich, Trans.). Minneapolis: University of Minnesota Press.

Trent, J., & Lim, J. (2010). Teacher identity construction in school-university partnerships: Discourse and practice. *Teaching and Teacher Education, 26*(8), 1609–1618. doi:10.1016/j.tate.2010.06.012

The United States Conference of Mayors. (2009). U.S. cities see sharp increases in the need for food assistance; decreases in individual homelessness: Mayors issue annual report on hunger, homelessness in cities [Press release]. Retrieved from www.usmayors.org/pressreleases/uploads/RELEASEHUNGERHOMELESSNESS2009FINALRevised.pdf

The United States Conference of Mayors. (2011). *Hunger and homelessness survey: A status report of hunger and homelessness in America's cities*. Retrieved from http://usmayors.org/pressreleases/uploads/2011-hhreport.pdf

U.S. Census Bureau. (2010). State & county quickfacts. Retrieved September 29, 2014, from www.census.gov/en.html

U.S. Department of Education, National Center for Education Statistics, Schools and Staffing Survey. Table 70. Percentage of public school teachers of Grades 9 through 12, by field of main teaching assignment and selected demographic and educational characteristics: 2007–08. Retrieved from http://nces.ed.gov/programs/digest/d09/tables/dt09_070.asp

U.S. Office of Housing and Urban Development. (2013, June). *The 2013 Annual Homeless Assessment Report*. Washington, DC: HUD Office of Community Planning and Development. Retrieved from www.hudexchange.info/resources/documents/ahar-2013-part1.pdf

References

Vagle, M. (2012). The anchor essay: Trying to poke holes in Teflon: Developmentalism; young adolescence; and contingent, recursive growth and change. In M. Vagle (Ed.), *Not a stage! A critical re-conception of young adolescent education* (pp. 11–38). New York, NY: Peter Lang.

Veit, R., Gould, C., & Gould, K. (2013). *Writing, reading, and research*. Stamford, CT: Cengage Learning.

Warren, D. (Ed.). (1998). *American teachers: Histories of a profession at work*. New York, NY: Macmillan.

Watson, C. (2006). Narratives of practice and the construction of identity in teaching. *Teachers and Teaching: Theory and Practice, 12*(5), 509–526. doi:10.1080/13540600600832213

Weaver-Hightower, M. (2003). The "boy turn" in research on gender and education. *Review of Educational Research, 73*(4), 471–498. doi:10.3102/00346543073004471

Welch, N. (1993). One student's many voices: Reading, writing, and responding with Bakhtin. *Journal of Advanced Composition, 13*(2), 493–502. Retrieved from www.jstor.org/stable/20865929

Wolcott, H. F. (2002). *The sneaky kid and its aftermath: Ethics and intimacy in fieldwork*. Walnut Creek, CA: AltaMira.

Yosso, T. (2006). *Critical race counterstories along the Chicana/Chicano educational pipeline*. New York, NY: Routledge.

Zeichner, K. (1996a). Designing education practicum experiences for prospective teachers. In K. Zeichner, S. Melnick, & M. L. Gomez (Eds.), *Currents of reform in preservice teacher education* (pp. 215–234). New York, NY: Teachers College Press.

Zeichner, K. (1996b). Teachers as reflective practitioners and the democratization of school reform. In K. Zeichner, S. Melnick, & M. L. Gomez (Eds.), *Currents of reform in preservice teacher education* (pp. 199–214). New York, NY: Teachers College Press.

Zeichner, K. (2010). Rethinking the connections between campus courses and field experiences in college-and University-based teacher education. *Journal of Teacher Education, 61*(1–2), 89–99. doi:10.1177/0022487109347671

Zeichner, K., & Miller, M. (1997). Learning to teach in professional development schools. In M. Levine & R. Trachtman (Eds.), *Making professional development schools work: Politics, practice and policy* (pp. 15–32). New York, NY: Teachers College Press.

Zeichner, K. M., & Liston, D. (1990). Traditions of reform in U.S. teacher education. *Journal of Teacher Education, 34*(2), 3–20. doi:10.1177/002248719004100202

Zeichner, K. M., & Liston, D. (1996). *Reflective teaching: An introduction*. New York, NY: Erlbaum.

Zeichner, K. M., & Tabachnick, B. R. (1991). Reflections on reflective teaching. In B. R. Tabachnick & K. M. Zeichner (Eds.), *Issues and practices in inquiry-oriented teacher education* (pp. 1–21). New York, NY: Falmer.

Zembylas, M. (2003). Interrogating 'teacher identity': Emotion, resistance, and self-formation. *Educational Theory, 58*(1), 107–127. doi:10.1111/j.1741-5446.2003.00107.x

Zetlin, A., MacLeod, E., & Kimm, C. (2012). Beginning teacher challenges instructing students who are in foster care. *Remedial and Special Education, 33*(1), 4–13. doi:10.1177/0741932510362506

Zlotkowski, E. (1996). A new voice at the table? Linking service-learning and the academy. *Change, 28*(1), 21–27. doi:10.1080/00091383.1996.10544252

Index

adolescence 102–4, 113, 118–19, 125–7, 135
Alsup, J. ix–xi, 7, 46, 49–50, 54, 65, 69, 94
answerability 74–5, 82–4, 124, 143
at-risk students 1, 3, 5, 7–11, 24, 62, 76–8, 96, 104, 121, 123–5, 128–31, 140–2
authoritative discourse 51–3, 56, 64, 77–9, 81, 97

Bakhtin, M.M. 3–4, 8, 11, 47–53, 56, 59, 63–4, 74–7, 79–88, 124, 139
borderland discourse 46
borderlands 46, 49, 65, 69

chronologies in teacher education 18–19, 146
community-based literacy 21
community field placements 1, 28–30, 69, 140, 146–7
Composition Studies 19–22, 110
counterstories/ counternarratives 2, 5, 54–5, 77, 106, 139
curricular constraint 6, 111, 118, 130–3
Curricular traditions: 108–10, 118–21; in cultural heritage model 110–12; in personal experience model 110–12; in skills model 110–12

Darling-Hammond, L. 14
Dartmouth Seminar 112, 118
Dewey, J. 85, 87
dialogism 2–4, 11, 48, 69, 74, 79, 82–8

discourse 46–8, 50, 53–4, 70, 145
double crisis of representation 128

English language arts: curriculum 56, 58, 60, 108–13, 118–21; teacher education 23–4
ethics of answerability 82–3

Family Partnership 9, 25–7, 34–5, 49–51, 55, 58, 60–1, 68–9, 90–2, 93–100, 101–8, 124–32, 135
Flower, L. 15–16, 21, 27, 100, 111
foster children/ students in foster care 37–8, 60

Gee, J.P. 7, 46, 53, 57, 100, 145
genre 4, 85–8
Gomez, M.L. 7, 32, 46, 48, 124, 128

heteroglossia 4, 74–6, 78, 87
history-in-person 105
homelessness in education 2, 9, 25–6, 33–5, 37–8, 58, 68, 125–6, 128, 131–2

identity: Bakhtin and identity 47–9, 63; research participants and identity 123; teacher identity 7–8, 24, 30–2, 41, 46, 50–1, 53–4, 59, 62–3, 78, 100, 138, 140; transitional state of identity 91
internally persuasive discourse 51–3, 55–6, 64, 76, 79, 81, 86
in-school vs out-of-school writing ix, 2, 24, 77, 130–1

Index

Kirkland, D. 130, 138

Ladson-Billings, G. 14, 128
Lefebvre, H. 5–6, 65
lodges 8–10, 28–9, 34, 37–9, 67–8, 111, 114–21, 132–5

Mettle Street School 8, 10–11, 28–30, 39–40, 66, 72–84, 86–8, 140
moral personhood 75, 86

narrative: as methodology 31–3; as story 32
narratives: of salvation 57–8; of self 47
New Times 53–4, 64, 78
'normal' students 81, 101–6, 118, 123–9, 131–5

pedagogical third space 130
place-based education (PBE) 64
Popkewitz, T. S. 7, 56–62, 94–5

reciprocal transformation 110–12, 119–20
reflection: as dialogic 84–8; in action 17, 146; in teacher education 84–8
reflective writing 145–6
reflexive pedagogy 84, 145
rhetoric of the future 77

Schön, D. 17, 84–5, 87, 139, 146
service-learning 15–18, 22, 24–7, 100, 110–11, 139
social turn in Composition Studies 20–1, 110
spatiality 2–3, 5, 11, 65

teacher: as authority and/or teacher as expert 18, 52, 90–1, 93–4, 100, 108, 140; as moral agent 75; as writer 27
teaching as feminine 99
teaching mythology 90–2, 100, 103, 108, 139

visible self 46

Writing Center 29–30, 39–40, 66, 76–9, 138

Zeichner, K. 14, 84–5